What I Remember

... and What I

Wish I Could Forget

By George Ducharme

ISBN: 978-1-7923-8122-5

Library of Congress Control Number: 2021923783

Cover design: Jacqueline Smith and Rebecca Flinn
Editing: Jacqueline.wordsmith, Rock Ledge Press

Three words to live by:

GET OVER IT!

Table of Contents

Foreword

Our lives are filled with decisions that we made or wished we would have made. My life was different.

Many decisions I made, I did not know why I made them. They seemed to be made for me by someone else ... someone, I later believed, who was watching over me. Things seemed to happen on schedule, too often to be a coincidence. For example, I would decide that I wanted to make a change in employment and presto – the phone would ring with a job offer. That happened three times. That is why I say my life is a Fairy Tale.

But I am getting ahead of myself. So let us begin at the beginning ...

Chapter 1

All Was Right in the World, Until it Wasn't

The year 1930 is not exactly a good time to bring a new life into the world. But here we are in 1930 in Hartford, Connecticut. March 1 to be exact. Just another day of struggle for most people as this was early in the Great Depression. But for Minnie and George Ducharme, this is a day of joy — a day to celebrate the birth of their child — a son. His name is George and later he would be called Junior.

During this worst of economic times in our nation's history — the closest we have seen since the Great Recession of 2007-2009 — everyone knew someone who was unemployed. It was a time when people struggled just to survive. Yet, they were happy to be alive. They managed as best they could. The worst brought out the best in people. Neighbors helped neighbors — everything from watching over children while parents were looking to earn a few bucks, to bartering with services instead of dollars. People accepted being unemployed as just one of those things one had to deal with. They believed better days lied ahead. They still had hope.

It was common to see children playing in the streets while neighbors kept a close watch over them. A neighbor did not hesitate to punish a child — any child — for misbehaving. A parent of one child was the parent to all.

If a child came home crying to tell their folks that Mrs. next door punished them, that child was punished a second time, by their parents. The adult figure was the authority figure and was always right. Back in those days, no one thought of suing the punisher — on the contrary. Parents actually thanked other parents for looking after their children. This was thought of as being respectful to others and children were taught to respect elders.

That respect carried over from one adult to another. I never heard anyone speak of envy or jealousy about someone who had a job or was better off than they were. There was respect and there was care. If an elder was ill, there was support from family, friends, and neighbors. People shared what little they had with others who had less. And no one thought less of those who had little.

These were different times. Women married early, raised a family, and their career was that of a homemaker. Graduation from high school for girls was rare. It was said that only those girls who could not find a man sought employment. Most people delayed having children until they could afford the expense of bearing and raising a child. In later years, I remember people saying they would plan to have a child when their furniture or even their car was paid off.

Yes, this was a different time. A time before credit cards. A time when people spent only what they had and not next week's salary. Most families purchased items on lay-away. These programs — brought back briefly during the Great Recession — allowed customers to purchase an item and would hold it until it was paid off. You could visit the store regularly and make a deposit toward the purchase price, until it was paid off. It was then, and only then, that you could take it home. Some stores and banks created Christmas Clubs, which allowed customers to save money during the year in order to buy holiday gifts. This was a slogan at the time — "Save your pennies and the dollars would take care of themselves."

Life was different. School was different. Children were taught how to save. There was a bank called Society for Savings that actually had a special savings program for kids. Parents opened a savings account in the child's name, and you could put as little as a penny in a plastic bag resembling today's sandwich baggies. The child had a bank account all their own and periodically the bank would add interest to the account. I remember getting one penny of interest and thinking it was a big deal. I think Monday was bank day at school. The children would compare their deposit with their classmates. Most deposits were a penny a week. In this way, it was hoped that children would learn to save and hopefully that habit would carry over into adulthood.

Life was hard but it seemed simpler. Meals were simple and basic. Restaurants were few. People cooked and ate at home. Girls learned to cook and sew. Making one's own clothing was a source of pride, not ridicule. Retail stores carried a large variety of sewing patterns. They came in packages with instructions and a picture of the dress, skirt, blouse, whatever. Mothers spent evenings listening to the radio while darning socks or mending damaged clothing.

I never felt deprived. That's because everyone I knew was in the same situation. We were poor, but we didn't know it. We were happy with the simple things in life. Today, they would call it "less is more." When my clothes did not fit me anymore, they were

3

given to someone who could wear them, and they were received gratefully. George and Minnie looked forward to the future almost unconcerned about the economic times they would face. They had a son, and all was right in their world. But not for long.

As teenagers, both of their parents objected to their marriage. Minnie's mother thought her daughter was too young to marry at 17. George's father opposed the marriage because of his son's health. He took Minnie aside one day after they had expressed their intention to marry — you did that back then — and told her in no uncertain terms she should not marry him because George had a serious heart condition. But teenagers always know best. That much hasn't changed over the years. The kids decided to ignore their parents' objections.

George's father's concern would soon be realized. Five years later, my dad, George, suffered a massive heart attack and died. Minnie, my mom, was just 22 and was now a widow with three small children — the oldest was not yet four-years-old. This would be a tragedy in anyone's life, but with the economy falling deeper into the Depression, this was a downright catastrophe. An eighth-grade education did not make Mom very employable. Another negative was her gender. At that time, no one would ever hire a woman over a man. After all, it was the man who was supposed to be the breadwinner and support his family.

Unable to find a job, Minnie got industrious and decided to take in boarders. The situation stabilized the family until the so-called "authorities" (that is what they were called) discovered that a young, attractive woman with three children was renting rooms to men. Mom could not persuade the authorities that the income from the boarders helped her family survive. Their solution? Put the children in foster homes. I was sent to one home and my two sisters went to

4

another until some enlightened social worker suggested that we be placed together.

Those authorities sent a very clear message: When Mom could support her children, she could get them back. So, not only had she lost the love of her life, but also her children were taken away as well. Understandably, she was in a state of deep despair. She continued to rent her rooms and the neighbors must have worked overtime gossiping. But she paid them no mind. She was strong. She was determined. And her next solution was simple: Find a man who would marry a woman with three small children.

In those days, marrying for security was very common. Love need not enter the picture. So, Mom embarked on her campaign to find the security she needed. And she found it in one of her boarders. He was a divorced man from Springfield, Massachusetts, named Emilio Bartolucci. He had left his five adult children to come to Hartford and start a new life. Little is known about his first marriage except that he kept in contact with his kids — frequently visiting them in Springfield or having them come to Hartford. Emilio was, of course, aware of Minnie's widowed status and, at the age of 49, was flattered that a woman (now 24) would find him appealing. I think, in order to end the gossip, he asked Mom to marry him, and she saw the opportunity as a way to get her kids back.

The authorities were made aware of her new marital status, but they looked askance upon this union because of their age difference. The authorities decided to wait awhile and see if the marriage would last. I was told that the authorities would regularly visit their home to check in on the marriage. Soon they saw that Mom was pregnant. The authorities were concerned that there would be yet another mouth to feed, but apparently didn't

5

make an issue of it. Nine months later, James was born. The marriage seemed more likely to succeed because both parents were delighted with the arrival of their new bundle of joy.

❀ ❀ ❀

Mom decided to ask the authorities to allow me to come home and be a big brother to James. After several meetings and discussions, her request was granted. It took a while, but one by one our family was being reunited. While there are no foster family horror stories to tell, it was nice to leave Mr. and Mrs. Negro — as I could live in a home where there was another boy.

James was an adorable child with big eyes and dark hair. He had dimples which seemed to be a topic of discussion every time anyone was introduced to us. When we were together, our difference in appearance and behavior were very noticeable. I didn't speak unless spoken to. Meanwhile, James had a bubbly personality that was infectious.

Just so you know, I did not know for several years that Emilio was not my father and that James was not my full brother. I should have figured it out. There was a recognizable difference in Papa's (Emilio's) behavior toward the two of us. It was obvious that James was his favorite. He held him on his lap and played with him. He smiled and laughed with him and raised him up into the air. He never smiled at me or held me that way. I did not know why. James wore new clothes while I wore hand-me-downs. James took dancing lessons. I was not asked if I wanted to take dancing lessons. Having to attend his recitals was especially unpleasant because it highlighted how differently we were treated. It wasn't until James went to school that I learned we had different last names. Go figure.

And go figure this — Emilio considered himself a candidate for sainthood because he was supporting someone else's child. He was the cook in the family, having been a chef earlier in his life. When we sat down to meals, he would hand me a plate already portioned out. James was asked what he wanted to eat and could have seconds. If I did not like what was on the plate, I was told it was that or nothing. Actually, that was a good thing. I learned to eat whatever was on my plate and continued to do so for the rest of my life.

I do not have many memories of those early years. I was told that when I was around four someone threw a large stone out of the sandbox where children were playing and it struck me in the left eye. I was taken to the hospital and had surgery. The doctors had to remove part of the pupil and I lost some of my vision. For years, I went through periods of wearing glasses and not wearing glasses. The doctors finally told me that if I didn't wear glasses, my right eye would get tired. So, I wore the glasses — silver-rimmed — just "perfect" for the no-personality kid that I was.

❋ ❋ ❋

Back to the family reunification. I told you it took some time. It was 1936 when my sisters were allowed to join us. I think I must have forgotten that I had two sisters until I noticed a dramatic change in Mom's personality. She smiled now — and even laughed sometimes. She was definitely a much happier person. That was about to change in a flash.

Emilio had developed what you could call an entrepreneurial spirit. He wanted to go into business for himself. Up until now, he had worked in a candy factory. He decided to lease the fourth and fifth floors of a five-story building on Main Street in Hartford. It was an ideal location for transients who wanted to live downtown.

When the authorities were made aware of his plans, they reneged on their plans to return my sisters. They were concerned that a rooming house was not a suitable home in which to raise young girls. When we could show that we had a suitable home for them, my sisters could come home. I would later wish I could tell them that it wasn't a suitable home for boys either — but more about that later.

Our new so-called home did not look like a home. Previously, we lived in a three-story apartment building on Morgan Street — just below Main Street. To arrive at our new home, we had to walk up four flights of stairs. That wasn't the only problem. At the head of the stairs, the first thing I saw was two bathrooms. Around the corner was a long hallway. The left side faced Main Street and the right side faced the roof of the building. There were six doors on the right and seven on the left. The difference was the exit that led to the roof. Go to the fifth floor and there were another 13 rooms. Each large enough to accommodate a double bed, a dresser, chair, and a closet.

Of the 13 rooms on the fourth floor, four were set aside for the family's living quarters. My parents' bedroom faced Main Street and across the hall was the kitchen and dining room. For some unexplained reason, the boys' bedroom was at the end of the hall just before the exit to the roof. Emilio planned to rent rooms primarily to men because he said they were less trouble than women (although he did rent to a few women). The men were now single, often having lived through failed marriages.

At my tender age, I certainly did not have a positive impression of marriage. I should add that my parents' union didn't help. I never saw my parents smile at each other or hold hands or even hug each other. Needless to say, I never saw them kiss. No "I saw Mommy kissing Santa Claus" here. It reinforced my later belief that Mom would have married anyone in order to get her kids back.

I was six years old when we moved to our new "home." There were 24 bedrooms that had to be taken care of every day. Mom had to make beds, dust floors, change linens and towels, wash windows and curtains, dust, and empty waste baskets. That was a full day's work.

Every Monday was wash day — and in those days all the linens were white. Mom would take the bottom sheet off the bed, place the top sheet on the bottom and add a clean sheet for the top. The bottom sheets were then taken to the kitchen where a ringer-type washing machine on wheels was rolled over to the sink. The sheets were then placed in the machine for the wash cycle.

When complete, each sheet had to be put through the ringer twice to remove whatever water remained. Now you know where they get the phrase "put through the ringer." The sheets were put through the ringer and so was I. That's because the sheets were placed in a straw basket that I had to carry up to the fifth floor via the iron stairway. It was my job to hang each sheet on the clothesline, which extended out about 50 feet. During the school year, I would do this chore after classes. This proved particularly challenging in winter because the sheets would freeze on the line and were difficult for a six-year-old to remove and carry down the stairs. When it rained or snowed on a Monday, we'd delay the process until the weather cooperated. I hated this chore. Laundry was heavy and wet and I had to struggle to carry the basket up and down those damn iron stairs.

Another tasking chore was taking out the trash. I had to take the barrels down four flights. Those barrels were heavy. I had to drag them down one at a time — plop, plop, plop. When empty, I would have to take them back up to the roof.

Oh, that's not all: The bedroom windows were washed once a month. For the Main Street side, Mom would sit on the windowsill and wash the outside while I washed the inside. For the roof side, I would wash both the inside and out.

If Monday was laundry day, Saturday was stair-washing day. I'd begin at the top of the fifth floor and work my way down to the street level. This was done with a pail of soapy water, rags and a brush. It had to be done and done right. Mom would inspect my work and it better be spotless or else I had to do it again. I learned at an early age that life was not a fairy tale (an interesting reference as I would learn shortly) and to do whatever I did to the best of my ability. I'd draw upon that lesson throughout my life.

So, you might be asking, where was James? Unlike me, he had lots of school friends and he was out playing with them. I was told that as the oldest, it was my responsibility to make sure the chores got done. Funny, I was always the oldest, so James was rarely involved in the hard work. Every once in a while, I would get to play ball with James and his friends. But I wasn't any good, so they didn't invite me very often.

It seems like the only time I got to spend time with my Mom was when we had to do chores. I know now that every time she looked at her me it reminded her that her daughters were not there. I don't think she realized how much I needed her. When I complained that I rarely saw her, she would say our work was saving money that would one day be enough for a down payment on a normal home. When I read the story in the Bible about the Prodigal Son, I understood very well how she felt and after that, I never complained.

I spent what spare time I had in the kitchen with Papa. As I said earlier, Emilio was the chef of the family. Three times a day, I would hear the speech about how lucky I was to have a meal. Sometimes, James would sneak me an extra slice of bread. That's one positive memory.

One Saturday, Papa took me shopping on Front Street for a new pair of shoes. I had holes in the old ones, so we went to push carts on Front Street where shoes tied to poles by the laces were sold. On this particular day, I would try on pairs until Papa said one fit. I told him that the pair hurt. Papa said they would stretch. When I said something to Mom, she said, "Of course, you are wearing two left feet."

Papa wasn't happy to have to make another trip to the "shoe department."

❀ ❀ ❀

Moving on — it is still 1936 — and the Connecticut River overflowed. My memory of this is vivid. As I walked to the Bulkeley Bridge which connects Hartford to East Hartford, I could see the water rising. There was a flooded parking lot, and a small house was under water. I could also see a boy I went to school with leaving that house in a rowboat. He was eating a jelly doughnut. I asked my mother how high would the water have to rise in order for me to have a jelly doughnut? I got slapped across the head for that one. The next day the water receded, and I forgot about the jelly doughnut.

I also vividly remember school. I listened, but rarely participated, unless called upon. It was custom at that time for the student to stand by their desk and answer a question when called upon. I would refuse to leave my seat in fear of giving the wrong answer and being laughed at. Because of this, I was a regular visitor to the principal's office.

"Not you again," he would say. My response was simple: Tell the teacher not to make me stand.

Here's something that won't shock you: I hated gym. I wasn't much of an athlete, and we had gym three times a week. After class, we were required to take a shower. Because I started school as an underdeveloped five-year-old, I was smaller than the other kids. They would stare at me. I later learned that I suffered from rickets, and it stunted my growth. My father was six-foot-four. I grew to be only five-foot-seven. Add to that my stepfather portioning out my meals, I didn't stand a chance. So, here I was with an under-developed body and let's not forget that eye surgery. Because I lacked peripheral vision and depth perception in my left eye, I couldn't see something being thrown at me until it was too late.

❊ ❊ ❊

So, when it came time to choose teams for football or baseball, I was always the last man standing — and that wasn't a good thing. I used to pray that a ball would not come to me. I had to endure a lot of ridicule and a lot of nicknames like four-eyes and sissy and the one that stuck: scarecrow.

One day when I was home, I stood in front of a full-length mirror and outstretched my arms. I did look like a scarecrow. The next time I was called scarecrow, I announced that I did look like a scarecrow. The kids did not call me scarecrow after that. I guess because it did not offend me.

One year, it was the last day of gym class. We played baseball and I got three hits. Don't ask me how. I was so excited; I spent the whole summer waiting to get back to school so that I could play baseball again. That excitement ended when I struck out three times.

Football was a whole other story. What position would I play? I wasn't strong enough for the line and could not judge catching the ball so I couldn't be a receiver. I had small hands and couldn't throw the ball, so quarterback was out of the question. So, they created a new position — that of water-boy. The joke may have been on me back then but later, who would believe that I would grow up to work for professional sports for 16 years?

I carried many a pail of water and I could also carry a tune. So, in sixth-grade music class, I was always seated in the last seat, the 5th seat, reserved for those who could carry a tune. When my teacher moved me to the 4th seat, I was furious, displaying Oscar-winning emotion. My teacher told me to stop screaming or I would be sorry. I did not know what she meant, but I stopped misbehaving.

Fast-forward to graduation day where we received a diploma, and some prizes were handed out. Suddenly, the principal shouted, "And the last award is for the Best All-Around Student."

There was absolute silence. I was not listening and the boy next to me poked me and said, "George, they just called out your name. Go get your award."

After the ceremony, that music teacher congratulated me and said that was the reason why I was asked to quiet down. I responded that I would have rather had my seat in the fifth row instead of the prize I had won.

Recalling this, I'm reminded of another life lesson learned in sixth grade — the school play. This particular year, it was "A Christmas Carol" and I was selected to play the role of Scrooge. I overheard teachers talking and they said that I was the only boy who could memorize all the lines that Scrooge had to learn. I immediately thought — me getting up on stage? Never.

For the next few weeks, we practiced, and I followed all the stage instructions. Everyone was excited about the play, except me. When the big day arrived, I was sick. Mom had to call the school to report my absence because I had a fever. She never knew I had the

13

role of Scrooge, so she was not suspicious of my illness. Here is that divine intervention that you will hear about throughout my life story.

Speaking of stories at school, we were reading fairy tales and this day, we focused on Cinderella. Each student read a portion out loud. When it was my turn, I realized the similarities in Cinderella's life to mine and shouted, "I am Cinderella!" The kids laughed and the teacher ignored my outburst. I don't know what I would have said if she had asked me to explain.

I liked fairy tales like Cinderella. They gave me hope for happy endings, but that was not to be for me. My princess never did appear.

Funny how I remember so much from sixth grade, as opposed to seventh or eighth at Henry Barnard Junior High. What I do remember is that that was the location in the summer from which the buses took off to take the kids to Camp Courant. To this day, it is an opportunity for inner city kids to see the countryside. James and I would board the bus early in the morning. For the first time, I got a glimpse of what other neighborhoods looked like, and I remember asking what those small buildings were — they were houses. James knew that because his friends lived in houses.

When we arrived at camp, it was in a wooded area. It was the first time I had seen real trees. We spent the day playing games. Some kids played baseball — I did not for all the reasons I've told you. Lunch was served at the same time each day – a peanut butter and jelly sandwich, a carton of milk, a couple of cookies, and a piece of fruit. In the middle of the afternoon, we had to board the bus to go home. We never left on time. That's because some kids did not want to go home, so they hid in the woods.

I should have been one of those kids.

• Chapter 2 •

The Rooming House Years

We lived as a family at the rooming house on 1097 Main Street for seven years. Except for trips to Camp Courant, my life was confined to the center of the city. Across the street from our building was a First National grocery store with a long metal sign above the entrance. During September 1938, there was a devastating hurricane which I watched from the 4th-floor window of my parents' bedroom. I was looking out from the window watching the heavy rain when suddenly the metal sign took off out of view. I called to my parents to come and see what had happened. They made me leave the room and I missed the rest of the hurricane. One of Papa's sons from his first marriage, Raymond, walked several miles to the McCook Hospital that night, where his first son was born during the hurricane.

During these years, there were eleven theaters within walking distance. Every major film studio had its own theaters where only its movies were shown. The Strand was owned by Warner Brothers, the Allyn by Paramount Pictures, the E. M. Loews by Columbia Pictures and the Loews Poli by Metro Goldwyn Mayer. Movies remained usually one week, then transferred to other theaters downtown and in the neighborhoods, where they remained until the audience declined. It cost 5 or 10 cents for children, and I think about 35 cents for adults. When "Gone with the Wind" was released, the price was 75 cents. I never heard a negative comment about the price because the film was such an outstanding critical success. There weren't any restrictions on children's attendance because language or graphic sex was not seen or heard in the movies at that time. Much was left to one's imagination, which I think made the scene more interesting than today's movies.

Speaking of language, I do not remember hearing swearing during conversation. I never heard the F word anywhere – not in school, on the street or in the rooming house. It was not spoken. At least, not when I was present.

Though only a child, I preferred dramas to musicals or Westerns. Bette Davis was my favorite screen personality. When her movies were shown at the Strand, which was just around the corner from home, my parents would have to come and get me out of the theater because I wanted to stay and see the movie again and again. She was unlike any other movie star ... unlike any woman I had ever seen. Every gesture and movement were exaggerated. I could not take my eyes off her. Her movies were always well attended, but I rarely saw anyone my age in the audience.

The State Theater was only a few hundred yards from the rooming house. It was said to be the largest theater in New England, seating 3,000 people on the main floor. There was a balcony, but I never knew why no one was permitted up there. This theater was unique among theaters. The top musical entertainers of the day appeared there in live performances; anyone who was popular or had a hit record appeared at the State. Singers, as well as the big bands of the time were featured. It was a time when singers were not only part of the band but also were now beginning to be personalities in their own right. In the '30s, '40s and '50s, all the popular entertainers played the State.

Every Sunday after lunch, I would walk to the State Theater and remain until I sat in the first row, aisle seat, right in front of the stationary microphone. Unlike musical performers of today who run back and forth across the entire stage, at that time singers stood in front of the microphone and did not move while singing. When I entered the theater, I would find a single seat in the rear. The stage show lasted about an hour and then a Monogram Western was shown on the screen. Most of the audience would begin to leave after the live performance, and I would push my way forward to find a seat closer to the stage. After three performances, I would arrive at my destination, the aisle seat in the first row.

Glenn Miller, Artie Shaw, Benny Goodman, Duke Ellington, and Count Basie were names I remember. Singers Patti Page, Johnny Ray, Ella Fitzgerald, Dean Martin and groups like the Mills Brothers, Ink Spots and the Harmonicats, to name a few, were others I remembered seeing from my front-row seat. Because of the size of the theater, all these performers appeared during the peak of their popularity, which made the State Theater the place to be on weekends. And because of the 3,000 seats, performers earned more than in other theaters in the country.

I saw Frank Sinatra three times from the front row center. Sinatra's first visit was an event. His first appearance at the State caused a city-wide traffic jam. It seemed that people from all over Connecticut and western Massachusetts had converged on downtown Hartford. Thousands came to the city to see and hear the first teen idol of the generation. The theater was located down Village Street, which connected to Main Street. People were standing in line all the way up to Main Street and then down Morgan Street to the entrance of the Bulkeley Bridge. People did not mind standing in line because they knew there were 3,000 seats waiting for them.

What I Remember …

After the last show, I thought about going backstage to see Sinatra and tell him I thought Columbia Records, for whom he recorded, was not doing right by him. I felt they were requiring him to sing songs that were well out of his range, and he seemed to be straining his voice to sing them. I did take a few steps toward the rear of the theater, and then changed my mind. Why would he listen to some teenager with a criticism like that?

When I arrived home, I was animated in conversation about Sinatra's performance. I kept telling them that he was going to be popular for a long time. No one seemed to be impressed with my enthusiasm or prediction. In their minds, this was just another teenage fad.

• Chapter 3 •

Always Hungry

When I wasn't in a theater, I was out on the streets making money. My first job, at 10-years-old, was selling the afternoon paper, The Hartford Times. Some of the other kids who also sold the paper would walk along the streets approaching adults who might want a copy. I thought I could sell more papers in a shorter time, standing in front of the entrance to the Travelers Insurance Company and waiting for the employees to leave after the workday. It took me only a few minutes to sell all my papers. The paper cost three cents. Employees would throw three cents at my pile of papers, grab one, and run for the bus which would take them home. One employee would grab a paper and run away without paying. He did this a few times. One day I waited for him. When he reached for the paper and started to run away, I tripped him, and he fell to the ground. He never cheated me again.

One summer I worked on a produce truck operated by an immigrant who spoke little English. Papa knew him and he offered him my services. The man would drive his truck, stocked with fresh vegetables and fruits, to the outskirts of the city. He would park half-way up a street and clang a bell to inform residents he had arrived. I would total the cost of a purchase, make change when necessary and bag the items. Sometimes I would get a nickel tip from the lady making the purchase when I carried the bag to her door. When all the customers were served, we went on to the next street.

When I was 13 years old, I applied for a shoeshine license from the city. My number was 13 and there were particular locations where one could shine shoes marked "BB," for bootblack. It cost five cents for a shine. I would approach servicemen in uniform because they almost always gave a five-cent tip. I set a goal of $4 for the day. When it was nearing darkness, I would seek out any male and tell him I could not go home until I had made $4 for the day. It always worked.

Funny thing, I could not make myself stand up in class to answer a question, but I did not have a problem approaching strangers to earn a nickel.

❁ ❁ ❁

During the rooming house years, I was always hungry. I ate what Papa put on the plate. When you are hungry, your stomach makes funny noises and you have difficulty sleeping. On these occasions, I would sneak down the hall to the kitchen and look for leftovers in the refrigerator that I could take and would not be noticed the next day.

There was always Jell-O, and if some of the Jell-O had already been eaten, I would place two fingers under the opening in the dish and take some. I overlooked the fact that the remaining Jell-O would slide to the bottom of the dish. No one seemed to notice the missing Jell-O. I would repeatedly let it be known how much I enjoyed Jell-O, and since Mom was the one who made the dish, I could always count on finding some in the refrigerator.

Italian bread was a staple at our meals. There was an Italian bakery just around the corner and whenever we needed bread, I would be sent to buy a loaf at the Moon Bakery. The one-pound loaf was twelve cents, and they sold a half-pound loaf for six cents. Fresh bread had an aroma like no other food. I walked home with the bread under my arm. I thought of myself as the William Penn of Hartford.

At mealtime, I became aware that Papa did not remove the entire loaf of bread from the bag, but took out just enough for the meal and sliced it. On the way home one day, I remembered this fact. I took the end of the bread from the bag and pulled off a hunk and ate away. Then I pulled out the remainder of the loaf, reversed it and placed it back in the bag with the missing hunk end inside the bag. I calculated that no one would notice it for several days. I thought it strange that he never commented on the missing bread.

Mom rarely ate meals with the family. She was too busy with her chambermaid duties. Because she worked day and night, we did not have to hire help and the money saved was set aside for a down payment on a normal home. Most important, it would mean the return of her daughters. I am positive that if Mom had eaten with the family, I would have had more to eat and would probably not have had the underdeveloped body I had. Also, Mom would not have tolerated Papa's telling me "how lucky I was."

Mom rarely raised her voice in anger, but there was a situation that always raised her temperature. When Papa would want to spend some of the savings, Mom would object loudly. "That's the down payment on our new home. Why do you think I work like a slave every day?" Her tone and volume put Papa on the defensive and he dropped the subject.

❈ ❈ ❈

An unexpected event would cause a dramatic change in our lives, as well as that of all Americans. It was Sunday, December 7,1941. James and I had gone to the movies. When we left the theater, there were lots of people in the streets talking about the Japanese attack on Pearl Harbor. The next day, when we were home from school for lunch, President Roosevelt was on the radio declaring war on Japan with his "all we have to fear, is fear itself" speech. I was now eleven years old and did not understand the seriousness of the attack.

Overnight, the country became incredibly patriotic. The people became much more serious. First came the draft of every eligible male. Before long, almost every family was touched by the war and had someone who was serving our country, either as a draftee or an enlistee. The Hartford area was one of the country's mobilizing centers. Pratt & Whitney, Colt's Firearms and other factories were converted to producing war materials. Around-the-clock employment was now available to women, as well as men, who were not serving in the military.

Every family received a coupon book for products that were being rationed, such as meat, eggs, butter and other items that were needed for what was called the "war effort." There was a grocery store nearby called Mohican Market that was famous for the baked goods made on the premises in full view of customers. In the center of the floor was an island surrounded by glass where customers could stand and watch bakery products being created. My favorite was cream puffs. They were huge and filled with freshly made whipped cream. They sold for three cents each but were sold only when the ingredients were available. There was not any announcement that rationed products would be available. It became known when lines would form outside the store.

I don't know how people knew there were rationed items available. It was as if people were hiding in doorways just waiting for the news. Crowds would build so quickly that the Mohican management had to restrict admittance to a manageable few at a time. Long lines of people would suddenly develop, seemingly out of thin air. Everyone carried their ration books with them at all times so they would be ready when rationed items were available. Trading coupons with others was prohibited. One could not remove the coupons in their book; only store personnel could do so.

After a while, if you were lucky enough to buy a hard-to-get item, you would do so even if you did not need it for yourself. You reasoned that you could trade it with someone who would.

There was a store on Main Street called Silver Slipper which sold women's hosiery. It was located on the second floor of the building and the only access was a long flight of stairs. Nylon stockings had recently been introduced and were very popular with the women. Since they were not a necessity, coupons for them were not in the ration book. You could buy them whenever they were available. Mom gave me money to keep and told me to watch that location for any sign that nylons were on sale.

One day, while walking along Main Street, I noticed women leaving that stairway with smiles on their faces. I knew something was on sale and I ran to the stairway. It was so crowded with women trying to get upstairs, that women who had made a purchase had to battle their way out to the street level. I was the only male in the stairway. As women tried to walk down the stairs, I would ask them what was on sale. It was nylons. The women laughed out loud when they heard me ask if 51 gauge were on sale. I did not know what that meant; I only knew that was what Mom wore and was what I should ask for if I should reach the counter before the "Sold Out" sign was put up.

❋❋❋

What I Remember …

Everyone seemed to be in a serious mood all the time, probably thinking about their loved ones overseas serving their country. Every sacrifice or change in lifestyle was accepted willingly. I don't remember any anti-war conversations or demonstrations or objections to the sacrifices people were asked to endure. Everyone who wanted a job could find one. People saved their money. What else could they do with it? Most everything you would buy for yourself, or your home, was not for sale in stores.

The radio and newspapers were the only source of information about the war. The radio announcers just reported the news; there wasn't any commentary. No opinions or discussion in print. The news was managed by the government, and no one seemed to object. It was a time when there was great trust in our leaders. Anyway, that is how it appeared to this 11-year-old. Names of casualties were not printed in the paper. When there was a huge battle somewhere in places I never heard of, the news sometimes reported that there were "hundreds or thousands" of casualties. Families dreaded receiving Western Union telegrams. They delivered the news that a member of the family was a casualty, missing in action, or dead.

Hollywood produced movies that were mostly propaganda and helped keep spirits high. When an American flag appeared on the screen, there was applause and cheers from the audience. If someone had even suggested burning our flag in demonstration against the war, I think a public execution would have followed. Anyone wearing a military uniform was treated like a hero. Some storekeepers refused payment for a purchase. Meals were on the house in many restaurants. Everyone knew that servicemen earned only $21 a month as a Private, with small increases as they were promoted in rank. While there were women in the Service, most people thought of the war as men fighting other men.

A new mailing system was announced. It was called V-mail. It was a very lightweight paper on which you wrote your message. With so many letters going overseas, and so little space on airplanes or ships, this method enabled more mail to be delivered in a short time to our loved ones.

❋ ❋ ❋

In the summer of 1943, I began what continued for four years – working on the tobacco farms in Windsor, a nearby town. The company truck would pick me up at 7 a.m. The workday was 8 to 5 with an hour off for lunch, which I brought from home in a brown bag. I was a picker of tobacco, and I would travel the rows on my knees. At the end of the day, my knees really hurt from the sores on them.

At lunch time, some of the boys and I went swimming in a dirty pond near the tobacco fields. When it was time to return to work, the supervisor would come to the pond and blow a whistle. On this particular day, as I swam to dry ground, I cut my hand on a board with a rusty nail and was rushed to the hospital where a large number of stitches was needed to close the wound.

The next day, over the objections of my parents, I was back on the job. I was not going to lose a day's pay. I wore a glove over my right hand and picked tobacco with my left hand. I was able to keep up with the slowest of the pickers. For years, I could see what I thought was a black spot where the stitches were. I would scratch at it but was never able to remove it. Some years later, still preoccupied with that black spot on my palm, I was able to grab hold of it, and I pulled out a black thread that was at least an inch long.

25

If that injury had happened in later years, parents would have brought legal action against the tobacco company for negligence. No one thought about lawsuits in those days, except maybe the more educated. Poor people accepted every negative in life. It was just part of living. It was a more or less "get over it" attitude, which I adopted for myself. That attitude helped me get through the rough spots in later life.

Chapter 4

A Real Home

We had now been living in the rooming house for seven years. It was 1943 and the war was continuing. Something dramatic was about to happen. A change in our living quarters was about to take place. The money that was being saved through Mom's work as a chambermaid was about to pay off. We now had enough money for a down payment on a two-family house in the north end of the city on Addison Street.

James was less interested in moving than I was. He had a good life and lots of friends. I knew how much this meant to Mom for it meant her daughters would finally be coming home to live with us. It had been twelve years ... twelve empty years for Mom. Years that would never be recovered. Years when her daughters were growing into young women. They were babies when the state took them from her. I was still too young to understand what a traumatic period these twelve years had been for her. I had my own reason for joy. Papa was not coming to live with us. He would remain at the rooming house, and we would see him on weekends if the business allowed.

Mom would now be the head of the household. Where Papa had been the chef in our family, Mom would now be preparing meals. It would be interesting to see what we would eat now that she was the cook. After all, she had not cooked a meal in seven years. I knew one thing – no more would I hear "how lucky I was" as each meal was served.

Our new home at 15 Addison Street was a two-family structure, with the previous owner continuing to live on the second floor until their new home in West Hartford was ready to be occupied. It was stipulated in the sales documents that the previous owner was building a new home, and it was expected to be completed in a few months.

Because of the war, a rent-control policy had been enacted by Congress to prevent landlords from taking advantage of tenants. New housing almost ceased being built during the war because those materials were needed for the war effort. Without rent control, landlords could take advantage of the shortage in housing and raise rents at will. I make a point of this because the previous owners made an application through the rent control office to remain where they lived and were repeatedly given three-month extensions. We did not know at the time how this would impact our lives down the road.

Our new home had five rooms. There was a living and dining room, kitchen and two bedrooms. Mom slept in the back bedroom and James and I shared the other one. There was a paved driveway along the side of the house, where cars could be parked. We did not own a car. The house was heated by a gigantic coal furnace in the basement, which I learned immediately to operate. There was a window adjacent to the furnace, and a large wooden enclosure where coal was stored and used as needed. The furnace was really a monstrosity with overhead vents that carried the heat to the five rooms above. The second floor had its own furnace on the other side of the basement with the same setup.

I had new chores given to me. During the winter months, in addition to taking care of the furnace, I would shovel snow off the sidewalks and the driveway. I took the garbage to the street each week. There was a small corner grocery store operated by a family, which I visited several times a day. I would buy only what I could carry home. Selection of items was limited, usually only one brand of each item. Nothing was priced. The owner would calculate the total cost with paper and pencil. Products had little or no nutritional information or warnings.

When supermarkets came into existence, everything changed. We shopped once a week and spent a lot of time looking over all the choices we had. The corner grocery store was visited only for items like milk and bread.

• **Chapter 5** •

New School, New Friends

Once a week, I would spend an afternoon after school sorting through the ashes that fell to the bottom of the furnace. It would not occur to me to cover my face or head and, after two or three hours of sifting through the ashes looking for pieces of coal that had not burned through, I was a mess. My face and hair were white with dust and my throat was very dry. Looking in the mirror, I commented that I would be distinguished-looking when I was an old man. I considered the afternoon time well spent when I could look at the pail, filled with small pieces of coal I had found while sifting the ashes. Each evening before going to bed, I would go to the furnace and place small pieces of coal over the larger ones in the furnace. By filling the spaces between the coals, they burned more slowly and hopefully would last until the next morning. If the fire burnt out overnight, I would build a new fire with paper and wood before going off to school.

With Mom now the cook in the family, our meals took on a different look. Papa had concentrated on soups, stews and pasta. Mom varied the menu and, for the first time on the dinner table, there were vegetables I had never eaten before. After I had eaten what was on my plate, I was asked if I wanted more to eat. That also had never happened in the past.

It was a new experience not to go to bed hungry. No need to sneak down the hall to the kitchen and look for something to eat after the others had gone to sleep.

❄ ❄ ❄

Living in a different part of the city meant I would be going to a new school for the 9th grade. I was enrolled in Northeast Junior High as a freshman. It was a difficult adjustment for me, being so shy and introverted. At Henry Barnard the students were the same ones I went to school with at Brown School. These students were not very welcoming to this newcomer. My appearance and personality did not help.

The change at the dinner table came too late to reverse the damage rickets had done to my body. My upper body had not developed normally. I was reminded of my appearance while I was examined by the doctor at the beginning of the school year. Before the doctor had come into the examining room, I was asked to take my clothes off from the waist up. When the doctor came into the room and saw me, he started to laugh and said softly to the nurse that he had never seen such a weak upper body on a 13-year-old.

One year later, I went to another school. This time it was Weaver High School, which was quite a distance from home. I had walked to Northeast Junior High, but now I would be taking a bus to Weaver. There were five of us, four boys and one girl who took the bus each day to Weaver. We sat together at the back of the bus, and they became my first friends. It was the first time I was with children, my own age, outside of school.

I was invited to their homes, sometimes for meals. We usually ended up playing cards. They taught me the rules. I was a serious card player and suddenly very competitive, wanting to win every hand, while the others talked and joked while playing. I would remind them to concentrate on the game. We would play for pennies. I had a paper route in the neighborhood and made $2 or $3 a week delivering the afternoon paper. I was allowed to keep my money and spend it as I wished. Usually, I would win or lose less than a dollar.

We moved our card games from home to home, sometimes playing late into the evening. One weekend we played all day Sunday until very late into Monday morning and did not go to school that day. I was a senior at that time and had not only never missed a single day of school, but also I was never late for school. When I did not appear, the school office called my home, concerned about my absence.

I did not tell my mother that I overslept, and she assumed I was in school. Even though the caller told her that my absence would be overlooked because it was the first time, Mom angrily told the caller to give me the strongest penalty for playing hooky. I was given a cipher, the only demerit for my three years and one which prevented me from being acknowledged at the graduation ceremonies.

• Chapter 6 •

The Nightmare was Real

One Sunday afternoon, we decided to play cards at nearby Keney Park. Someone brought along a blanket, and we spent the afternoon playing pinochle. I had a terrible day, losing game after game, until my losses exceeded the incredible sum of $10. The winners allowed me to give them I.O.U.s, at which time we called it a day and went home. My losses meant I would be without petty cash for a month or more. I could not believe the bad luck I had all day.

Some weeks later, Lenny, who was not a player at the pinochle disaster, and I were having a silly argument over nothing and the subject of friendship came up. Lenny remarked that he, not the others, was my best friend. He explained to my amazement that my losses at Keney Park were not due to lack of luck. The others had collaborated on a plan to cheat while playing the games.

I was devastated. I did not want to believe that anyone would do such a thing. I was not mature enough to understand what had happened. Why would anyone do such a thing to a friend? These were my first friends. I thought friends were someone special in a person's life. It really hurt me. It was an emotion I had not felt up to this time. I was so naive and trusting and so very angry. I tried to rationalize what had happened. Did

I do something to make them want to teach me a lesson? This was the first time anything like this had happened to me. How was I to deal with it?

I left Lenny and walked home all the time trying to make some sense of it all. I was in a daze. What should I do? Should I just ignore it – say nothing – go on as before? I knew I could never look at them the same way. I decided to end what was left of this friendship. I sat alone in the front of the bus. I declined invitations to the movies, bowling and especially the opportunity to play cards. I would simply remove them from my life. I would have nothing to do with them again. It never entered my mind to confront them, so if they wondered why I was suddenly unavailable, no one said a word. Every so often, James or Mom would inquire why I was not spending any time with my friends. I would make up some excuse that seemed to satisfy them.

A behavioral pattern developed as a result of that incident. Whenever I had a serious disagreement that could not be resolved but was so serious as to make future communication difficult, I would simply end the relationship. I would just dismiss that person from any future involvement. Some would say that was immature of me, and maybe it was, but it was certainly less stressful not to waste time with someone with whom I preferred not to associate. It reinforced my belief that the only real solution to such matters lay in three simple words — GET OVER IT.

✿ ✿ ✿

Life in our new home was good. Life without Papa was *really good*. When he would come home on the weekends, I was a different person. All he had to do was walk through the doorway, and I would crawl back into my shell, the shell I hid in during all those rooming house years. I cannot explain my reaction to his presence. After all, he never abused me physically. I do not know what caused me to fear him, but I was much happier when he returned to the rooming house.

❖ ❖ ❖

One Saturday afternoon in July of 1944, while picking tobacco, the supervisor suddenly whistled for us workers to come out of the fields. We were going home. As we boarded the truck, we were told that there was a fire in Hartford where the Ringling Brothers Circus had set up its tent. The location was on Barbour Street, about a mile from our home.

When I arrived at home, I learned James had gone to the circus. Mom was a basket case, worrying about her baby. I left the house and ran up Tower Avenue. I could see and smell the smoke but could not get near the tent for all the police and fire personnel and equipment parked along the road. I was told to go home. When I returned home, James was there. He had intended to go to the circus and try to sneak in under the tent, but he was caught by circus personnel each time. He said he went around the entire tent looking for an opening but could not find one and just gave up and started walking back home. On the way, he met some boys that he knew, and he stayed with them before continuing on his way. He said he could hear the sirens and see the smoke, but never thought it was coming from the circus tent.

Later that day and into the evening, the radio broadcast the names of those lives lost in the fire. The list kept getting longer as more bodies were found and identified. To us boys, it was just a list of names. Mom was in tears and turned off the radio, knelt on the floor and prayed. James and I did not appreciate the horror of that fire until we recognized the name of a neighbor and her daughter. Over 150 people died in that fire. Circuses were not

35

allowed to play under tents in the state after that. In the future, the circus would play at the State Armory and later, the Civic Center. I went once, but it was not the same.

A few days later, I went back to work at the tobacco farm. As with my shoeshine money, I gave my tobacco money to Mom. One day Papa asked for some of the money and she refused him, saying it would buy me new clothes for school, money that he would not have to spend. I guess she felt that would make a bigger impact on him. He understood that message and the conversation ended.

❋ ❋ ❋

Up to now, this story has been mostly about what I remember. Now it is time for some of what I wish I could forget. James and I slept in a double bed in the rooming house at the end of the hall near the exit to the roof. He slept on the side of the bed nearest the door, and I slept nearest the window. It was summertime, and our windows were wide open.

I was about 8 years old, and asleep, when I awoke to find someone at the side of the bed with his head bowed down. It was a man ... a man I did not recognize. He lifted his head and asked me where Mary's room was. Mary was a divorced woman who lived on the 5th floor. He asked me to take him to her room, and I took him up the back fire escape to Mary's room.

I came back to my room and went to bed. I had an unusual feeling but could not explain it. In the morning, I asked James if he had heard anything the night before and he said he had not. For the longest time, I believed I had dreamed the incident even though my body told me something unusual happened. I did not mention it to James, because I did not know what to tell him. And if it was a dream, what was the point?

It was four years later that I knew it was not a dream.

I had gone to the Allyn Theater that afternoon. The theater itself was nothing unusual, except for the staircase leading to the men's restroom. It was very wide, and I enjoyed running up and down those stairs, taking two and three at a time. During the movie, I needed to visit the restroom. I arrived in the restroom and was alone at the urinal when, a few seconds later, I realized there was someone on either side of me. That seemed strange because the room must have had a dozen urinals, so I wondered why would anyone stand next to me? Before I could zip up, I was turned around by two teenage boys. Each grabbed an arm, and one put his other hand over my mouth and told me not to yell. Two other boys were there, with one standing at the entrance playing security guard and watching for anyone who might be coming.

The other boy went to his knees and performed what I would later come to know as oral sex. After a few minutes (which seemed much longer), they changed places. Then the "security guard" spoke up. Someone was coming. They let go of me and all four ran up the stairs. I ran into one of the stalls. I was shaking and almost to tears. I was bewildered.

Why did they do that? They did not hurt me, but I kept wondering ... why did they do that? I sat there for a long time, afraid to leave, for fear they might come back or be waiting for me upstairs or outside the theater. When the movie ended, the restroom filled with several men. I waited for them to leave and followed them up the stairs and ran home.

At age 12, I did not have any knowledge whatsoever of the word sex. I don't think I ever heard the word. Unlike today's culture that has children having children at that age, I

knew nothing about it. I did know that I experienced
something that would have to be my little secret. I wondered
if it happened only to me or if other boys also had the same
experience. Who could I talk to about this weird happening?
Since at that time I did not have any friends or even
associations with other boys, there was no one to talk about it.

• **Chapter 7** •

It Would have to Remain My Secret

In one way, I was pleased, because now I knew that something did happen four years ago. I was not dreaming. I was sure of that, because that strange feeling I felt four years ago had returned, and I now knew that man had performed oral sex on me, a boy of 8 years old. This time it was young boys, and the first time it was an adult. I was mystified why they did what they did, and why they did it to me. Is this something all men do as they grow older? Nothing made sense to me.

Today, at the sight of a "men's room" sign I relive the fear of that day. To this day, if I should walk into a men's room and find myself alone, I would immediately leave. I did not know one could relive a time in the past as though it were happening now. My body would be trembling. I would have to remind myself that it was my imagination ... it was not being repeated this day. Of course, I did not mention this incident to anyone. I did not know how to explain it. What would Papa say if I told him what happened? Would he punish me if I told him? I decided it would have to remain my secret.

Years later when I saw the movie "Gone with The Wind," the scene where Clark Gable carries Vivien Leigh upstairs to the bedroom reminded me of that day and the staircase in the Allyn Theatre. I relived that scene with the four boys. I had to leave my seat, because I started to get emotional and was afraid the other patrons would notice. I have seen that movie many times since, and that scene always brings back the memory of that strange and terrifying occurrence.

I could not know that an even more horrific incident would occur a few years later.

• **Chapter 8** •

The Teenage Years

As I approached my 13th birthday, I was beginning to come out of my shell. I joined in conversation with the family, I felt free to voice an opinion when speaking with others. I no longer considered myself a "Cinderella."

When I was asked, as most children are, "What do you want to be when you grow up?" I would answer, "I don't know, but whatever it is, I am going to be good at it." I cannot imagine why I would say such a thing because I was not good at anything. I didn't have thoughts about the future; I took every day as it came, never thinking about tomorrow.

In school I studied just enough to pass the course, not interested in getting an "A." I paid attention in class, but rarely participated unless called upon. I would refuse to stand by my seat to answer the question. If I did not know the answer, I was afraid the kids would laugh at me. I was a regular visitor to the principal's office. "Not you again," he would say. I would answer that he should tell the teacher not to require me to stand.

Mom had completed only the 8th grade and did not place much emphasis on school. I believe she sent me to school because that was the law. She did ask regularly if I had done my homework. I usually answered that I did it in school during a study period. I did listen to the teachers in class and had a good

41

memory, so I did okay on tests. I was not competitive in class the way I was when playing cards.

I was fortunate to attend Weaver High because most of the students were Jewish and were serious students planning on attending college. Jewish holidays were days off for Jewish students. In the Latin class, I was the only student on those holidays and thought I was the one who had a holiday. The Jewish boys rarely participated in sports outside of gym class, the way the other boys did. One boy told me that Jewish parents were very strict about studying. They wanted their children to attend a college to prepare for a career that would achieve financial independence for them.

In my family, attending college was never a subject of discussion. College was for rich people. No one in our extended family ever attended a college, much less graduated. No one in the neighborhood ever spoke of going to college when they graduated from high school. I could not even tell you where a college was located in Connecticut.

Now that we had a real home, what the family did discuss was the expected arrival of my sisters, Marion and Estelle. Marion was 16 years old and Estelle 14 when I saw them for the first time. While I did live with them as a baby, I did not remember them at all. Living in a rooming house, and not having neighbors in the center of the city, I don't think I ever heard the word "sister." Mom always referred to them as her daughters. I was told that my sisters had the same mother and father that I did. James had the same mother, but a different father and last name.

Mom was a different person. It was obvious that the expected arrival of her daughters was a real big deal. Whenever we had visitors, she spoke of them coming home soon. She was animated

... a different person than the one I had come to know. For the first time, I saw a smiling and happy woman.

Except for an occasional visit to the foster parents' home, Mom did not have any real contact with her daughters for more than 12 years. She missed all those wonderful moments parents cherish watching their children grow up. The depth of her loss was not apparent to me until much later in my life. I had led such a sheltered life as a youth that I did not appreciate the pain of having one's babies raised by some strangers. Just a few days before they arrived, Mom bought a new bedroom set for the back room and moved her bedroom into what had been the dining room. In the future, we would eat in the kitchen. I knew now that these girls were special.

Marion soon found a job at the Travelers Insurance Co., and Estelle and I became close, very close. We took the same bus to Weaver High, and I suppose she looked after her younger brother, trying to make up for lost time. I am sure Estelle knew more about me than I knew about her. We never discussed what it was like for them, knowing that even though their mother was close by, they rarely saw her.

Mr. and Mrs. Negro were exceptional foster parents. They treated my sisters as though they were their own daughters and years later, on special occasions when the Negro family was invited, they were especially friendly to me. Mrs. Negro always remarked how proud she was of me. They remembered my birthdays with gifts. I began to think of them as a second family. For all the time that Marion and Estelle lived with them, and until their deaths, they always addressed their foster parents as Ma and Pa. The fact that they were Italian made the transition easier because Mom and Papa were also Italian.

43

Estelle was beautiful … a natural beauty. In fact, the first time I saw Hedy Lamarr in the movies, I said to myself, "She looks just like Estelle." This sister of mine was a free spirit and a tomboy. In the summertime we occasionally went to a state park for a Sunday outing. Baseball was always on the agenda. Estelle was a joy to watch. She could hit and field as well as any of the boys or men playing. It would not surprise you that I did not participate.

I say Estelle was a natural beauty because I never saw her fussing around with a mirror or makeup. In the morning, she was the last one out of bed. I would leave the house to catch the bus and call to her to hurry or she would miss the bus. The bus driver, usually the same one every day, would pull the bus to the corner so he could look up the street to see if Estelle was coming. When he saw her coming around the corner, he would yell out to the passengers that she was on her way and the students would start cheering for her to run even faster. When she boarded the bus, applause and whistles greeted her. The bus driver would tell her, "You make my day!" This routine was almost a daily occurrence.

Marion had a boyfriend who was in the Marines. Pat was not only handsome in his uniform, but he also had a winning personality. What a catch for any girl, I thought. But what is it they say? Life is what happens to you when you are planning other things. And life did just that to Marion.

The three-month extensions that the Carusos (the aforementioned previous owners of our new home) had sought from the Housing Authority during the construction delay on their new home in West Hartford, turned into years. Extension after extension added up to over three years. During this time, my parents were helpless because they were told by their attorney that they could not appeal the decision. The situation became even more complicated when Justin, the son of the Carusos, returned home from the Navy after the war was over.

Justin, or Chet as he was known (don't ask me why), took a liking to Marion and now she was being courted by a Marine and a former Navy man. Unfortunately for Pat, he was away on duty, while Chet was upstairs developing a relationship that became serious. Chet was nothing like Pat. Where Pat was friendly, warm, considerate, and respectful, and had the unanimous approval of the family, Chet was temperamental, emotional and had a short fuse. He could be violent at times, too. Both families tried in vain to discourage the relationship.

During an argument with his mother, who did not think Marion was suitable for her darling son, Chet struck her, and she fell to the floor. His excuse for his behavior was that he was defending the woman he planned to marry. I was only 15 years old at the time, but I advised Marion to put an end to the relationship. I told Marion that anyone who would strike his mother would someday do the same to her. It seemed the more the family disapproved of Chet, the more she defended him, and they soon announced their engagement.

Apparently, love does strange things to people. No sensible person would trade Pat for Chet. Our family was devastated. It must be among the strongest pains for a mother, to have to watch your child make a serious mistake and be powerless to do anything about it. Why was it so clear to all of us, but not to Marion?

The even bigger decision lay ahead. How to tell Pat, who is fighting in a war, that the woman he was fighting for, and planned to marry, had chosen another. I don't know how she did it, but somehow, she found the words. His family was worried about Pat. How would he accept the news? In a war, one has to be on his guard all the time. Would this most unexpected news affect his concentration?

Now, our two families would be united by marriage. Chet's mother Lucy was a loud-mouthed gossip that I took a dislike to immediately. It was obvious Chet took after her. Lucy's husband, Joe, was a gentle, quiet man. Talk about mismatches. I could hear her on many occasions screaming at him, but never heard a response. He drank a lot, who could blame him? There was so much tension in that family. Sometimes the yelling was so loud, I would hide in the bathroom just waiting for violence to occur. I guess the liquor helped him tune Lucy out. I believed the less I had to do with her, the better.

• Chapter 9 •

Alone & 16 in New York City

When I was 16 years old, I asked Mom if I could go to New York City, after school closed, to celebrate that milestone. As I had said previously, personal safety was not an issue, and I did not have any fear of travelling to the big city by myself. I had seen an ad in the Hartford Courant promoting $2 a night at the Allen House. With savings of about $20, I thought I would have enough money for travel, food and room for two days. So sometime after school closed, I took the train to NYC with a small overnight bag and went directly to the Allen House. It was a tall building just off off-Broadway. After I registered, I took my bag up to my room and decided to tour Times Square.

I walked up and down Broadway, taking the side streets where many of the theaters of Broadway were located. On the corner of 49th Street and Broadway was a restaurant called McGinnis', which featured roast beef. About waist-high the brick had been replaced with a sliding glass window. A passerby could stand there and watch a chef carve roast beef and place it on a small dinner roll, which sold for 49 cents. I stood at the window watching the chef do his thing and he noticed me. I must have looked like a starved homeless person because he handed me a sandwich, saying "here kid, you look hungry." I would continue my travel and return to McGinnis' every hour or so and stand at

47

the window. I did not have to buy supper that evening because the chef fed me every time I stopped there.

Finally, it was getting late and I was tired of walking up and down all those streets, so I headed for the Allen House. I was not only tired but also feeling very greasy because of the city air, so I decided I would take a shower before going to bed. As I walked down the hall to my room, I noticed a light in an open door and looked in to see a shower room with about a dozen shower heads. At the time I did not realize that I did not have a shower or bathtub in my room. So, I undressed, wrapped myself in a towel and headed for the shower room. As a child in gym class, I had faced the wall while showering because the other kids showering were staring at me and my underdeveloped body.

I finished my shower and turned to get my towel when I saw, on the other side of the room, a huge Black man looking at me. He had this weird grin on his face that was eerie, and he kept sticking his tongue out and passing it over his lips. I was immediately uncomfortable and took my towel and left the room without drying off. Hurrying down the hallway, I reached my room, put the key in the door and there he was, behind me. He pushed the door open, and shoved me forward, so that I landed on the bed. I was experiencing a fear I had never known. I thought I was going to die in this hotel and if he took my wallet, I would not be identified. I was panicked, breathing heavily.

I cried out, "I don't have much money, only enough to get back home."

He answered in a Bela Lugosi voice, "I don't want your money, I want this." He pulled the towel off me, turned me over, and grabbed my crotch. He was smiling, seemingly satisfied with what he saw. He knelt down beside the bed. He was so aggressive, I thought he might chew it off. I began screaming and the look he gave me silenced me instantly.

The emotional state I was experiencing made it impossible for an erection and after some time, he angrily gave up his attempt at oral sex and got up and left the room. I got up from the bed, rushed to the door and locked it. I put a chair under the door handle (I had seen that done in the movies) and planned to get dressed and leave the hotel that very night. I was still trembling and sobbing at the same time. I changed my mind about leaving, fearing the man might still be on the floor and who knew how he would react at seeing me. I waited out the night. I could not sleep. Whenever I closed my eyes, the guy was there licking his chops.

The next morning, I put my things together and checked out of the hotel. I had planned to stay another night, but after last night I couldn't wait to leave and get home. I did not mention the incident to the desk clerk because all I could tell him was that a big Black man had attacked me. Looking around the lobby there were several large Black men, none of whom was my attacker. I had unknowingly booked a room at the YMCA. No wonder it was only $2 a night.

The train ride home seemed to take forever. There were many empty seats. Not much traffic on a Saturday morning travelling from New York City to Hartford. It was a good thing there were not many travelers because every so often I would start trembling and crying, reliving the night before.

When I arrived home, Mom asked me why I had shortened my visit. I told her I had seen everything I wanted to and, under my breath added, more than I wanted to. However, recalling that incident, even now as I write this story, brings back that terrifying night as though it were yesterday. For several years, whenever I

49

passed a YMCA while driving, I would pull over to the first space I could find, while I tried to recover from the memory of the horror of that evening.

❊ ❊ ❊

Let us return to the rest of my story.

It is June 1947 and another graduation. It was a very hot June evening. The senior class, all 388 students, would be sitting on the stage of the Bushnell Memorial Hall – a venue without air conditioning. There was overhead lighting that increased the temperature, adding to the discomfort for all of us.

The one thing I did notice and did not understand was that every time a Black student accepted a diploma, there was loud applause and even some cheers and whistles. It wasn't until later in life that I realized what a tremendous achievement graduating high school was for a Black inner-city child at that time.

After graduation, I went to work for Bryant & Chapman Dairy. I had a part-time job there in my senior year. I would be working in the office as the Accounts Payable clerk, responsible for auditing and paying the invoices for all the dairy's expenses. Although I had almost failed typing class at Weaver, I learned to type well while performing this position.

• Chapter 10 •

Lessons in the Army Air Force

Nine months later it was March, and I was 18 years old and eligible for the draft. Although the war was over, the draft of every 18-year-old was still in effect and would mean that I would be a member of the U.S. Army, if called for duty. Never could I picture myself with a rifle over my shoulder, trudging up a muddy hill. I looked at the other services. I knew the Marines were out; I could never pass the physical. The Navy was out because I would get seasick in the bathtub. That left the Army Air Force. Down to the recruiting station I went and after being informed of all the opportunities that lay ahead, I considered enlisting for four years, but not before I was assured I would always be stationed where there was electricity. I had begun to shave, and I used a new invention, an electric razor.

The call to duty came in October, when I left by Pullman for San Antonio and Basic Training at Lackland Air Force Base. If I thought by leaving home, I had escaped Papa, I was sadly mistaken. A new figure would replace him and add to my insecurity. He was called a DRILL SERGEANT.

It was 6 a.m. on the first day of Basic Training when 60 Privates were called out for Roll Call. The drill sergeant was as red-necked an individual you could ever meet, who despised anyone or anything that came from the Northeast. As far as he was concerned, I was from New York – a YANKEE. He called my name out and pronounced it, I think intentionally, "Dutch Army." I politely corrected him saying "my name is Ducharme, Sergeant." For the 13 weeks of basic training, five days a week, he called me "Dutch Army." In addition, he assigned me to KP at least four times a week, instructing the cook to have me clean the large pots. The other airmen were assigned only one day a week.

These were the pots in which soups and stews were prepared and some of them seemed as tall as I was. I had to crawl inside to clean them. The grease on the inside of the pots was so thick it stuck to my fatigues, especially the collar, and did not wash out at the laundry. I developed a rash on my neck that caused me to scratch until I bled. The rash remained for years after I left the Air Force. I visited doctor after doctor looking for a cure.

One doctor told me to sit in a tub of water up to my neck. I had to buy a thermometer that would float. The temperature of the water had to remain at 98.6 degrees. After a time in the water the temperature would drop, and I had to add hot water until it read 98.6 degrees. I did not take too many baths before I realized that I was washing the oil out of my skin and my dry skin began itching all over my body. I looked for another doctor until a dermatologist found the cure. A special lotion that, at that time, cost about $5. I used that lotion for over 20 years until the price rose to $50 a bottle.

In the seventh week of Basic, we were given Saturday afternoon to go into the city of San Antonio. The base was at the edge of the city and the bus would be empty as it began its trip downtown. I do not remember why I was late, but I did not take the bus with the 59 other airmen in the squadron. I took the bus alone. We had been told not to speak to the "niggers" when we got to town, but it was not clear why we shouldn't.

I was the only one as I boarded the bus and took a seat. As we approached downtown, the bus took on more passengers. A little old man, a Black man, sat next to me even though there were other seats available. I thought that was unusual, because if we were told not to socialize with them, they also must have been aware of the policy. He asked me where I was from and when I said Connecticut, he started a conversation with me. He was curious about life in Connecticut. I did not realize until a few minutes later why he was so curious about rules of conduct.

I could tell we were close to downtown and decided I would leave the bus to walk from that point on. I reached for the buzzer to inform the bus driver that I wanted to depart at the next stop, and there it was, a sign, above the door, COLOREDS TO THE REAR. I turned to my right and saw only black people sitting in the seats. I left the bus and just stood on the street trying to understand what I just saw. I started walking ahead and approached a brick building at the corner. There was a door with a sign above it, COLOREDS ENTRANCE. I walked a little further and approached a restaurant with a sign in the window, WHITES ONLY. There were two water fountains on the sidewalk one labeled WHITES ONLY, the other, COLOREDS ONLY.

Where am I? I was in uniform as I asked myself, "Is this the country I am supposed to defend?"

Living in Connecticut was very different. I was sure that in high school classes I had read that the Civil War was fought to free slaves, and it was over, but apparently not in Texas. Why had not the federal government outlawed this behavior? While it was a warm sunny day, I felt a cold chill through my body. I started asking questions, learning the Democrats controlled the South and we really were two countries. Why had not a Republican president put an end to this horrible situation? I was not proud to wear my uniform from that day until the Civil Rights Act was passed 100 years after the Civil War ended.

At the end of the 13 Basic training weeks, we would be promoted to Private First Class and receive an increase in pay. All but one of the class received the promotion – guess who did not. Having been trained well by Papa, I was accustomed to being considered inferior to others, so I did not even question my failure to be promoted.

In spite of the promises made by the Recruiting Officer, I was sent to Clerk Typist school in Cheyenne, Wyoming. If there was one school I did not need to attend, it was Clerk Typist school. My training as Accounts Payable Clerk for Bryant & Chapman was more than enough training for any clerical job they had to offer. My education at Weaver was a plus also. It was not a complete waste of time though because I learned that the top three students could select their choice of future assignments in the Air Force. I decided that day that I would choose the Adjutant General's department in Washington, D.C. and hopefully, one day, become a lawyer. For the first time in my life, I was looking forward to the next 13 weeks and a chance to prove I was no longer a "reject of society."

For 13 weeks I would attend five classes a day starting at 8 a.m. My first class was Typing. The instructor came into the room and said he had some housekeeping to do, and we would spend time becoming familiar with the keyboard. I was totally familiar with the keyboard so I took a piece of paper which was on the desk, put it in the typewriter, opened the manual on the desk and started to type. I was typing on a manual typewriter. I do not know if electric typewriters existed at that time.

A few minutes later, the instructor was at my desk, snatched the paper out of the typewriter and said, "What are you doing?" I have always had trouble answering stupid questions, so I said nothing.

He looked it over and said, "Where did you learn to type?"

"I had a job that required some typing," I said.

"What do you mean, you had a job?"

I told him that I had gone to work after I graduated high school and had worked 15 months before I was called up by the Air Force.

"How old are you?" he asked.

"I'm 18 years old."

"What are you, some kind of quiz kid?" he sarcastically asked as the other students in the class laughed out loud. He said I would be a distraction in that class, and he did not want to see me here again.

I thought not having to attend Typing class was a positive. I could sleep an hour longer each day. As the weeks passed, I was doing well in the other four classes. I became more confident each day that I would be the top student in the class, or at the very least, one of the top three students and therefore qualify to choose my future assignment.

Tomorrow is Graduation Day and a new beginning for yours truly. I could not sleep this night. I was so excited about what was going to happen tomorrow. What do you think of me now, Papa? The next morning, I wondered why I was not tired having stayed awake the entire night. It was to be a morning ceremony that I would find boring until the top three students were named. The speaker raised his voice telling the audience he was about to make the announcement of the top three airmen. I leaned forward. I thought I was going to have an anxiety attack if he took much longer. Then he began speaking. The number 3 student's name was called. Of course, it wasn't me. Then the number 2 student's name. No surprise here … it was not me. The number 1 student is … and then he paused, building up suspense. I could not wait to hear my name, this time pronounced correctly. I jumped up out of my seat and he shouted out the name. It was not me. He did not call my name. I was in shock. The audience was laughing because I was standing, and it was not me.

Oh no. This time I would not accept the news quietly. They are not going to get away with it this time without an argument from me. I took a couple of deep breaths and headed for the speaker.

"Sir, I think you made a mistake. I was the top student in this class. I received perfect scores in every quiz and test." I knew he merely read what was on the paper that was handed to him. He said just that and added that he would look into it and contact me later.

Two days later, I was called into his office for the result of his investigation. "You came in fourth," he said. As I pleaded my case, repeating that I had perfect scores in every measure of performance, he was looking through my file on the matter. I waited for some further explanation for the error. Looking up from the file, he said, "I see what the problem was, you had an incomplete in one subject."

"Incomplete, what does that mean?" I said.

"You did not complete one class."

"What class was that? I never missed a class all 13 weeks."

"You did not complete your typing class."

I exploded. I could not contain myself. "How could I receive an incomplete for a class I was told not to attend because I was overqualified, and I would be a distraction? I should have received a perfect score for that class." The Officer apologized and added that there wasn't anything that could be done now.

So once again, I was on the wrong end of the deal – was this going to continue to happen to me all my life? Would I ever receive fair treatment? Nothing like that could happen today without the airman demanding a correction. But it was a different time then. I told myself it just was not in God's plan that I should become a lawyer. I would have made a damn good lawyer.

Like a good airman, I put the matter behind me. It was the beginning of my GET OVER IT policy.

Later that day, I was assigned to Kelly Air Force Base where I would await a permanent assignment. During this waiting period, I worked in the squadron office doing clerical work. In a few days, my new orders arrived. I would have a permanent position as Chief Clerk of a squadron in San Bernardino, California. I was still a Private. I was told that everyone who held that position in peace time was a Sergeant, up to a Master Sergeant. The C.O. of my squadron had been made aware of what happened to me in Clerk Typist school, and he promoted me to Corporal. So now I was probably the only Chief Clerk in the Air Force who was a Corporal.

The duties of a Chief Clerk were similar to being an office manager who was familiar enough with the day-to-day routine that he could replace any absent personnel. One responsibility I had was to process applications of airmen who sought a transfer to another position at another location. Notices were posted regularly and once in a while I would notice an opening that interested me, and I would submit an application for myself. Oddly enough, where other applications seemed to be almost routinely approved, whenever I submitted one, it was rejected, or I assumed it was rejected because I did not get a positive response. At first I ignored it because a few other airmen had also not received responses.

The months went by and I performed, I thought, up to standard with the C.O. complimenting me from time to time. I was happy during this period because I was doing something I knew how to do and I thought, doing well. I got along with the other office personnel and the airmen in the Squadron probably because I was efficient and accurate in doing what was asked of me.

From time to time when I saw new assignments that interested me, I would file an application for transfer without any success. One day while taking papers to the C.O. for his signature, I mentioned the rejections to him and asked him to look into the matter. He hesitated before answering me, and then to my surprise, he told me he had not submitted my applications for consideration.

"I don't understand, why not?" I asked.

He explained his refusal very simply. He said my performance as Chief Clerk had been excellent, and he was planning to promote me to Sergeant. But I knew there was a "but" coming and was trying to anticipate what possible reason he could have for not submitting my applications.

"As I have told others, in all my years as C.O. I have never been more satisfied with a Chief Clerk. I trust your work. I am retiring next year, and I refuse to have to train someone who probably will not perform up to your standards. I want my last year to be free from any pressures caused by my Chief Clerk's performance. On my last day as C. O. I will approve an application for any transfer you wish and will add a personal recommendation to boot."

I walked out of his office as angry as I had ever been. Now I was being mistreated because I was too good at what I did! When is this treatment going to end? As I sat at my desk, I became more angry by the minute. This was going to be the last time I would tolerate being discriminated against.

I was staring at papers on my desk, but my mind was elsewhere. I remember the phone ringing, taking the call, but nothing about the conversation. On my desk was the day's mail. Among the mail was a notice from Headquarters informing airmen that the Army Air Force would now be known as the United States Air Force, with new uniforms and pay scale etc. In bold print was a statement that airmen who suffered financially by this change could apply for discharge. I realized I would be losing 55 cents a month under the new pay scale. I was smiling because I was amused by the possibility that I might be eligible for discharge under this new regulation. I was skeptical that a 55-cent loss would qualify me for discharge, so I called Headquarters to have the information verified. I was told that I did qualify.

I decided to apply for a discharge. The problem was how would I get it by the C.O.? I pondered this question overnight. The next morning, I had some correspondence for the C.O.'s signature that I had failed to bring to his attention the night before because I was lost in the news about my possible discharge.

I handed him the correspondence and waited for him to sign them. That's when I remembered that he never read anything I gave him for his signature. I watched as he signed one letter after another, each time only lifting up the bottom of the page enough to see the signature space.

I walked out smiling and hurried back to my desk so I could fill out the discharge request. I would include it with the correspondence for the day that needed his signature. Later that afternoon, I nervously brought him the papers for signature with my application for discharge in the middle of the pile. With my fingers crossed behind me, I waited for him to sign them hoping he would not look over the letters. He did what he always did, just sign without reading them. I prayed that someone from the Processing Department would not call and mention that I was being discharged.

So far, so good. No calls and the application was on its way to being approved. Every time the phone rang, I anxiously answered it expecting some flaw in the application or anything that would delay or reject it.

My fear was allayed when a phone call from my mother informed me that Papa had died of a coronary thrombosis, whatever that is. That was great news. Now my chances for discharge were dramatically improved. I could add "hardship" to my application. I was the oldest child in a family and would be needed at home to help support the family. Hooray, Papa finally did something good for me. HE DIED.

With Papa's funeral only a few days away, I could have asked for Emergency Leave and returned after the funeral and await the processing of my discharge. I don't remember the specifics, but I think the Air Force decided it was a waste of their money to send me home to Connecticut for a funeral, return to California and then have me return to Connecticut after I had been discharged. The bottom line is I would leave California for the funeral, a discharged member of the Air Force.

There was one more thing to do before I would leave – that was to say farewell to my Commanding Officer. I walked into his office with my discharge paper in my left hand and extended my right hand to him. He was sitting behind his desk, reading something. When he noticed my hand in front of him, he said "what is that for?"

I answered that I wanted to say goodbye on my last day in the Air Force. He looked at me quizzically, and said, "What are you talking about?"

I then handed him the discharge paper and said rather happily, "You sir, are the last person to dictate my life for me. From now on, I am in charge." I took the paper from his hand and walked out without saluting.

Damn, did that feel good.

Chapter 11

A Loyal Dodgers Fan

The news of Papa's death left me relieved. There wasn't any feeling of loss or sadness. I felt absolutely nothing. Years later, I saw the Broadway musical "A Chorus Line" and heard one of the numbers entitled "Nothing." I empathized completely with the character.

The years when we lived at the rooming house Papa had treated me so much like property. He would play with his son, hug him, toss him in the air, joke with him and show his affection for him just by smiling while he talked with him. He never smiled at me or played with me. He so destroyed my self-esteem that I think I really believed I was inferior to other children, a reject of society.

I remember that Louise, the wife of one of Papa's sons by his first marriage, soon after the funeral said to me, "It is all over now. He can't do anything more to you." After that, whenever the family gathered and she was present, she would tell anyone within earshot how miserably I was treated by her father-in-law. She told me how proud she was of me because, in spite of my childhood, I was becoming a successful adult.

I came home from the Air Force a different person than when I had left. I was more self-assured. I began to trust my own feelings and judgment in making decisions. And there were a few decisions that had to be made. First of all, there was the matter of employment. I visited Bryant & Chapman and was told that they did not have any openings. I did not know, until someone informed me, that as a returning serviceman I had to be rehired at the same or comparable position. Suddenly an opening in the office was found.

I was paid 75 cents an hour, which was minimum wage, even though it was the same position I had held for over a year before I left for the Air Force. With confidence in my performance growing each day, I soon asked for an increase in pay and was given a $3 raise and told I would be reviewed every three months. I received a $3 raise every three months, increasing my pay to $39 a week. On my first anniversary back on the job, I was called into the Assistant Manager's office and told I was being increased another $3 to $42 a week. That was good news of course, until I was told that it would be my final increase. I was now the highest paid employee in the office.

"Are you telling me that at age 21, I have reached the peak of my earning power?" I asked. I looked around the office of maybe 40 employees, some of whom had been employed longer than my age. "What about your job or the Office Manager's job?" I added.

"You cannot have those positions because you are not a college graduate and Sealtest, who owns the dairy, does not hire anyone for management positions who does not have a college degree," I was told.

College was something I never gave a thought to, but I made a decision right there on the spot and said to Mr. Laird, "keep your $3, I am going to college." I came home from work and told my mother that I had quit my job and was going to college. She said that was a good idea. Neither one of us had any idea what my decision would mean. No one in our family or extended family had gone to college or even thought about it. No one in the neighborhood that I knew had ever gone to college. Our family thought college was for the wealthy, which we certainly were not.

❀ ❀ ❀

It was the month of May. I was a Brooklyn Dodger fanatic, having been so for almost five years. Jackie Robinson was my hero. I so admired his talent on the field. He could play any infield position. That he had to perform in a circus-like atmosphere only added to my respect for him. Sixty years later, I still regard him as my hero. Being a Dodger fan helped me accept adversity. That may sound silly, but it is true. Although they were the class of the National League during this period, they had never won a World Series. That team in the World Series could turn victory into defeat like no other. I could never relax until the final out in the 9th inning. I learned to deal with negativity, or so I thought.

In this year of 1951, the Dodgers had a fantastic team and were leading the league. I decided that before I went to college in the fall I would not go to work until the baseball season was over. I wanted to be able to listen to every game on the radio. This was going to be "our" year, and I did not want to miss an inning of it. I read the daily sports pages, subscribed to the Sporting News, and if you can believe it, the Brooklyn Eagle, the Dodgers' hometown paper in Brooklyn. I could not read enough about my team.

In the meantime, I knew I had to register at a college. I did not know where a college was located, except for Yale, in New Haven. In the Yellow Pages, to my surprise, there was a college in Hartford, called Hillyer. Today it is called the University of Hartford. One day I decided to visit Hillyer College and register for the coming year. I was handed several pieces of paper, told to take them home and fill them out and bring them back. I asked if I could fill them out right there and was told I could. Minutes later I walked up to the counter with my completed pages and handed them to the lady. She said they were in order, how would I like to pay the $500 tuition for the first semester, beginning in September?

I yelled out, "$500? I don't have $500!" In fact, it did not occur to me there would be a financial expense involved with going to college. Why would I? There wasn't any charge for high school. I did not realize that everyone in the office could hear me. Another lady sitting at a desk behind the counter came over to me and said, "Why don't you try the University of Connecticut? They have a branch here in Hartford and the tuition is only $75 a semester."

That was better. I could afford $75. I intended to find a part-time job after the baseball season ended. I left the office at Hillyer and walked to the university. It wasn't much to look at, just two floors of classrooms. I found the office and asked about registering for the next set of classes in September. Again, I was given forms to complete, which I did while standing at the counter. The $75 was due sometime before classes would begin in September. Because it had been four years since my high school graduation, I was required to take an entrance exam to prove I could meet their standards for enrollment. I was nervous about the exam until I saw the questions. Nothing to worry about, just some simple math and English questions, which I breezed through in a few minutes.

Mom had gone to school through the 8th grade and really wasn't in a position to counsel me. That was not a serious problem because in my first two years, I would be taking only required courses, no electives. There wasn't anyone I knew who could advise me. I was on my own to make whatever decisions that had to be made.

What I Remember ...

All set for college, I would look for a job later that summer. I could now concentrate on the Dodgers. I would listen to every game for the rest of the season. In August the team was 13 games ahead of the next team in the division. They were a cinch to win the Division. I would begin my search for a job. It did not take long before I was hired to work at Mead Clothes on Asylum Street, a men's clothing store owned by, believe it or not, two Brooklyn-born brothers, Dodger fans to be sure. I would work in the office afternoons from 1 p.m. until 6 and Saturdays from 9 to 6, eating my bagged lunch while working, for a total of 34 hours a week.

As the baseball season was coming to an end, the New York Giants were on an extended winning streak and the season ended with the Dodgers and the Giants in a tie for first place. It meant they would have to play a three-game series to determine who would represent the National League in the World Series. These three games would be the most important of the season for both teams and just my luck, I would not be able to listen to the games because I would be working at Mead Clothes.

The Giants won the first game, the Dodgers won the second and the third game would decide the winner. Not a single customer came into the store while the games were being broadcast. It seemed that even traffic by the store was at a standstill. There was tremendous interest in the final game. When I arrived at 1 p.m., the brothers left the store to listen to the game and would return every few minutes to keep me up to date on the progress of the game.

Later, I was told that it was the ninth inning and the Dodgers were ahead 4 to 1. Only three outs to go. In a few minutes the game would be over, and the Dodgers would be in the World Series. The minutes dragged on. I wondered why it was taking so

66

long to get three outs. The minutes flew by like hours, and still no news. So maybe the Giants scored a run or two, even so, it should not take this long to end the game.

Something was happening and it would not be good news. I was sure of it. Then the brothers ran into the store yelling, "You won't believe what happened!" I did not wait to hear the news; I put on my coat and walked out of the store.

"Where are you going, we did not tell you what happened," yelled one of the brothers. I did not have to walk but a few steps to learn that the Dodgers had lost the game by a score of 5 to 4.

I was in a trance. I did not remember getting on the bus to go home. I do remember turning on the radio when I did arrive home. Switching from station to station, every announcer was saying the same thing: The Dodgers lost the game in the bottom of the ninth inning when Bobby Thompson hit a home run to end the game. That blasted home run went only 296 feet into the stands, a pop fly in every other ballpark. I kept moving the dial, hoping one announcer would have a different outcome to report.

My brother asked, "Why are you torturing yourself, turn off the damn radio." I just had to hear that news again and again. It did not sink in. I would not believe that it really happened. Maybe in the paper tomorrow morning the result would be different. I was 21 years old, acting like I were 5. I was in a world of sorrow I had not visited before today. The Dodgers were not just a baseball team to me, they were the most important thing in my life at that time. My mother chimed in, "You are acting like a child." That was an understatement.

The next day I went to class but was still preoccupied with the Dodgers' loss. I sat in class but did not hear anything. I was in a no-man's land. I kept reliving that score – 5 to 4, 5 to 4.

Disappointments when you are young can be a learning experience. I learned that life went on and you have to get over it. I tried to tell myself it was just a ballgame, but it was much more than that to me. It was days before I began to act like an adult again.

❂ ❂ ❂

My grades as a freshman college student were fair considering I had been away from studying for four years. My schedule of classes was such that I had time after classes to study before going to work at Mead Clothes. The college library was the place I found most suitable because it was quiet. If there was any noise or distraction, I would not remember what I had just read and would have to read it over again.

One day that would turn out to be a milestone in my life. I was studying in the library, when a group of students came in and sat at the other end of the room. Soon they were talking loudly, and I could not concentrate on my reading material. Normally, I would walk out of the library and find a vacant classroom. However, this day, I did not. What followed, I could not explain, not then or even now.

I walked over to the gathering and told them I could not study because of all the noise they were making. I don't know why, but I did not then walk back to my seat. Instead, I asked what all the commotion was about. They were lamenting the fact that they were only nine students and they needed ten to seek election to the Student Council. Almost in unison they shouted, "Will you be our tenth person?"

I answered that I would not be of much help because I did not know any of the other students. I told them that I leave the school after studying in the library to go to work. I added that I was not a member of any extra-curricular activities and probably would not

68

get them a single vote. They were not deterred. Without a tenth person they could not seek election, so at the very least I would qualify them.

If just adding my name would make them eligible to seek election to the Student Council, why not do it? I told them they could include my name in any forms necessary to apply. Again, I did something out of character. I sat down and visited with them and before I realized what I was doing, I was planning the campaign. They told me that they did not know of any restrictions on campaigning. That was good news to me, and my imagination started working overtime.

My commonsense approach to most things told me we had to advertise our team in places that would be seen by the student body. I suggested hanging signs below every classroom clock. Most students look at the clock frequently during class. I also suggested putting our material in the restrooms. If you were standing at a urinal, there was a sign, eye level, promoting the "Cheer Party." That's what we called ourselves. If you went into one of the stalls and shut the door, you were looking at one of our signs. The planning session ended when I realized what time it was and said I had to leave for work. We regularly met in the library to continue discussing ways to reach the students.

A couple of weeks later, our creative approach to advertising and our enthusiasm was rewarded when the student body reacted favorably by electing our team. With the election decided, I could now go back to my normal routine, or could I?

The next day after class I was in the library studying when the group arrived and asked me to join them. I was caught off-guard when they asked me to be their President. They said I had been their leader during the campaign, and they could not have

69

been elected without me. I was flabbergasted. Me, a President! They want me to be their President. I was just beginning to come out of my shell. I did not think I was ready to lead anyone or anything. I was flattered to think they wanted me. I thought of the times in gym class when no one wanted me on their team. Now, THEY REALLY WANTED ME! To be wanted, what a wonderful feeling. Something I had not known before today.

I asked what would be required of me as President. No one in the group knew specifically what the President's duties and responsibilities were. How difficult could it be? Would it interfere with my studies? I had promised myself that I was going to college to get a piece of paper that said I was who I already knew I was. I was told a college education would open doors of opportunity in the future. I think I agreed to be their President because I enjoyed the feeling of being wanted. It was a new experience for me.

No sooner had I agreed to be their President, than in walks the Director of Student Activities to congratulate the group on its victory. He had praise for our imaginative campaign. Then he asked if we had elected our officers. He wanted to know who would be President. When told I was, he said he assumed as much. He congratulated me and said he wanted me to be in his office at 9 a.m. the next day. We would be reviewing the items that would have to be included in the speech I would be making to the entire student body in a few weeks.

"Whoa!" I shouted, "I have to give a speech before the entire student body? I cannot do that." He saw how excited and overwhelmed I was and attempted to calm me. I explained my fear of public speaking. I told him when I was in school, I would refuse to stand at my desk to answer a question. He told me I was much younger then and that I could do this. He said that he never knew a student who wasn't nervous when told that public speaking was a part of being President. He said that they all reacted just as I did. He repeated that I could do this. He even said he had confidence in me.

Wow, what is happening here? First, the students want me to be their President and now the Student Activities Director is saying he has confidence in me. I am not accustomed to this kind of talk. This is me, "a reject of society," you are talking to. I mean, I liked hearing these things, but honestly, I don't know the person they are talking about. "What would Papa say now? Could I have overnight become a different person? If they all think I could, maybe I do not know myself at all."

The speech I had to prepare was a welcoming speech to the student body. I was given an outline of subjects to include and was left to put the remainder of the speech in my own words.

When I was satisfied that I had written what I wanted to say and reviewed it several times, I began to practice reading it aloud, then in front of a full-length mirror. I never liked being read to by teachers. I thought they should know their material well enough not to have to read it to the students. I was determined not to read this speech to the students.

By the time the big day arrived, I think I had memorized the entire speech, but to be on the safe side, I took a pen and wrote down key words of each paragraph on the palms of my hands. The Director of Student Activities called the students to order and made a short statement introducing me recalling the imaginative campaign. The students roared with approval. He then said something about my fear of speaking in public and that I had

71

never done this before. He encouraged the students to show their understanding and support. Which they did to loud applause.

Then it was my turn. I walked to the podium, looked out at the students, and could not remember the first word of my speech. I had anticipated this and was pleased I had written words on the palms of my hands. I looked at my palms and thought I would faint. They were SOLID BLUE. The ink had run from perspiration, so that I could not read a word. I looked at the audience again, then back down at my hands. I wanted to disappear. The next few minutes were a blank. I know I was talking but did not have any idea what I was saying. For almost 20 minutes, I kept speaking and could hear laughter and applause from time to time.

I knew I had finished speaking when the audience rose to their feet cheering. The Student Activities Director walked over to me to shake my hand. I held back; I could not give him my blue palm. Instead, I just raised them so he could see. He praised my performance and said I was a natural public speaker ... that the words just rolled off my tongue and I did it without referring to notes. I thought to myself, if you only knew what I was going through. The students were still standing and applauding as we walked off to the wings. How did I do that? Another case of DIVINE INTERVENTION?

I think that morning was a turning point in my life. I had conquered the demon I had lived with for years. I now believed I could do anything I was determined to do. I was really proud of myself, even though I did not know a word I said. I hoped it was the speech I had written. That prolonged student ovation erased all the insecurities I had lived with in the past. I was a different person ready to face the world with a new confidence.

❄ ❄ ❄

Those two years at the Hartford Branch were not what I expected them to be. My grades were more than satisfactory, but my involvement in student activities was a complete surprise. Not only was I President of the class, but also I was the male lead in the annual stage production. I remembered what happened in the 6th grade when I did not appear for the role of Scrooge in "The Christmas Carol." No panic this time.

The memory of this performance makes me smile. My role was that of a proper English gentleman and in the last scene, I proposed to my leading lady. In rehearsal, I merely spoke the lines. On the stage that evening, I was lost in the character. I took out a handkerchief, placed it at my feet and then knelt down to speak my lines. Someone in the audience was amused by the maneuver and started to giggle, then laugh out loud. I recognized the laugh as coming from my sister Estelle. She was uncontrollable and her laughter was contagious. Others joined in. Soon, it seemed the entire audience was laughing. There I was on my knees, waiting for them to stop so I could continue with my proposal. After what seemed like eternity, the laughter ended, I spoke my lines, and the play ended to loud applause. Had it not been for Estelle's laughter, I thought the performance would not have been noteworthy. Thank you, Estelle. The next day the students were talking about the lady with the laugh. I did not tell them it was my sister.

During summers, I sought employment to raise funds for next year's tuition, which was $750. My first summer was spent as a bookkeeper for Eastern Paper Company. When it was time to look for work for my second summer, the economy was such that there were almost no jobs for part-time work. When I realized it was unlikely that I would find a part-time job, I decided to seek a full-time job. I needed the money for next year's tuition.

I applied for a job at a factory called Niles Bement Pond in West Hartford. When I told a little white lie, that I had left college to help support my family, I was hired for a position that had me working from 6 p.m. to 6 a.m. five nights a week. It took about an hour by bus to get to the factory. I would leave my home at 5 p.m. and arrive home the next morning at 7 a.m. I went to bed immediately and slept until about 3 p.m. This schedule left little time for myself, but it meant that I would be saving almost all of my take-home pay. I saved enough money that summer to pay for my tuition the remaining two years. I graduated without owing any money for my education.

I worked between two men in their 40s who had been employed at the factory for many years. The three of us did the same job, which could not be more boring. I took a metal item from a container on my right, placed it in the machine in front me, turned a dial forward and backward, removed the item and placed it in a container on my left. After a while, I could complete the operation with my eyes closed.

The men on either side of me spent time complaining about the job, the company and the working conditions. One evening, after a few weeks of listening to them complaining all night long, I blurted out, "If you are so unhappy with this job and this company, why the hell are you still working here?"

Almost in unison, they answered "I would lose my pension." I asked how much their pension was and was shocked to learn that neither one knew the value.

I vowed that evening that I would never remain in a job that I did not enjoy. Money would be secondary.

❄ ❄ ❄

Before the beginning of the third year, I had to select a major for the balance of the two years. I knew I wanted something in the Business School. I had a choice of Sales, Marketing, Insurance and Finance. Below the word Finance, was a statement "Students would daily receive a free copy of the Wall Street Journal." That's how I chose my major, Finance.

Life on campus at Storrs, Connecticut, was very different from the Hartford Branch. I was assigned to 7B, the only male dorm amongst all the women's dorms. My room was located on the side facing the women's dorms and every night the students who had rooms across the hall, would come in for the show the women put on for the boys, pretending they were unaware the shades had not been pulled down. Try studying in that atmosphere.

I mentioned it to one of my classmates one day and he suggested I move to his fraternity, where there were a few rooms that could be rented to non-fraternity members. I had heard negative things about fraternities and was skeptical about moving until I was told most of the members were Science and Engineer majors, who studied all the time. It was a very quiet dorm with a capacity for 60 students, two in a room, on four floors. I had a room on the 3rd floor.

The members were pleasant guys who I always said "hello" to when I passed them on the stairs. At mealtime, we ate in the dining room where meals prepared in our own kitchen were served. We had our own chef. We had a house mother, an elderly widow, who was there more or less as a chaperone. She really was not needed because it was a house of serious students who were there to learn and prepare for the future.

A few weeks after I had been living there, Dave FitzSimmons, my roommate, and the one who suggested that I move into the fraternity house, told me that he was asked to offer me membership in the fraternity. By this time Dave and I had become good friends. The invitation was totally unexpected. I had heard stories in the past of the rowdy parties in fraternities, but this one was very different. If it was good enough for Dave, it was good enough for me. I accepted the invitation and was soon a member of Phi Sigma Kapp.

Life at the fraternity house was very pleasant. The fraternity brothers were friendly, and I enjoyed being a member for the almost two years that I lived there. The time passed quickly and soon we would be facing Graduation Day.

You would think that Graduation Day would be a memorable occasion. After all, I had spent the last four years with one objective –- to obtain a piece of paper that said I was who I already knew who I was. Today I would have that piece of paper in my hands, a diploma from the University of Connecticut.

It rained on Graduation Day so the ceremonies were transferred to the Jorgensen Auditorium, which seated several thousand. Students from the various schools would be joining those from the Business School. We were seated down front on the left side of the auditorium. I thought that meant we would be among the first to receive our diplomas. I just assumed that the students would walk to the stage, receive the diploma, shake a few hands and return to our seats. When it came time in the program for the students to receive their diplomas, we were asked to stand as a group, someone said a few words I could not hear, and that was it. I waited for someone to make the sign of the cross, or do something ritualistic, but that was it. Nothing at all.

Where was the diploma I expected to have in my proud hands? It was at the office of the Business School, which was some distance from the auditorium. We had to walk there to receive it. When we arrived, the diplomas were laid out in alphabetical order. No ceremony, no handshake, no nothing. I don't know what procedure was followed for the other schools. I was very disappointed as were the other graduates. But with our families waiting outside, we did not have time to dwell on that now. I think due to the strange way we received our diploma, there wasn't that moment to remember. No moment for the family to react. No one saw us receive our diploma. When I graduated from high school, there was applause and sometimes cheers as individuals shook the hand of the Superintendent of Schools.

I do not recall any family gathering, aunts, uncles and cousins, that sort of thing. My mind was elsewhere. I was thinking about the decision I had made of accepting a position with Sears, as a management trainee.

In my senior year, companies from all over the country visited universities and other institutions of higher learning to interview the future graduates for openings in their companies. There was a listing every day of companies coming to campus with information regarding interviews. The interviews would be scheduled at 15-minute intervals. One of my fraternity brothers was Edgar Platt, whose father was employed by Sears, Roebuck & Company. He and Mrs. Platt visited Edgar frequently and included me in whatever plans they had made for the day. During every one of those visits, Mr. Platt would tell me that I was "Sears material." I was not quite sure just what he meant by that statement, but when I saw Sears name on the list of future visitors, I felt obligated to make an appointment.

77

What I Remember ...

Prior to the Sears appointment, I already had several interviews. These were companies I wasn't interested in, but I wanted to get some experience on the routine and what to expect. I thought it would prepare me for those interviews that were of interest to me. I found these interviews not very informative, enlightening or challenging.

The Sears interview was different ... much different. I had become accustomed to being asked the same questions, almost in the same order by men in business suits, in their 30s or 40s. The representative from Sears was a much older man. He wore a sweater and slacks and loafers without socks. I thought, this one is going to be different. He asked me to sit down, and then shocked me with his opening statement. Very calmly, he asked, "Why the fuck should Sears hire you?" I was dumbfounded, but not for long. For the next 45 minutes I told him why Sears should hire me.

I left the interview thinking what a waste of time. Leaving the room, I saw students who were angry that I overstayed my allotted time. I told them they were in for a shock and left. Returning to the fraternity, I looked for Edgar to tell him of my 45-minute Sears interview and that it was a waste of time. "Tell your father I went to that interview just for him."

When Mr. and Mrs. Platt again visited Edgar, I told them of my interview, minus the four-letter word. To my surprise, Mr. Platt was impressed that I had held the attention of the interviewer for about 45 minutes. He said he thought that was a positive and that I could soon be receiving a job offer in the mail. I dismissed his prediction. I expected I would receive a form letter, similar to the ones I had already received, thanking me for taking time to speak with their interviewer, but all openings had been filled, and that they would keep my name on file should an opening occur in the future. I could not have been more wrong.

A few weeks later, there it was, a letter from Sears. "We are happy to inform you that you are one of the men we would like to have enter our employ following your graduation. Therefore, this letter is a firm offer of employment to you at a starting salary of $75 a week."

I screamed, "I don't believe it!" and went running to look for Edgar to tell him of the offer.

"My father told you that you would get an offer," Edgar said.

"Why do they want me? I don't know why they want to hire me," I answered. That interview, in my mind, was merely a waste of time. All the interviewer knew about me was that I could talk and he should have known that before he interviewed me.

I did receive an offer of employment from another retailer, G. Fox & Company, located in Hartford. Two offers, coincidently from retail companies. One, Sears, the largest retailer in the world at that time, and the other, the largest privately owned department store in the country. For some reason, retailers were attracted to me. They both saw something in me that was to be prophetic when some 20 years later, I would open and manage a retail store, the Whalers Gift Shop, for the Whalers Hockey Club.

I accepted the Sears offer even though I was baffled by it. I rejected the G. Fox offer because I wanted to leave home. In my letter of acceptance, I asked to be assigned for the training program at a location away from my home. Their reply to my letter acceded to my wishes when it said I would be sent to West Virginia for training starting on June 20. Acknowledging the location and date, I asked for a week off in October to attend the World Series in which the Dodgers would be participating. I think they accepted the request because the odds were on their side that I could predict in June who would be the National League representative in the World Series in October.

On Monday, June 20,1955, I entered the Sears store in Huntington, West Virginia and asked the first person I saw where the Manager, Mr. Winters', office was located. I was told that he was on vacation. I thought that odd since he probably knew months before that I would be arriving today. Even if he had a previously scheduled vacation at that time, I would think he would have asked someone to greet me. I did not know what to do. The person I talked to was the hardware department manager. He solved the problem for the time being when he said he knew I would be assigned to a retailing department sometime in my training period. Why not spend it with him in his department until the manager returned from vacation? I had to smile because I did not know a wrench from a screwdriver.

For three months, I remained in the hardware department and spent most of my time taking inventory, counting nuts and bolts of different varieties. Most customers coming into the hardware department had a problem at home and wanted the salesclerk to solve it. I had difficulty understanding the Southern dialect, and not knowing how to solve their problem when I could determine exactly what it was they were saying, I was useless in trying to serve customers.

I had expected that Mr. Winters would look me up when he returned, but he did not. The other store personnel ignored me. I knew only two people, the manager of the hardware department and his other employee. Not a single person working in the rest of the store ever came over to meet me. I wasn't invited to lunch or to anyone's home or even for a drink after work. It took me a while before I realized I was in the South and I was from the North, a Yankee, if you will. I was positive that I had learned in high school that the Civil War was over. Apparently, these employees did not know that.

The same was true of the home where I lived. I visited the local Catholic church for suggestions where I might find a room in someone's home. They suggested a three-story single home owned by an Irish widow with nine – I said nine – children, the eldest about 16. I paid $10 a week for the room on the 3rd floor. It was the beginning of the summer season, and it was hot up there. The only time I saw the owner was once a week when she came up to collect the rent. The children must have been told not to speak to me because none of them did.

One Sunday afternoon, my day off, I walked to a local swimming pool and after swimming a few laps, sat in a lounge chair and promptly fell asleep. I was awakened by someone tapping on me and saying, "Mister, I think you had better get out of the sun." I then realized my body was really hot. The next thing I noticed was my red hands and legs. When I arrived home, I looked in a mirror and saw my red face. I actually had rosy cheeks. That was a first for my olive skin.

On the way home I stopped at a drug store and was told I should purchase some Johnson's Baby Cream. I applied it as I continued the walk home. I was still several long blocks from home. When I was about to pass another drug store, I realized the jar of cream was empty. My hot skin had absorbed it all. I bought another and before I made it all the way home, I had bought four jars of the cream. Not surprisingly, I did not sleep that night. The next morning, I was still red all over but I went to work anyway.

There was a considerable difference in my appearance because of the sunburn, yet not a single employee commented upon it.

On the last day of my 13 weeks in the hardware department, I was anxious to learn what department I would be assigned to for the next phase of my training. It was late in the afternoon and I had yet to hear anything.

Then a man came into the department and said to me, "On Monday, I want you to come in wearing your work clothes. You will be working in the receiving department."

I answered, "I am wearing my work clothes, who are you?"

"I am Mr. Winters, the store manager."

This was the first time I had seen him since my arrival 13 weeks ago. "So, you are Mr. Winters," I said rather sarcastically. "You are the one who was supposed to meet me on my arrival from Connecticut. You are the one who was supposed to be my mentor, the one who was supposed to help me find a place to live. The one who was supposed to be there for me whenever I had a problem getting adjusted to working in the store, and I meet you for the first time after 13 weeks in the store. IF YOU ARE AN EXAMPLE OF A STORE MANAGER, THEN I DON'T WANT TO BE ONE. I am leaving and calling Philadelphia and letting them know what a sorry excuse for a store manager you really are."

I left the store hoping to find a pay telephone along the way home. I did find one, but I was too late. Mr. Winters had already called and told them I was insubordinate and should be fired.

I had an angel on my side and did not know it at the time. Apparently, the interviewer at UConn had given me high marks and on the typed report of my interview he had handwritten, "Don't let this one get away." That old man's opinion was highly valued, since several of his past recommendations later became Vice Presidents of the company. I was invited to the Philadelphia office where I told my side of the story. When I had my say, I was offered an apology, saying Mr. Winters was not typical of store managers, and that his behavior probably was due to cultural differences. I was told I would not be fired, I would be sent to a Trenton, New Jersey, store where I would begin "traveling auditor" training under the guidance of the Controller.

Before leaving West Virginia, I contacted my priest friend, the one who answered the door of the Rectory the day I arrived. During my three-month stay in West Virginia, I had become friendly with him. He had told me he was from New Jersey and when he learned I would be transferred there, he thought we should get together when he returned home to spend his annual vacation with his parents.

Arriving in Trenton, I went to the nearest Catholic church, asking for assistance in finding a room in a private home, same as I did in West Virginia. I was referred to a family nearby, who greeted me warmly and invited me to have dinner with them after I was settled in my room. The Cassidy's reception was in marked contrast to that of the Irish widow with nine children. We spent the evening getting acquainted and I knew immediately that I was going to enjoy living there.

The following morning, I walked into the Sears store and asked for the Controller's office. You would think I would remember his name since he was the opposite of what I had experienced on my first day in West Virginia. He took me up to his office, introduced me to his staff, then to the Managers' office for more introductions and then on to the selling floor where I met every employee working at that time. He told me to take a day to find a place to live. When I told him I already had a place to live, we went back to his office.

There he told me that he had been made aware of my treatment by Mr. Winters. He wanted to assure me that Mr. Winters was not typical of store managers. We then got right down to the business of my next 13 weeks and the training to become a traveling auditor. He handed me a manual about six inches thick and said, "I am told you are a self-starter, that I should inform you what was expected of you, and let you go at your own pace." He told me his entire staff was told to assist me in any way as I worked through the manual. I thought, wow, what a difference in style. This training was going to be fun.

❖ ❖ ❖

The baseball season was coming to an end and guess who was representing the National League in the Series … the Brooklyn Dodgers! I had asked for time off to attend the World Series when I agreed to accept the Sears offer of employment. I cannot remember how I was able to obtain tickets, but I did, for the 7th game. I invited my brother-in-law Dan, Estelle's husband, to attend with me should there be a 7th game. The Dodgers would be opposed by the New York Yankees, a team the Dodgers had never defeated in a World Series. Dan was as much a Yankees fan as I was a Dodgers fan and we had many a friendly discussion about the rivalry. If there should be a 7th game, I wanted to have a Yankees fan with me so I could gloat a little … I had earned that. The Series did go the distance and Dan and I took the train to New York for the game that would decide the winner of the World Series. I would be leaving for Trenton following the game.

The Dodgers went ahead 1-to-0 early in the game, and I began to perspire. My hands were wet and no matter how many times I tried to wipe them dry, it didn't do any good. I kept waiting for some idiotic error by the Dodgers which would blow the lead, because that was their pattern against the Yankees in a World Series. My team went ahead 2-0, remained ahead and finally it was over … Johnny Podres had pitched a shutout. The Dodgers had won the game and their first World Series, and I was there in Yankee Stadium, with a Yankees fan, to see it happen. I remember a news report about telephone lines being jammed in Brooklyn as fans congratulated each other on their team's success.

Dan left for Grand Central Station, and I headed for Penn Station for my trip back to work. I think I was smiling all the way to Trenton. I was 25 years old, but I was a kid again. This was the happiest day of my life. When I returned to work, the employees, who had by this time been aware of my loyalty to the Dodgers, were eager to join me in my happiness.

❈ ❈ ❈

One evening, while I was in my room upstairs, Mrs. Cassidy called to me and said I had a phone call. It was my sister, Estelle. As I walked down the stairs, I wondered why she would be calling. No one from home had ever called before this and I feared it was bad news. Estelle spoke hesitatingly and she seemed to be searching for the right words. "You must come home, Mama needs you," were her first words.

I tried to question her why I should come home, what had happened. She was not making any sense. Finally, she told me that James had been in an accident, and I was needed at home. She could not or would not elaborate on what kind of accident … something to do with glass was all I could understand. She kept repeating that I must come home. I put the phone down and said

85

to Mrs. Cassidy, something is wrong at home, I must pack a bag. Her son drove me to the train station.

Trains were running on schedule and soon I was on my way to Grand Central Station where I would transfer to a train leaving for Hartford. It was a three-hour trip; the train was a local, which meant we would be stopping at every town along the way to Hartford. I kept reviewing the conversation with Estelle, trying to make sense of it when I suddenly had the answer. James was dead. Whatever kind of accident it was, he did not survive. I started planning the funeral. It was past 2 a.m. when I put my key in the front door to find the entire family waiting for me. There were hugs and kisses and lots of tears. No one said that dreaded word.

"James is dead, isn't he?" I said.

He had started the day before working as a truck driver at a glass company. He and a co-worker were delivering glass to a construction site. James had little experience driving trucks and he parked his truck on a slight embankment. The sheets of glass were held stationary against the sides of the truck and tied on each side with a rope. The co-worker asked James to help him unload the glass, a request which was against company policy. The driver's role was to drive the truck, not unload it.

As they untied the rope, the glass fell forward touching James' windpipe and killing him instantly. The co-worker was a few inches taller and the glass falling against him broke a few ribs. James was 24 years old.

James' freak accident was front page news the next morning. It fell to me to identify his body before it could be prepared for burial. Entering the funeral parlor, an attendant escorted me to a door. I saw a winding iron staircase. It was like a scene in a horror movie. I was escorted down the iron stairs. At the end of the staircase was an open door with a light on. As I took each step hesitatingly, I could see the feet of a body lying on a gurney. With each step down the staircase I could now see more of the body, the knees and then the waist. Alfred Hitchcock could have had a field day with this scene.

It was James, nude, except for his shorts, lying on a gurney. I looked at him. He seemed asleep. I told the attendant that James did not look dead. He pointed to a scratch about an inch long on his Adam's apple and said that he had the wind knocked out of him. He added that James did not suffer.

James' wake was a circus. The front-page news of this unusual death brought out the curious who came to see the family in pain. They would stare at Mom, seemingly hoping she would react bursting into tears or screaming in pain. I sat in the front row facing the casket with a woman on either side of me. To my right was James' ex-wife. They were recently divorced, after five years of marriage. To my left was a woman who claimed to be his girlfriend. Throughout the hours of the two-day wake, the two women talked over me, each claiming to be the love of his life.

In those days, people who went to wakes stayed for the remainder of the visiting hours. The room was filled with people standing along the walls. A line of people extended beyond the room out to the street. From time to time I could hear crying and sobbing coming from those seated behind me. Mom did not show any emotion. She was still in a state of shock. Her baby was dead. No visible expression of any kind. She was just there. She had said earlier that the worst pain a parent could experience was the loss of a child.

In spite of the circus-like atmosphere, from time to time I could hear people talking and saying Mom should sue the company because James' death was due to the company's negligence. James was hired as a truck driver and should not have been asked to help unload the glass. Others would join in the discussion saying James parked the truck incorrectly. Others answered that he had only worked one day and was not fully trained in his job.

My Uncle Mike was more familiar with lawsuits than any member of the family and he sought the advice of an attorney he knew. The attorney then was asked to represent my mother in a suit against the company. During the case heard before a judge, the company did not take responsibility for James' death but did agree to pay funeral costs and give Mom a small cash settlement. I wanted to fight the decision with another attorney, but Mom wanted an end to the matter. "No amount of money will bring James back," she said. Sometime later, the attorney was arrested for, I think, embezzling funds from clients' accounts. My uncle would know that kind of lawyer.

It did not escape my mind that this kind of lawyer might be the type of lawyer who most likely would accept money from the company to not pursue the case. At a time of crisis, most families want the matter to be over. It is later, when the pain is manageable, that the client becomes angry and regrets not pursuing the case. It isn't about the money, it is more about justice and making the guilty party pay a penalty, in this case, a prison sentence.

I remained at home for nine days, until things quieted down, and Mom could understand that I had to return to work in Trenton. The Cassidys were very comforting when I arrived, and we talked for several hours before I went to bed. The next morning, I lay in bed. I was awake but could not move. I was paralyzed from the neck down. I called out to Mrs. Cassidy that something was wrong with me, would she please call a doctor. Doctors made house calls in those days and in an hour or so he was in my room examining me.

The doctor checked my pulse and temperature and then asked what was going on in my life lately. When I told him about James and that I had just returned from nine days at home, he told me that my body was reacting to the stress I had experienced. I would be okay in a few days. His diagnosis proved accurate. Each day, from the neck down, I had feeling beginning to return. By the fourth day, I was back to normal and ready to go to work. I telephoned the Controller and asked him to please talk to the employees and ask them not to speak of my personal loss. I asked that they ignore the fact that I was away for two weeks. I knew I was not ready to deal with others' sympathy without getting emotional. The employees did what I asked and sometime later, I was able to discuss James' death without becoming emotional.

James' death caused me to become philosophical. That he was only 24, told me I should treat each day as if it might be my last. Never go to bed angry about anything. Never let a disagreement fester. Continue to adopt a "get-over-it" attitude. Never fail to express love and affection for others. I think that I matured significantly in just a few weeks.

❖❖❖

Eight weeks into my 13-week training, the Controller called me into his office to tell me he had informed Philadelphia that I was ready to go out on the road as a traveling auditor. He said it was a good decision to allow me to proceed at my own pace. He told me that my personality would be a plus in my new role and that I would make a fine auditor for the company.

He told me that I would be missed by the employees who had grown to respect me.

I was surprised, but happy, at the news. Happy to be going on to a real job and that the training stage was over. At the same time, I was sad to leave Trenton and my new friends there. It had been a wonderful experience and I would always fondly remember my time there. I said goodbye to the Cassidys and to Trenton and returned home to await my first assignment as a traveling auditor.

• **Chapter 12** •

The Late 1950s

I did not have to wait too long for the letter assigning me to Long Island, where Sears had 29 stores. I would spend one week at each store. I would be staying at the New Yorker Hotel, near Times Square, from Sunday evening until Thursday evening. I would have an expense account without limits on everything but meals. I would be allowed $1 for breakfast, $2 for lunch and $3 for dinner. (Remember, this is 1956 prices.) Honestly, the designated amounts were more than I needed. For all other expenses, I was to use reasonable judgment.

This was truly exciting news, to be assigned to New York City. By this time in my life I had become very interested in the entertainment world, reading "Variety" weekly. This period was to become known as the Golden Age of Broadway. I would now have the opportunity to see Broadway shows and any other of the performing arts in the city. This was going to be a hoot.

The first store that I was assigned to was located at Riverhead, at the very end of Long Island. I spent three hours each day, one way, on the Long Island Railroad. I left the city at 7 a.m., arrived at the store about 10 a.m., worked until 3:30 p.m. and was back in the city about 6:30, in time to plan my evening on Broadway. I smiled as I remembered my earlier requests of Sears, to assign me where I would not have to travel a long distance. I did not object to my new schedule because I was living in New York City and that made all the difference in the world.

One night after work, I walked into a ticket broker's office and was undecided how I wanted to spend the evening. It was suggested that I see the new musical that had opened the evening before to rave reviews. It was "My Fair Lady" with Rex Harrison and Julie Andrews. I was more interested in drama shows and rejected the recommendation, choosing another show instead. For the time I spent in NYC, whenever I met someone and the conversation got around to Broadway shows, "My Fair Lady" was always the show talked about. I was told that I had to see it before I left the city. Honestly, I was tired of being pressured into seeing that show. Nothing could be that worthwhile.

One time, when the subject came up again, it was said that it would run forever. In that case, I said that I would attend the last performance on Broadway. Some six years later, long after I had left Sears and NYC, the announcement was made that "My Fair Lady" was closing. I sent for tickets for the last performance and was so lucky to purchase them. It turned out to be one of the most exciting nights I had spent in the theater. Judy Garland, repeating her Carnegie Hall concert in Hartford, was the most exciting night I have ever spent viewing a live performance. More about that later.

Back to "My Fair Lady." During its seven-year run, the musical numbers had become well known to the public. Most of the most popular singers and bands had recorded them. The audience that night was in a festive mood, greeting every musical number with a standing ovation. It felt like they were saying "goodbye" to each number. I knew I had made a gigantic error in not seeing it earlier. I believed I would have returned again and again while I remained in the city. But no matter how many times I might have seen it, nothing could match that last performance and the audience's response to it. When the performers came out for their curtain calls, the audience responded with cheers and whistles. I don't think anyone was applauding because our hands were hurting from all the hand clapping during the evening. It was a night to remember, and I certainly do remember it some 50 years later.

❊ ❊ ❊

The auditing job was beginning to become routine, but I did enjoy meeting new people in each of the stores I visited. I was told often that I was a different kind of auditor. I even smiled. I had discovered early that store personnel were terrified of auditors. I could not understand why. If I find a mistake, what of it? No one is perfect. I tried to calm their fear by being extra friendly. I would joke with the employees and try to put them at ease. It worked. I was invited to lunch regularly and learned things I never would have found for myself during the audit.

Though I was performing satisfactorily as an auditor, I could tell the time was coming when I would want a new challenge. It was a pattern with me that when my work became routine, I would get bored and want a change. I thought I should think about asking for a possible position as a Controller of a small store or Assistant Controller in a large store. I would be making that decision much sooner than I realized.

Going through my usual routine at one of the stores, I discovered a serious irregularity that needed further investigation. Before long, I had found proof that the manager of the major appliance department was stealing merchandise by creating delivery authorizations for merchandise for which there wasn't a

93

sales record. Further investigation showed that he was shipping merchandise to locations where he would then retrieve it and sell it himself.

This was my first situation in which theft had occurred. The total loss to the store was in the tens of thousands of dollars. I took my findings to the store manager who was shocked to learn that his most trusted employee of long standing was a thief. I told him I would report the news to Philadelphia for guidance on how to proceed.

To my amazement, the store manager asked me not to report it. The thief had a large family, and they would suffer for his "mistake." The manager told me I would be destroying a family. I WOULD BE DESTROYING A FAMILY? What about the father who had committed the crime? Naturally I could not go along with his suggestion. I told him that I was not the judge or the jury. I was merely the reporter of what I found, and it was up to someone higher in management to decide what action should be taken. I decided I could not write up the incident while I was in the store for fear someone might look over my shoulder and see the contents.

When I returned to the hotel that evening, I asked to see the manager. Because I was a regular customer at the hotel, I was known by the staff. I asked if I could use a desk with a typewriter to prepare a report. I worked late into the evening, writing the report and double-checking my facts to be sure I was making an unbiased statement with just the facts. I did add a statement that made the store manager's position known. I mailed the report at about midnight.

When my report was received in Philadelphia, I was called there to discuss it. I thought about calling the store manager to tell him I would be absent for a time and decided against it. When I arrived in Philadelphia, I was ushered into a room where several men and women were present. They asked me a number of questions. They wanted to be sure that all the facts in the report were beyond dispute. They were particularly interested in how I discovered the irregularity in procedure. I left the meeting with a "well done" from the group. They were satisfied with my responses, and I was told to return to the store and complete the audit as if nothing had happened.

I don't think I ever thought about finding such a situation. I suppose the possibility was always there, but I did not see myself as an investigator, but merely a reporter confirming that company policies and procedures were being followed. I did not want to be put in a position of destroying someone's life. That reaction by the store manager made me uneasy. I did not find joy in discovering a thief among the employees. Now I was uncomfortable in my role as an auditor. I went to each store hoping I would not find a similar situation. It was time to make a change. I would resign.

In the two years since graduation I had kept in contact with Mr. Neisloss at G. Fox, visiting him in his office whenever I went shopping at the store. He was the Assistant Controller of the store and the man who interviewed me at UConn and who had later offered me a position. During every one of these visits, Mr. Neisloss would ask me when I was coming back home and going to work for him. He apparently knew that sooner or later, I would grow tired of living out of a suitcase. I decided to visit him and hope that this time he would ask me the same question.

He greeted me with a big smile and a handshake. We sat down for a visit and chatted, small talk. And then he said the magic words. "When are you going to come to work for me?"

I answered, "What would you have me doing?" He told me that recently an opening became available in the audit department, and he thought I would soon tire of traveling. For that reason, he planned to keep that position open until he saw me again. The salary would be $125 a week. Since I had visited him regularly for the past two years, he thought he would have his answer soon.

My Sears audit experience would make me a perfect fit for that department. I was now earning $5,000 a year at Sears and this offer would take me to $6,500 and I would not be living out of a suitcase anymore. I tried not to show any reaction to his offer, instead I said, "If you had made me that kind of offer two years ago, I would be working here now."

He smiled as he said, "You were not worth it then, but with two years of Sears experience, your value to G. Fox has increased."

"May I have time to think it over? When would you require a response?" I asked.

"Take your time, the position is yours if you want it," he replied.

We chatted for a few more minutes and I left to do some shopping, knowing I had found a new job. I would send a formal resignation letter to Sears and give them reasonable notice to replace me. My resignation letter was brief. I simply said that after two years of living out of a suitcase, I wanted to plant my feet somewhere and stay put for a while. I knew my return home after the death of my brother would please the family.

When my resignation letter reached Philadelphia, I received a phone call asking me to complete the audit of the store where I was working and then come to the headquarters the following Saturday for an 8 a.m. meeting. I saw the visit on Saturday as some sort of exit interview. What a surprise I had in store for me.

I arrived at the headquarters on time and expected to spend 15 or 30 minutes and leave. I then planned to visit the city of Philadelphia, starting with the Liberty Bell and look around until it was time to catch the 6 p.m. train back to Hartford.

Although this was my second time at the headquarters, having recently visited to discuss the theft I had discovered, I did not get to see much of the building. This time I was taken to another part of the building, which had a long corridor with many offices on both sides. There were signs on the wall indicating the occupant of the office.

A lady ushered me into the first office on the right where I was introduced to a Vice President. I met so many people that day I cannot remember names. The conversation was very friendly and not the formal one I had expected. Much of the conversation dealt with the possibilities for a future with Sears. There was praise for my performance, but nothing that would suggest I was leaving the Company. Where was the "Thank you for your service and good luck to you in the future" sentence? Then the visit ended, and I was taken to another Vice President's office.

When that conversation ended, it was on to the next office, where a similar conversation took place. It was the beginning of a calculated plan to entice me to reverse my decision. I never got to see Philadelphia because I spent the whole day visiting with one executive after another. We didn't even stop for lunch, which was brought in and the VPs I had previously met, joined us.

The entire day was spent trying to persuade me to stay. "I had a great future ahead of me with Sears." That was the message of the day. I did suggest that I might accept a position as a Controller, depending on the location. I would refuse a store in the South where I might have to relive the Civil War again. A

97

position as Assistant to the Controller of a large store might also be acceptable.

When I realized it was 5 p.m., I stood up and said that I really had to leave to catch my train. I told them that I had enjoyed my time at Sears, but I wanted to stop traveling. I thanked them for the very complimentary comments made during the day, but unless they had a position that would meet my requirements, my decision was final. At that time there was not such a position available. We shook hands and my time with Sears was over.

It was a very strenuous day for me having to defend my decision to resign. I wondered if others had experienced the same tactic when they had resigned. I was exhausted and could not wait to leave that building and board the train for home. The train ride would give me time to relax, and I certainly needed that. Thank God, the train was on time. There were not very many passengers traveling to Hartford on a Saturday evening, so I just about had the car to myself.

I reflected on the day just passed. I thought to myself, "I don't know what you have George, but I think you are going to have a very interesting life." I must have something, why else would so many high-powered executives give up a Saturday to try to persuade me to stay with the company? I thought about what the college interviewer reported, "Don't let this one get away." I could never dream that there would be a fairy tale of a life ahead for me.

Chapter 13

What I Thought Mom Needed

I had written to my priest friend in West Virginia of my intention to leave Sears and return home, and any invitation to visit with him and his family would have to be postponed until I was settled. I knew that G. Fox was closed on Mondays and thought any visit would have to be a Sunday and Monday, rather than the typical Saturday and Sunday. Father said that was not a concern because he would be staying at home for at least two weeks. I would let him know when I would be available, and he said he would schedule his vacation at a time convenient to both of us.

The family was more than happy to see me back home. I realized immediately that James' death had made a considerable change in Mom's personality. She was a different person, quiet, lost in her thoughts and rarely smiling. I suggested to my sisters that maybe a new location would help her adjust to life without James. There were so many memories in that home, a change of scenery could help bring her back to the Mom we had known in the past.

Marion and Chet lived in West Hartford. Estelle and Dan had bought a home in Windsor Locks. So Mom was living alone at the time I returned home. While I someday wanted to own my own home, I thought it best that for the time being I would live at home and look after Mom. The girls and I investigated real estate agents and, having selected one, I asked my sisters to begin the search. I wanted the new home to be something Mom would like. I thought the decision needed a woman's touch, so I left it to my sisters to make the decision. I had narrowed my choice to a location just south of Hartford. I really did not want to leave the city, but a change of scenery was necessary for Mom. I decided that our new home should be in Wethersfield.

Weeks went by without any decision on the move to Wethersfield. I was getting impatient with my sisters, who seemed unable to make a decision. I thought it was time I should insert myself into the decision-making process. I told the girls I would meet with the real estate agent and hopefully find a suitable new home for Mom. I called the agent and asked to meet with her to look over properties available in Wethersfield. It was a Sunday afternoon that we met and headed to Wethersfield via Maple Avenue. It wasn't much of a trip to get to Wethersfield and soon we were on Ridge Road heading south. There were houses on the right side of the street and undeveloped property on the left side. We drove a few hundred yards on Ridge Road and she turned left at the first street.

It was called Oakdale Street. We headed down a hill and she stopped at a stop sign at the first corner. She took the key out of the ignition and pointed to the corner house to my right. That property was for sale. A small seven-room cape, with beautifully landscaped grounds. There was a sidewalk dividing the property leading to the front door. On either side of the sidewalk were tall trees, a white birch on the left and blue spruce on the right. There was a line of trees at the property line on the right and two apple trees on the other side of the house.

We went inside. It was like a cute doll house. There were a number of cut-outs in the walls where figurines were placed. There was a fireplace and above it another cut-out which held a large framed painting. The room was warm and friendly. Evidently, the builder had customized the property to his liking. I saw a kitchen and a small dining room and there were two bedrooms on this floor. Upstairs were two unfinished rooms. I thought they could be my rooms. Mom would have the first floor, I would have the upstairs. I then headed for the door which led to the basement. It was also unfinished. The next step was to walk around and see the outside.

The back of the property had a line of very tall maple trees. There was a beautiful crab apple tree in the center of the property. The agent said it bloomed in the springtime. There was a rather small garage attached to the left side of the property. There was an enclosed sun porch. Although there were seven rooms, it really was a small house. I thought it was perfect for Mom. I made the decision right then to buy it.

It was owned by a soldier and his young family. He had only owned it for about a year when he was again transferred. He had planned to finish the upstairs rooms for his children when they were a little older, but never got around to doing the work.

"I'll buy this property," I said to the agent. Prepare whatever papers are needed for my signature and work out the details with the owner.

• **Chapter 14** •

Two Cars

W^{hen} I returned home, my sisters were there visiting Mom. I proudly announced that I had bought a new home. They were panicked. How could I make an important decision like that so quickly and without their knowledge? I was the one buying the house and I did not think I needed their approval. I wanted their input, but they had delayed too long to satisfy me. If I had some doubts, I would have sought their opinion. I did not have any doubts. This was a done deal.

It became almost a trademark of my behavior in the future. I made major purchases instantly. Too many times in the past I had heard of people delaying a decision and when they had decided to buy whatever it was, someone else had already made the purchase. Some people like to bargain, I don't. If it is something you want and can afford, go for it.

Mom and I lived in that home until she died, 46 years later, and every time someone would visit for the first time, they too, described the home as a "doll house."

Buying that home in Wethersfield was not as reckless a decision as it appeared to be. There were so many special features, I saw a one-of-a-kind property, beautifully landscaped. I was told that the original owner was the builder and he had customized that property to satisfy his taste.

We sold our home on Addison Street to a Black woman with children. She was unable to secure a mortgage for the total selling price, so we took a second mortgage for the balance. We had been advised not to do so because "Blacks were unreliable mortgage payers." I was impressed with this woman. She seemed honest, had a strong personality, and I thought her to be a person determined to make a better life for her family. So I ignored the advice I was given. She never missed a payment and years later, when I happened to drive by the property, it looked much better than when we owned it. Most people just need an opportunity to prove themselves.

I was now 26 years old, and probably one of the few at that age who did not have a driver's license. When I was 16, the age when one was able to have a license, I could not afford a car. What did I need a license for without a car? Besides, I could get anywhere I wanted to by bus. Once we moved to Wethersfield, that was a different story. There was a bus that went to Hartford, but no way to travel around Wethersfield. The first Sunday morning, getting dressed for church, I suddenly realized we did not have transportation. We were able to hitch a ride with a neighbor. Now I not only needed a license, I needed a car.

My Uncle Tony was living with us at that time, and I asked him to take me to Taber Cadillac, a firm with an outstanding reputation. Having worked for Sears and now G. Fox, I learned how important it was to do business with trustworthy companies. Both of these companies had excellent reputations for customer service. I had $1,500 to spend. We walked into Taber's and I told the first person I saw that I needed a used car and I had $1,500 to spend. Mistake number one. The first car I was shown, coincidently, was priced at $1,500. I would never make that mistake again.

Actually, this was not the first time I would be buying a car. Some years back, my Uncle Mike came to me for money to buy another car. He had recently divorced my aunt and wanted to go to Texas and start a new life. He did not think his present auto was safe to drive that long a distance. He had seen a Mercury for sale and wanted to buy it, but he needed $750 more than he had.

I went upstairs to find my bank passbook and was pleased to find my balance was $760. We went together to the bank where I told the teller that I wanted to withdraw my balance. She suggested I leave $10 to avoid having to open a new account sometime in the future. I withdrew $750 and gave it to my uncle. A few days later, he left for Texas and I felt good about having had a part in helping him start a new life. He later remarried and they had a son. My new aunt was a wonderful person whom I came to love. Uncle Mike and Aunt Clara had a happy life together until his death years later.

While the salesman was completing the paperwork for the sale of my car, an Oldsmobile, I told him this car was my first one and that I had not yet learned to drive. He stopped working on the contract and said he had something he wanted to show me. We walked through the entire lot and there, way in the back of the lot, was a black hearse-like looking Cadillac. He told me the sales price of this car was only $750. I remembered that was the amount I withdrew from my bank account to give to Uncle Mike for his new car and wondered if this might be a good omen.

The Cadillac had been owned by a doctor's wife, who decided after nine years she wanted a new car. My first reaction was negative. How could I drive a Cadillac, even if it was nine years old? Besides that, it looked like a hearse. That make of car was owned by rich people and I certainly was not rich. However, I did know the difference between $750 and $1,500, the price of the Olds. I bought the "hearse." It would be ready for delivery in a few days. I would need two people to drive it home, one to take us to Taber Cadillac, and Uncle Tony, who would drive it home to Wethersfield.

A few days later, we went back to pick up my car and take it home, where it would remain in the garage until I learned to drive and applied for a driver's license. When we arrived home, there were several cars parked on the street which I recognized were owned by friends who were visiting Mom. They had waited to see my new car. I got out of the car and went inside. Everyone came to the front door to see my car. Someone remarked, "What are you doing with a Cadillac?" When I told them the price, they all agreed that I had made a good decision.

Before I had gone inside the house, I had asked Uncle Tony to put it in the garage. Sometime later, when the guests were leaving, they wanted to say goodbye to Uncle Tony. I thought he was upstairs in his bedroom, but he wasn't there. Maybe he was outside having a smoke. I went outside and walked around the property, but he was not outside. I noticed the garage door was raised and walked over to lower it when I heard Uncle Tony from inside the car, calling to me, to tell me he could not get out of the car. He was a Mr. 5-by-5 and the small garage did not allow the door to be opened wide enough to allow him to get out of the car. I told him to back the car out of the garage and someone else, who was smaller, would drive it in the garage. Everyone laughed their heads off when told where he was. Everyone that is, except Uncle Tony. He did not find any humor in the incident.

105

What I Remember ...

Once I had my driver's license, I realized that I would be Mom's chauffeur and that idea did not sit well with me. Mom was now 57 years old. I told her it was time that she, too, learned to drive. Naturally, she resisted for all the reasons people her age would give. When we reached a stalemate, still refusing to learn to drive, I solved the dilemma by giving her driving lessons for a Christmas present. I had the company put an expiration date on the certificate, although their policy was to honor it anytime in the future. I knew if the gift did not have an expiration date, it would sit somewhere and not be redeemed.

As the deadline approached, I kept on reminding her that I had spent over $200 for those lessons. I had asked the instructor how many lessons did the slowest-learning customer need before qualifying for the driver's test. I then asked for one more than that number. I knew Mom would never let $200 of my hard-earned money be wasted and so the last week before the expiration date, she agreed to the lessons. Weeks later she completed the course, passed the test and I bought her a used Chevy.

The next day she invited a neighbor to take a drive in her new car. Off they went heading toward Massachusetts. When they approached the state line, Mom surprised the neighbor by telling her it was her first time behind the wheel by herself. "Not bad, for the first time driving by myself, don't you agree?" The neighbor later told me that she could not relax all the way home.

Mom was fearless with her Chevy. She was like a kid with a new toy, driving to church, shopping and even taking weekend trips to Windsor Locks to visit her daughters and grandchildren. There is something special about being behind the wheel of your own car ... having control of the vehicle in your own hands ... a unique feeling of independence. I think all new drivers feel that same emotion when they drive their car for the first time without someone in the passenger seat watching every move you make.

One evening my Aunt Lilly, my father's sister, came to visit us. She was the only member of my father's family who kept in touch with my mother from the day he died. I did not know her well, but I remember liking her very much and enjoyed listening to them reminisce about the good old days. At one point, while Mom was out in the kitchen preparing refreshments, Aunt Lilly whispered to me that she wanted to tell me something. I knew, whatever it was, she did not want Mom to hear that conversation.

Aunt Lilly wanted me to know what it was like for my mother when she lost her childhood sweetheart and her three children at the same time. She had been close to Mom and knew the details of the discussions and debate that resulted in the placing of us children in foster homes. I learned for the first time the horror of that experience and the unimaginable pain my mother had to live through. Aunt Lilly said that there was a time she thought Mom would be hospitalized with a mental illness. No one could comfort her. She cried all the time.

I thanked Aunt Lilly for telling me about that time, wishing we had had that conversation a long time ago. At last, I knew why she rarely talked about the past. What few times I asked about my father, wanting to know something about him, she would simply change the subject. I was only nine months old when he had his heart attack, so I did not know anything about him … what he was like, what kind of work he did, all the questions a child would ask of a deceased parent. It was a time in her life she did not want to relive. And now I knew why.

I went to bed that evening promising myself that my mother would never again be without her family. I decided then that I

107

would live at home and look after her. When I bought the house on Oakdale Street, I planned someday to have my own home, but that evening I changed my mind. I would see that her grandchildren knew Gram and Nana. They would not be told in the future, "I wish you knew your Gramma and your Nana." We would attend every family event together, from births, recitals, birthdays, graduations, and of course, holidays.

I liked our new home. I did not like having to spend so much time keeping the beautifully landscaped grounds in the condition I found them. I could spend the whole day mowing the lawn, raking leaves, burning the leaves, trimming the shrubs etc.

When I was finished "gardening," I would stand at the front steps and look over my day's work and be satisfied that I did a good job. A week later I had to do it all over again. I longed for the day when I could afford to have a landscaping contractor do the work.

• **Chapter 15** •

The Exception

I did have one loose end that needed attention. I wanted to fulfill my agreement to visit the priest's family in New Jersey. I wrote to him telling him I was now settled, and we could plan that weekend. Several letters later we agreed on a date and I looked forward to seeing him again and meeting his parents. I would travel by train, arrive early in the afternoon, and leave the next day. Although I had to transfer in New York City to Penn Station, the ride was really enjoyable.

I was met at the station by the priest and he took me on a tour of the coastline near his parents' home. When we arrived at the home, I was impressed beyond words. It was a large old home, with mahogany wood beams and staircase. It was beautiful, so different from my home in Wethersfield. His parents were delightful, soft spoken and very friendly. We had a wonderful get-together and dinner that evening.

It was about 11 p.m. when the mother decided her day was over and she left for her bedroom upstairs. Her husband followed soon after. I was tired too, so a few minutes later, I excused myself and went up to my room which was next door to the parents' room. It had been a very enjoyable day, and I looked forward to a good night's sleep.

What I Remember ...

I had removed my shoes and socks and most of my clothes, when without warning, the door flew open. It was the priest. He shut the door, looked at me but said nothing. Then he came at me, forcing me to fall back on the bed. He tried to get hold of my private parts, and we started to wrestle. He was my size, so I was equal to the task of defending myself.

We had turned over and I was on top of him as I whispered, "What is wrong with you? What are you doing here? Did you forget your parents are in the next room? Don't you think they can hear us scuffling?" I was not concerned about this being a sexual attack because I believed I would prevail if he tried again. I was more concerned about his parents possibly learning that their son, the priest, was a sexual predator. I could not even imagine the reaction when a parent of a priest learns that about their son. We stopped wrestling and I got up from the bed. He got up from the bed and left the room without saying a word.

I was breathing heavily as I tried to make some sense of what had just happened. It had been 10 years since I was attacked in that New York City hotel when I was celebrating my 16th birthday. That time, I was afraid for my safety because the man was huge, and I was no match for him. I had no such fear this time. This time was different. It was a priest in his home with his parents within earshot. Is that why he invited me here? There was nothing in our past relationship to indicate he was that way. I would not have agreed to the invitation if I had any idea what he was up to.

Thoughts raced in and out of my mind. Was he friendly to me all this time, just waiting for an opportunity? Had he tried the same with others in West Virginia? Did his parents have any idea he was the way he was? I began shaking a little. I could not get it out of my mind that he was a priest. I grew up looking at priests as unique individuals who had given their lives to promoting the word of God. Their behavior was unlike any other males. They were not interested in what this world had to offer. They took a vow of celibacy.

I was a mess. In the hotel, I locked the door. There wasn't a lock on this door. Why would there be? I could not leave the home; I was stranded in that house. Then I began thinking about tomorrow. How would I face him at breakfast? Did the parents hear anything? Would the priest speak to me? He certainly could not apologize in front of his parents. I wished that tomorrow would never come. I did not know how I would face the day. Would all my questions be answered? What answers could there be?

I lay back in bed, shutting my eyes and trying not to relive the past few minutes. However, just as in the hotel room, when I shut my eyes, the giant was there repeating the horror, this time the horror was magnified. It was a priest attacking me. It was a long night of minutes asleep and then minutes awake, remembering what I wanted to forget.

I was asleep when there was a tap at the door. I did not answer, fearing it was the priest wanting to apologize. I was not ready for that just yet. Another tap at the door; it was the priest's mother saying Father was going to say Mass in the dining room and they would wait for me.

Wait for me? I cannot go down there and face him saying Mass. That is more than I can handle. What could I do? Should I respond that I wasn't feeling well and would skip Mass today? That would lead to more lies when I finally did appear. I would have to go downstairs sometime. I could not stay in my room forever. If I ever needed advice, this was the time.

What I Remember ...

I thought about the three words that I lived by – "Get over it." I did not think I would ever get over this. The minutes preoccupied with my dilemma seemed like hours. Finally, I came to the sensible conclusion that I had to go downstairs and somehow attend Mass as if nothing had happened. I had to do this for his parents.

I knew it was Sunday and thought we would go to Mass at their parish. It never occurred to me that Mass would be said at home. I dressed and was still wondering how I would get through the next hour, what would be one of the most stressful hours of my entire life. I walked down the stairs, still unsure of my behavior when I saw him. The dining room was rearranged for Mass. The table would serve as the altar. Chairs were placed in a row in front of the table. I would have a ringside seat for this performance. The mother asked me if I had slept well. "Oh yes, very well," I answered.

My chair was right in front of the center of the altar. How could I not look at him? Suddenly, I had the answer. I would fix my eyes on his hands, never looking up for any reason. If I did not have to look at him, maybe I could get through this. And then I realized, the worst moment was ahead, when he would give me communion. Stay fixed on his hands, do not look up at him. I was perspiring as we approached communion. I was reliving last evening, trying to ignore the fact that this man in front of me had broken his vow. Attempting to do what he tried to do, was the same as doing it.

Communion time had passed, now Mass had ended and I was still in one piece. One had to be a Catholic to understand how stressful that hour had been. A new thought entered my mind. Should I tell him I plan to notify the Bishop of his behavior if he

112

did not resign? Leaving the priesthood would not guarantee his behavior would change. At least it would not someday be an embarrassment to the Catholic church. I would have to spend more time thinking about that.

It was now time for breakfast. I would position myself so that I would not have to look at him. He spoke not a word. I directed my conversations to the parents. The time was made easier when he left the table saying he had things to do. I kept looking for clues to the question, "Did they hear anything last night?" I concluded they did not.

After breakfast, I helped with the dishes, telling them I did it at home all the time. Another white lie to give me something to do to pass the time. It was a beautiful day and they wanted to show me around the grounds. As we walked the area, I thought I was in the middle of a flower show. So many varieties and there was a story to each one.

It was afternoon now and time for another meal. His mother had prepared a light lunch and had also packed something for me to eat on the trip home. Now my thoughts were of the drive to the train station. It was time to leave. We hugged and I thanked them for their hospitality and of course the flowers. As if on cue, Father appeared. He would be driving and there would be just the two of us in the car. I knew I would not speak and hoped he would not also. It was silence all the way.

At the station, I gathered my things from the back seat, shut the rear door and then the front door and walked away, not saying a word and definitely not looking back. I was pleased it went so well. It was over. Or was it?

My normal routine at home played out. On Sunday Mom and I went to church. When it came time for communion, I

113

remained seated. Mom had the aisle seat and rose to go forward to the altar for communion. I did not follow. She looked back at me quizzically. I looked forward pretending not to notice. After Mass, Mom asked me why I did not go to communion. I told her that was not a question she should ever ask anyone. I am sure that she mentioned it to my sisters, but neither one ever said anything to me. I think it must have been about a year before I went to communion. I guess I finally came to the conclusion that it was immature of me to let one priest's behavior affect my attitude toward all in religious life.

For months I did not go to confession or receive communion and it really bothered me that I had let this incident control me. I decided to go to Confession, but not in Hartford. I took the train to NYC and went to St. Patrick's Church to have a priest hear my confession. I told the Confessor of my experience with the priest, and he began to condemn me for causing the incident.

"What did you do or say to that priest to cause this situation?" I could not believe what I was hearing. He went on and on that I was to blame. "Did I touch the priest improperly?" and questions like that. I left the confessional with him still berating me.

Then began days of questioning myself. I would go to bed thinking about it, waking up thinking about it. Finally, I decided to see a psychiatrist. What a mistake that was. He just happened to have a brother who was a priest and was defensive, that among other things, I was suggesting that a priest had done what I said he had done. Again, it was my fault. It wasn't until news out of Boston years later of priests' behavior with children that I began recovering from the guilt both the Confessor and psychiatrist had planted in my mind.

114

From that day, I have looked at priests in a different way. Now they are just men in a unique career. I attend Mass regularly and at Communion time, I look only at the hands when receiving Communion.

Sadly, I have not entered a Confessional since that weekend. I confess my sins directly to God, who I believe understands. While most of my life I have lived by three words – "Get over it" – this is the one exception.

Chapter 16

G. Fox & Friends

My first day at G. Fox would be memorable. Mr. Neisloss walked me around the two floors of the office. He introduced me to dozens of men and women. I met the two auditors with whom I would be working, Karl Kochman and Jack Litter. On the return to his office, he said that he did not expect me to remember anyone's name, but he wanted them to meet me because, as an auditor for the store, I would have occasion to visit them sometime in the future. I said, "I remember one."

"Who?" he asked.

"The lady on the 4th floor, Ann Uccello."

"Why?" he asked.

I answered, "I do not know." I could not know that she would directly or indirectly lead to my fairy tale of a life that was to come.

Miss Uccello was a few years older than I. There was a professionalism about her that I noticed right away. She had a very responsible position and was probably the only employee who met with the owner, Mrs. Auerbach, whenever she was in the store. One day she called to invite me to lunch. She asked if I was a Catholic because there was an organization, of which she was a charter member, called the Catholic Graduates Club, consisting of about 500 Catholics who had recently graduated from colleges all over the country. They had returned home after graduation and, like me, most had lost contact with former friends. She assumed that was my situation also.

Catholic Graduates Club was a cultural, social, as well as religious organization. I was very happy to learn of its existence because, as Ann assumed, I did not know anyone in Wethersfield and had long ago lost contact with my high school neighbors. There was something planned for every evening, one could make it a way of life and I did, even was elected president some years later. Because the meetings were held in the evening and on weekends, it was ideal for me as I wanted to find new interests and meet new people. Many meetings were held in the members' homes and soon I was holding meetings in my home.

It was at my home where I hosted the Discussion Group meetings that I met Sal Palazzolo. He lived with his parents, a couple of blocks from me. His parents were Old World Italians and charming beyond words. They, as immigrants before them, had come to America to make a life for themselves and their three children, all boys. They treated me like another son. One Sunday at Mass I introduced Mom to them, and another friendship was born. I still see Mrs. Palazzolo's beautiful genuine smile when she opened her front door, and I was standing there. Sal and I became good friends and I was so happy for him when sometime later he told me he had found the woman he wanted to marry and be the mother of his children. Toni was also a member of the club. They would bring three daughters into this world.

Speaking of friends, my very first friend was Nataleno Coco, called Nate. We attended grade school together and he was my protector when others picked on me. Today we call it bullying. He was very popular, and it only took a few words from him to stop others from mistreating me. When I visited his home, it was the first time I had seen the inside of a normal home. The rooming house was not a home, but merely a collection of rooms. I had a new meal called Pasta Fagioli at his home. It was a simple soup with macaroni, kidney beans, celery and tomato. Delicious. Whenever I eat that meal, I think of those times at the Coco kitchen table and the warm feeling I had for that family.

Nate had an older brother, Joe, who operated a newspaper stand in downtown Hartford. Joe put Nate through college and law school. I would visit Nate when he worked at the newsstand and chat between customers. The two of us wanted to live each other's life. When he was in college, I had a job at Bryant & Chapman. He wished he were me. He was still in college when I enlisted in the Air Force. Again, he wished he were me. He was going to be a lawyer, something I could only dream about.

Nate asked me to be his Best Man when he chose to marry. His reputation as a lawyer earned him an appointment as Assistant Corporation Counsel of the City of Hartford. He died too young for a person with such promise for the future. I think for me, his death was almost as traumatic as James' untimely passing.

Meanwhile, the work as an Auditor at G. Fox was nothing to write home about. My very first task was to read the mail. I was told that this was such an important task that Mrs. Auerbach, herself, had to approve the person assigned to do it. I saw that statement as a public relations gimmick to make me feel better about reading mail. I did not realize that I had to be approved in person.

I was sent up to the 11th floor to Mrs. A's office. Of course, I was happy to be able to meet the owner of the country's largest privately owned department store.

She was tiny. Sitting behind her desk, all I could see was her head. She played the role well, coming out from her desk to sit with me on the couch. Grandmother-like, she held my hand as she spoke to me. I was naturally a little nervous, but her charming manner disarmed me. She was pleased to meet her newest Auditor, of whom Mr. Neisloss had spoken of so highly.

Mrs. A made it very clear that she believed reading the mail was probably the most important single task in the store. It was how she learned what the customers were thinking. She said quite emphatically that her trusted subordinates "kept things from me." She went on to say that I would be her eyes when I read the mail.

"You are to send to me any correspondence that is a serious or long-standing complaint." She said if anyone reprimands you for doing so, you can say you made a mistake by putting it in the wrong slot. Then she winked at me. She told me to think of myself as the owner of the store when I read the mail and I would know what to do.

We stood, shook hands and she said that she would be looking forward to reading the mail I would send her. I left her office feeling much better about reading mail and very happy that I had that time with the owner of the store. I probably set a record for putting mail in the "wrong slot." To tell you the truth, after that meeting with Mrs. A I really enjoyed the 90 minutes I spent each day reading the mail.

Auditors spend their time in a series of boring tasks: checking policy and procedure and recommending changes where necessary to protect the company's assets and reputation. One of these boring tasks was to examine the sales checks of transactions each day. It was a task undoubtedly set aside for the newest member of the Audit department. The checks were not examined each day, but instead set aside and stored in boxes waiting for a dull time in the workday. At that time, cash registers were not used to complete a transaction. Instead, a system of tubes was used to send the sales check and payment through pipes throughout the store that found their way to the Tube Room.

The Tube Room was in the basement of the store, where employees spent their day opening the containers, validating the sales check and making changes where necessary. Then the sales check and any cash would be placed in the container and sent back to the department. At day's end, the validation machine would show a total of money received and it would be compared to the money in their drawer. Discrepancies would be noted in the "over and short book."

The Auditor would examine each check for the validation that should match the total of the merchandise purchased. It was a task so boring, one could easily fall asleep while doing it. It was difficult to concentrate for long periods of time. I had to look away to refocus every few minutes. But it was a task that had to be done and today it was my turn.

I began thumbing through the stacks of sales checks. Not surprisingly in this particular store, there were thousands of them. I had been looking at sales checks for about an hour, when something registered in my brain, but I wasn't sure what it was that caused me to hesitate. I went back to look at the checks that I had already seen and sure enough, there was a check without a validation. I took it over to Karl's desk. He looked at the check and reached for the "Over and Short" book. If there was a difference in the cash in the drawers and the validation totals, it would be noted in the book for that day. There wasn't any difference noted on the day of the sales check we had pulled without a validation.

While Karl was examining the "Over and Short" book, I went back to my desk to continue looking at sales checks. There was another without the validation, then another and another. I yelled out to Karl, I think all of us ought to look these over. Karl and Jack joined me, each taking a box. When we had completed examining all the sales checks in the boxes, we had thousands of dollars in missing validations that were not reported in the "Over and Short" book. All the missing validations were on checks processed by the same person. There was only one conclusion: Someone was stealing money from the store, and lots of it. Karl complimented me for discovering the "irregularities." He then took the checks and the "Over and Short" book and we all went to see the Controller.

This was a very serious matter. The Controller was visibly upset. Not only was he upset about the losses, but also he believed his department would be criticized for not having discovered the situation earlier. He told Karl that Mrs. A should not be told of this matter and as far as we were concerned, our work on this matter was completed. We were not informed how it was resolved, except we knew Mrs. A was never informed of the matter.

Working with Karl and Jack was a learning experience. It was the first time in my life that I wasn't on my own. I worked with people who knew more than I did, and I could learn much from them. These two men were exceptional in so many ways. They were intelligent, well-read and informed, tolerant of others and especially witty.

Jack was the funnier of the two. He had a dry humor that sometimes took a few seconds to realize the humor in his statement. Whenever I look back on those days with Jack and Karl in the Audit department, one moment always comes to mind.

Our office was located in a corner of the floor. We had windows. One winter day that was especially windy, a female employee whose desk was a short distance from our office came into the office and asked Jack to shut the window because it was so cold outside.

Jack, at his wittiest, answered, "If I shut the window, will it be warm outside?" In utter disgust, the employee turned and walked away.

At lunch time many days the three of us would leave the store and walk a few blocks to Putnam & Co., a local brokerage house, where we would watch the tape of current stock prices on the New York Stock Exchange.

In the winter I always wore a topcoat over my suit jacket. Neither Karl nor Jack owned a topcoat or overcoat. The cold did not seem to affect them in any way. When I would suggest that they might catch a cold, Karl would answer that one did not catch cold from the cold, but from germs. Who could argue?

• **Chapter 17** •

The Early 1960s

As much fun as it was to work with Karl and Jack, after I had discovered another thief I had the same feeling I had with Sears. I did not want to be a detective. I lost interest in remaining in the audit department. I decided to talk with Mr. Neisloss about a change of assignment. He said he knew I would regularly want a new challenge and he offered me the position of Inventory Coordinator. That person was responsible for the taking of the store-wide inventory twice a year. It was a two-month project, taking me out of the audit department for four months each year.

Taking twelve floors of inventory was a monumental undertaking. First, there was the creation of instructions on how to take inventory which would be distributed to all the employees in the selling departments. Then there were meetings and more meetings with employees and department heads. Once taken, the pages of inventory were placed in pads of 25 and given to me. Now it was my task to compute the value of each department's inventory. This was especially important because the result directly affected the bonuses of the department managers. The book value of the inventory (purchases minus sales added to the opening inventory) was known to the department manager in advance of the taking of the inventory. When the pages were calculated, they had to come close to their book figure. Losses would reduce the profit of the department and, in turn, the bonus figure for each.

Naturally, the department heads were anxious to know the results which were computed by approximately 60 comptometer operators. (A calculating machine that computed the inventory in dollars and cents.) The personnel department hired part-time workers to do the computing. I was their supervisor and responsible for training them. Computing the value of the store's inventory took about two weeks. We were set up in the auditorium on the 11th floor and the part-timers worked varied schedules from 8 a.m. to 9 p.m. On Saturday, they worked until 5 p.m. The workers were full-time employees of other companies, and housewives wanting to make a little extra money.

Each operator would first establish that there were 25 pages in each pad. When there were fewer, I would contact the department and a search to find the missing sheet or sheets was conducted. Operators were taught to look for unusual quantities or prices. Whenever one was pointed out to me, I would again call the department for a confirmation that the information was accurate. Apparently previous Inventory Coordinators just had the operators compute what was on the paper, not questioning anything written on the pages.

By calling the departments with our questions, we gained their respect. In the past, large discrepancies between the book value and the inventory result were always blamed on the comptometer operators. That was no longer the case. They appreciated our concern for accuracy.

I did not know it at the time, but word started to spread about the new attitude and the one responsible for it. I was beginning to be the "fair-haired boy." I say "boy" because my employers in the past and now in the present always called me "Georgie." Don't ask me why. No one outside of work ever called me "Georgie." It was particularly amusing when the person calling me "Georgie" was younger than I was.

We were on their side and they no longer questioned the results given to them. In addition, Mr. Neisloss was happy because he did not have to deal with managers, twice a year, complaining about his personnel. The fact that I had reduced the cost of computing the inventory by a third also added to the growing positive reputation I was developing.

I looked forward to the inventory work. Twice a year it took me away from the boredom that was auditing. But after three years of dual positions, I again was ready for a change. So, it was time to talk to Mr. Neisloss.

He was ready for me, apparently knowing me better than I did myself. This time he had a new position for me, a full-time position, the Assistant Budget Director. It would be a newly created position, which had to be approved by Mrs. A.

The Budget Director and I reported weekly to the top-level management. He had veto power over the hiring of personnel in the store. Every request for personnel had to have his approval. Each department was allotted personnel dollars as a percentage of their sales. My job would be to maintain that percentage. The cost of personnel was the largest variable expense in the store. It directly affected the bottom line. I took my new position seriously and frequently disapproved requests. The director was more lenient than I and rarely disapproved a request. Where I had gained a reputation for being on the side of these managers when I was working as the Inventory Coordinator, suddenly I had changed spots and was seen as not so friendly to them.

125

My meeting with Mrs. A was friendlier than the first some six years ago. Maybe it just seemed that way to me because I think I was a little nervous then. This time I was much more confident of my ability. We sat side by side on a couch as she spoke of the importance of my new position. She told me I would be challenged, especially by the long-time department heads (she referred to them as prima donnas) whenever I would reject a request for additional staff. "You have to gain the trust of these individuals, the way you did while working as Inventory Coordinator," she said.

I was a little surprised that she was aware of my performance in that position. She raised her voice as she added that I should not allow myself to be intimidated by any one of them. She told me that she would back me up in any decision I made, but I better have my facts straight.

As she stood ending our conversation, I was unprepared for her closing statement. She smiled as she said, "Frankly George, I am kinda looking forward to your battles ahead. I think my prima donnas will have met their match." We shook hands and I left her office, excited to begin my new challenge.

It would not be too long before that closing statement would be tested. A request for additional staff was made by the cosmetic department, which I rejected. This department was the most profitable one in the store, and because of that fact the department head was a powerhouse. Nobody argued with her. I was told that she always got her way. The battle lines were drawn. It was the latest version of David and Goliath.

When the Personnel Department received my rejected request, the head of that department came to my office to offer some friendly advice. He thought I was unaware of the consequences for taking on this woman. He told me that she would go directly to Mrs. A and I would be forced to admit I had made a mistake. I told him to inform the Grande Dame of my decision and I would face the consequences. With the Budget Director on vacation, I was on my own.

I did not have too much time to prepare myself when there she was, at my door. The diatribe began. In a voice one could hear throughout the entire floor, she insulted my lack of experience in retailing, my age, my short time in this new position, etc. She covered all the bases except the important one: Why did she need more staff? I listened but did not say a word until she came up for air. I simply said that my decision was firm. She would take the matter up with none other than Mrs. A. and she left, I assumed for her office.

She must have taken an express to Mrs. A's, because it was only a few minutes later that my phone rang. It was the boss, herself. When I assured her that I did have a good case for the rejection, she suggested I take the initiative and go to the department to further discuss the matter. I told her I would. She closed the conversation saying, "You are taking on the number one prima donna. Good luck, you will need it."

I knew that this situation could be a turning point for me as Assistant Budget Director. If I could win this one, the other department heads would have more respect for me in my new role. I had an ace up my sleeve, but it wasn't a sure winner. I would need some good luck on my side.

In my frequent travels throughout the store, I would sometimes stand on the mezzanine floor which overlooked the main floor. The cosmetic department covered almost the entire first floor. I would often notice the salespeople congregating at one end of the island, completely oblivious of customers waiting to be served at the other end.

I telephoned the Grande Dame and asked her to meet me on the mezzanine level. I was praying that some of her salespeople would again be ignoring the customers. As we looked over her vast department, I asked if she saw anything against company policy. Her response was negative. I then pointed to a specific island where customers were standing at one end of the island, while her salespeople assigned to that island were busy chatting with each other at the other end. She left me before I finished what I was saying.

Returning to my office, my phone was ringing. Guess who wanted to see me? In a few minutes she arrived and to my surprise, apologized for her behavior earlier. I thought it a mark of her professionalism to make the apology in person, rather than on the phone. She thanked me for calling that situation to her attention. A second time, she apologized for her disrespectful attitude. She shook my hand and in so many words, praised my calm demeanor throughout the incident. I never had a problem with her after that. You might say we became friends.

The Personnel Director congratulated me for standing my ground and winning the argument. I don't think it was a coincidence that the number of requests for personnel that I received declined after that episode. Mrs. A was effusive in her praise of my performance, closing her comments with, "it is about time that someone took the measure of that 'old broad'."

In my new position I attended, with the Budget Director, the weekly high-level management meetings. I found myself a customer advocate, disagreeing with management when I thought the latest suggestion would not be customer friendly. Although I was new and certainly the youngest person in the room, I felt I was being treated as an equal. I was enjoying my new role and satisfied I had found a position I would want to hold for some time.

Months later, I was called to Mr. Katzen's office. He was the Controller of G. Fox. Except for the weekly management meetings, I rarely saw the Controller and I don't think I ever had more than a few words with him whenever we would see each other. It was the Assistant Controller that I dealt with for the past seven years. Mr. Katzen asked me to be seated and proceeded to discuss my work since coming to the store in glowing phrases and sentences. Something was up, I thought to myself. He went on and on with praise for my work and the respect others had for me.

"I am very happy to tell you that you are being promoted to Budget Director of G. Fox. At 33, you are the youngest person ever to hold that position. You should be very proud of yourself." Did I just hear right? This position would put me near the top of management in this world-renowned retail store. Mr. Katzen continued, "I have just spoken to Mrs. A and she is in full agreement with your promotion. She undoubtedly will want to speak to you herself." I was stunned. I think all I remembered was that I would be the youngest person to ever hold this position. I wondered if I would still be called "Georgie."

Mr. Katzen asked me if I was pleased by this news. I certainly was, but as much of a shock as the news was, I wasn't so shocked that I would overlook one important detail: salary.

With a smile on my face, I asked Mr. Katzen if he had overlooked this "insignificant" item and with a straight face, he quickly answered that I would be receiving a $10 increase in salary. Did I hear him correctly? A $10 increase to head one of the most important positions in the store? Was he joking? I waited for a smile, a smirk, something to indicate he wasn't serious. I wasn't satisfied with his answer that I would, of course, receive increases in the future after I had performed in this new role for a reasonable time. I had trained myself to count to 10 when I was about to explode. I was boiling inside. We seemed to be playing a game of "chicken." Who would be the first to speak?

I waited for what seemed like an eternity of silence. He waited for me to say something. I was wondering how I would tell him that he could take his promotion and shove it. Of course, I would be more tactful than that, but I wanted him to get the message and get it clearly that I would not accept his offer. I felt that I was being treated as "Georgie," and not "Mister." I learned a long time ago, compliments are nice, but it is the money that tells you what a company really thinks of its employees. I waited long enough; I would speak first.

"Thank you, Mr. Katzen, for thinking of me for this position," I said, "but I cannot accept your offer as presented. I find a $10 increase in salary, following your glowing recap of my work, to be inconsistent and almost insulting. If I am half the person you described earlier, then don't insult my intelligence with a $10 increase. A $50 increase would be more than justified. For your information sir, I have been performing as the Budget Director for some time and you do not need 'a reasonable time' to assess my performance. You have offered the position to me because I am already qualified and capable to hold it. I cannot accept the position under the terms you have offered. I do, however, thank you for the offer. Give the position to someone else, and I will remain as the assistant." I stood up to leave the office. He said very firmly that I should sit down.

He glared at me. I glared at him. His next statements completely overwhelmed me. Angrily, he said, "I did not ask you if you WANTED the position. I told you that you would BE the Budget Director. If you do not accept the position I have just offered you, you will be fired. You do not have a choice."

I jumped out of my seat and headed for the door. Holding the door open, I turned and forcefully said, "SIR, I ALWAYS HAVE A CHOICE," and left the room. Wow, in just a few minutes that conversation had become a wrestling match and he was on top.

I walked around the store for about a half-hour thinking in a matter of a few minutes my emotions had run the gamut from elation to anger. I headed back to my office to be met by a trio of past and present superiors, the Budget Director, Mr. Kochman and Mr. Neisloss. They, one at a time, tried to restate in a more professional manner Mr. Katzen's angry response to my refusal to accept the position.

They all agreed I was a perfect choice for the position, and I should not let a few dollars cause me to reject the offer. I refused to budge. We had a stalemate brewing here. Mr. Katzen would be seen as weak if he consented to my demand. I thanked them for their opinions and told them that I would sleep on it.

That evening I thought over what had happened with Mr. Katzen. Then I remembered my last day at Sears, and how all those executives tried to change my mind. That time, I stuck to my position and resigned. That was the right decision at that time. Should I do the same thing this time? I liked the statement he made that I would be the youngest person ever to hold the position. That would look good on my resume. Had Mr. Katzen made a mistake in saying he would fire me? How could he retreat from that? It was I who had to come up with a solution. I really did not want to leave the store. I enjoyed the position I had.

How could I consent to what I thought to be an unreasonable offer, and not give in completely? He said that my salary would be adjusted later. Why not consent to him, but on my terms? Why don't I determine the time and the amount for any future increase in salary? Tell Mr. Katzen I would accept the position, but in two months I would want a $40 increase. Any lesser amount and I would resign. I hoped he would see in my counter offer a strong executive, but one who was reasonable and open to compromise. Tomorrow I would make my suggestion known. What would I do if he refused? I would worry about that later. Mr. Katzen accepted my plan. I felt I had won in the end.

I wonder what I would have done had I known what I later learned. Mrs. A had decided it was time to turn over the management to others. She was now in her 70s and knew she was unable to perform up to her standards. She would name three vice presidents to manage the store. The Budget Director and the Controller were two of the three. However, she told them that an announcement would not be made until replacements had been named for all three positions.

By refusing Mr. Katzen's offer, I was delaying that announcement and Mrs. A was getting impatient. Now I understood Mr. Katzen's angry outburst. It was an emotional one. Naturally he wanted to be a vice president, and little old me was standing in the way. He probably would have consented to any compromise I made. Maybe I should have asked for $100 instead of $40.

• **Chapter 18** •

An Unexpected (for some) Victory

L ife, since coming back home, was good. Mom had her job at the Travelers and I at G. Fox. With her driving license in hand, she was now an independent woman. I was busy with the Catholic Graduates Club, whose activities were filling most of my evenings and weekends. Every once in a while, Mom would say that I did not live at 51 Oakdale Street, I merely slept there.

In addition to Karl and Jack, I had become friends with Ann Uccello and Mary Barry, both employees of G. Fox who had introduced me to the "Grads" club. I shared my lunch time with the four of them, some days with Karl and Jack, the others with Ann and Mary. As a member of the "Grads" I had found new interests and was developing my social skills. My career was on a steady upward path and in the "Grads" club I had been elected President.

I had a full life and was enjoying every minute. I could not imagine that a phone call would change my life and send me in another direction.

Every workday, I rode the bus, usually arriving before 8 a.m. This particular morning, the phone was ringing as I approached my office. It was Mary. I thought it was odd that she would be calling me so early in the workday. "Guess who is running for City Council?" she asked. City Council, I thought to myself, I don't know anything about the City Council. I was not the least bit interested in politics.

"I have no idea," I responded.

"Ann," she said.

"Ann who?" I answered.

"Ann Uccello is going to run for the City Council," was Mary's unbelievable response. We talked for a few minutes and the conversation ended.

Ann Uccello was the last person I knew who I would think of as a politician. I put down the phone and prepared for the workday. Suddenly, my mind was elsewhere. I could not stop thinking about Mary's call. Ann Uccello, a politician? She was not the kind of person I had become accustomed to, in what little I knew about politics. My impression of a politician was an outgoing, back-slapping, running-off-at-the-mouth individual. Ann was none of these.

I left my office and went to Ann's. "What is this I just learned from Mary, that you are seeking political office?" I asked. She smiled and said that she had thought about it in the past and her interest grew when she became a member of the Republican Town Committee. (I did not know what a town committee was.) She added that the store was closed on Mondays and the City Council met on Mondays, so she talked it over with Mrs. A and she told me that I should do it.

"If you don't, you will wonder for the rest of your life if you could have succeeded in politics," she added.

I told Ann that I knew very little about politics, but I did know that politics was considered a man's game and that was why few women were ever elected to office. "What makes you think you can succeed in that world, and doesn't it take a lot of money to engage in a political campaign?" I said.

Ann interrupted me and said "Oh, the Party is taking care of all that."

"The Party?" I shouted, "You mean the Republican Party? Are you serious? Hartford is a Democratic city. I cannot remember who was the last Republican mayor." The conversation continued and it was more like a debate. The more we talked, the more I was convinced that Ann was headed for a disaster.

I went back to my office, but I could not concentrate on my work. I kept reliving the conversation with Ann. I must call Mary and schedule a private lunch, just the two of us. This "Ann thing" was bothering me. Mary and I met for lunch in a quiet corner of the employees' cafeteria. I explained my concern that Ann was going to fail. She was naïve to think the Republican Party was going to guarantee victory.

What they would guarantee is that three of the four candidates would be elected to the minority seats and those three would be the three men running with her. We had to do something. Mary agreed. Both of us were blank on just what we could do. We agreed to think on it and meet in a couple of days with our ideas.

In the meantime, I had a few more conversations with Ann. She told me that they were going to call themselves "The New Republican Party" and the four of them were going to meet at her home to develop ideas for the campaign. I asked if I could attend, and she said I could.

That evening after work, I went to the main library to research the past local election. It was a foregone conclusion that the Democrats would win, so the media did not cover the campaign extensively, at least not the two local newspapers. Why should they, there wasn't any story there. I learned that the Democrats won elections because they had a four-or-five-to-one lead in the voter registrations. I read what little coverage there was and looked over the results by district. There was a story the day after the election that included the fact that the turnout was in the low 30 percent. That number jumped off the page at me. That meant there were over 60 percent of eligible voters who stayed home. That was the answer, bring out more of those voters. The question was how to do it. Isn't that the main purpose of every political campaign? Could it be that the public apathy was due solely to the fact that the winners were already known?

Would there be more interest this year because of The New Republican Party? I would think the media would have something new to cover, but the result would be the same, because there were only four of them and it took five winners to take control of the Council. Each voter could cast a ballot for up to six candidates. Whoever they voted for, the Republicans would again have the three minority seats. I had to find some way to see that Ann Uccello was one of the three.

I don't know why I should be so interested, but I was. Her victory was all I could think about. I went to sleep thinking about it and woke up thinking about it. Maybe I would get some ideas at the meeting at Ann's home when the four of them would discuss the campaign.

Ann called me at my office and said they were meeting that very evening at 7 p.m. I told her I would be there just to listen. The four would-be councilmen met in the kitchen at Ann's home. I had been there many times, so I was really quite comfortable in that home. Mrs. Uccello joined the group and chimed in often with her opinions. I learned that the top vote-getter was automatically elected as Mayor, and the 2nd highest vote-getter was elected the Deputy Mayor.

As the evening passed, I noticed that whenever Ann had an opinion, she was interrupted by one of the men. However, when Mrs. Uccello had a comment, she was allowed to state her opinion. Who was going to argue with her, after all, it was her home? On the way home after the meeting which lasted about three hours, I was convinced that Ann was merely window dressing. The men were going to win those three seats and they acted as if they had already won them.

The next day I called Mary to meet me after work at the White Tower. We had a couple of hamburgers while I told her what I had observed the night before at the Uccello home. I made it clear that I believed the three men were out for themselves. I told her about the low turnout and that we had to find a way to bring out more voters. I believed that whoever we persuaded to vote, would vote for Ann. My idea was to travel the city, visit every home, every retail business and every factory. In other words, spread the word, so that every person we came in contact with, would be aware that Ann was a candidate.

Ann was virtually unknown to the voters, so our job was to dramatically increase her name recognition. When you have six votes, anything is possible. Just ask the voters to "give one of your six votes to Ann." Mary commented that we were looking for votes for Ann and neither one of us could vote for her because Mary lived in West Hartford and I lived in Wethersfield. Fortunately, the two of us knew many people. Mary was very active outside the store. We both knew many people who worked for G. Fox. Most importantly, we had 500 Catholic Grads, and

137

between the two of us, we knew almost all of them. They would form the base of "Ann's Army."

I suggested creating lists from Christmas cards and membership lists of clubs that Mary had. Even though many people on those lists lived outside of Hartford, we believed that almost every one of them lived in Hartford at one time or knew people who did. We had our Catholic Grads lists. Then there was the G. Fox weekly bulletin, which was distributed to 2,000-plus employees. We would have an article with her picture placed in that bulletin. Everywhere we went in the store we would talk about Ann's attempt to become a Councilwoman. We were beginning to put it together.

A couple of days later, Ann showed me the proofs of what would be her campaign photo. They were dynamite, all of them. Those photos spoke to me. They said character, honesty, integrity, all the good words we say about people we like. And most of all, it said, "Why does this lady want to get involved in politics?" Further, it said to me, maybe someone like this could make a difference. I was getting excited. I had the vehicle for recognition. That photo was going to be seen everywhere, hand delivered. Then I calmed down. What would they do with it? Every candidate's photo was in their campaign material. I did not want to distribute position papers, the usual "what-I-will-do-when-elected" baloney. Most people just glanced at it and threw it away. I wanted her photo on something that people would keep.

It was Sunday and Mom and I went to church. I could not concentrate on the Mass, my mind was on that photo. And then, just before Communion, it came to me: A photo that people would put in their wallets because something useful would be on the reverse side. Every time you pulled it out of your wallet, there was

Ann. What would be so useful that someone would want to keep it? The answer: telephone numbers of hard-to-find numbers in the phone book. In those days, the phone book, distributed to every home and business by the phone company, was the reference for every phone. We had only one phone company and their book was the main source of that information. People could call information 411 and get the number, but we were encouraged to look in our own phone book for the number.

I began to think of what numbers should be listed on the back of the photo. The numbers should be those we seldom call, but when we do, finding them in the phone book could be exasperating. What was the phone number for the main library, City Hall, the bus and train station, Social Security and the IRS? After minutes of unsuccessful searching for numbers like these, we would call 4ll. The more I thought about it, the more I was convinced people would keep the card and put it in their wallet. There it was, "Ann Uccello's Useful Telephone Numbers." We would have "Ann's Army" distribute them all over the city.

We also had the lists we compiled. Post cards were printed. On one side, Ann's photo and a place for the address. On the other side, a message asking the addressee to "consider voting for my friend Ann Uccello in the upcoming primary in September." We had made arrangements with Monsignor Daly, who was the chaplain of the "Grads" and the Pastor at St. Gabriel's church in Windsor, to use the basement of his church for a meeting. On the walls we Scotch-taped the city of Hartford's voting lists. We invited people to look through the voting lists for names and addresses of residents who they knew and address a postcard to them. Over 5,000 postcards were mailed to city residents.

Step number 2: Schedule "Ann's Army" to canvas the city's streets, house by house, knock on the door, hand the phone card to whomever answered and ask them to consider voting for Ann in the primary in September. Most of our volunteers had never worked in a political campaign and they eagerly approached this project. They were young, smiling and enthusiastic campaigners and their enthusiasm was noticed by the residents.

Step number 3: Schedule the army to position themselves in front of traffic centers – grocery and other retail stores, large employers of businesses and factories. Smile, greet the people entering or leaving the businesses and hand them "the wallet-sized card."

I didn't tell Ann too much about what we were doing. She told the "boys" that some of her friends were campaigning for her. They did not think too much of our effort, because as they put it, "what did they know about politics?" To be underestimated was a positive. They called us the "private effort." All the candidates could do what we were doing, but didn't. The Democrats didn't because they were assured of victory. The Republican men didn't because they believed they would be the minority on the council.

To remind you how little Mary and I knew about Hartford politics, we both had forgotten all about Betty Knox. We spoke of Ann as though she was the first woman to be seeking a Council Seat. Betty Knox, we learned, was seeking her 6th term on the Council. She was a member of a wealthy, highly regarded, family whose interest in Hartford was well established long ago. Betty was an Independent politician, but she ran as a Republican every election and was clearly going to win again. That bit of knowledge meant that only two seats were available to the New Republican Party, making Ann's chances even slimmer.

I did have a small concern: How would the large Hartford Italian population react to an Italian woman in politics? How would Italian men, who were mostly Democrats, react to a woman in politics, a Republican woman, at that? How would Italian women react to a woman in what was considered "a man's world?" In most Italian households, the women followed the lead of the male when it came to voting on Election Day. Would it make a difference to Italians that Ann was a Republican?

There was only one woman in local politics at that time, who coincidentally was Italian. She was the Secretary of State, Ella Grasso. The key word there was "Secretary." Many did not think of her as a politician and legislator, but as a secretary, who did office work.

Step number 4: Put Ann on Italian radio. There was an Italian radio program on Sunday morning that had a small but dedicated audience. We would take advantage of the large Italian population and put Ann on the radio with a campaign statement. I thought we would get a sense of the support Ann would get, if any. This idea was controversial.

I believed Italians or any other immigrant would be proud of anyone of their nationality who was successful. That was the reason they came to America. I lived in an Italian household, and I saw how my family's friends reacted with pride when one of their own had been promoted at work. Now they were going to hear a female voice on radio with whom they could identify. Another plus was the fact that, at least in our area, female voices were not heard on radio. Ann would be a novelty that would bring more attention to her candidacy.

Someone in the group knew of Enzo DeDominicis, the owner and President of WRCH, a radio station with the second largest audience in the area. He enthusiastically agreed to coach

141

Ann in what was commonly known among Italians, as the "beautiful Italian." Ann would write her statement for a 30-second commercial and have Enzo not only translate it into the "beautiful Italian," but also coach Ann with pronunciation and delivery.

We had our answer after Ann's very first commercial was heard on that Italian radio program. A star was born in the Italian community. Ann received rave reviews for her 30-second spot. The radio station was overwhelmed with calls inquiring about the female voice on the Italian program. It caused a sensation among Italians, who wanted to know who the woman was that was speaking so well in their native language. We were told that in Italian circles, she was the subject of much interest and pride.

First generation Italian-Americans spoke many dialects of the language, but most everyone could recognize the "beautiful Italian" when it was spoken. To hear their native language on the radio, spoken so well by an obviously educated and Italian woman, was a source of tremendous admiration and respect. We got the answer to all our fears. Italians, though many were life-long Democrats, would support her attempt at a seat on the City Council.

There was to be a primary to reduce the number of candidates to eighteen who could compete on Election Day. Although the word was out that Ann's supporters were all over the city campaigning, the male candidates and the media paid little or no attention. We were the "private effort," but nothing significant would come of it. After all, they were the professionals, what did we know about politics? Our effort was laudable, but of little value. Oh, to be underestimated by an arrogant elite … a marketing and public relations dream.

On primary day, we assigned Ann's Army to cover the 45 polling places in Hartford. Some were assigned from 6 a.m. until they went to work, then returned after work until the 8 p.m. closing of the polls. Ann's family and friends who were available filled in the hours not met by Ann's Army. We pretty much covered all 45 districts for the full fourteen hours of voting time. None of the other candidates of either party covered all 45 sites. Ann and I visited all 45 districts to thank our volunteers for their efforts.

That evening, Mary and I joined the Uccello family at their home to wait for the results of the voting. There were 22 names on the ballot, which had to be reduced to 18 for the final vote in November. I was positive all four of the New Republicans would be among the 18 that survived, but I wanted Ann to be the highest vote getter among the Republicans and be among the first nine, because there were nine seats on the Council.

The family listened to the returns, not sure of what to expect. The returns came in slowly and when it was over, Ann was the highest Republican vote getter and finished 9th in the voting. There was lots of noise and satisfaction at the results and everything, just as I had hoped for, had happened. Our "private effort" paid off.

Step number 5: Mail a note from Ann to all the volunteers, thanking them for their time and support. They all were reminded that the real test would come on Election Day and they should continue working as they had been, covering the city with Ann's wallet-sized card with the Useful Telephone Numbers. They did not need any encouragement, the success on primary day was more than enough motivation to continue.

On Election Day 1963, I again drove Ann to the 45 polling places. We spent the whole day, from about 7 a.m. until about

7:30 p.m. visiting and revisiting polling places. We arrived at the Uccello home in time to listen to the voting results. This time, those gathered were excited – this was the one that counted. Ann improved her 9th position and was the 7th highest vote getter and now had a new title, that of City Councilwoman.

This group of well- meaning but inexperienced volunteers had made history by electing another woman to the City Council. We had proved that in this country, anything was possible.

What was overlooked by the professionals and the media, was that this victory was accomplished with little money. It was accomplished with the best advertising ever devised, WORD OF MOUTH.

Chapter 19

Where Were You When

November 1963 would also be remembered, but this time, sadly remembered. Karl, Jack and I had gone to Putnam & Company after our lunch in the G. Fox cafeteria to watch the stock market doings. I was standing with my back to the ticker-tape machine, a few feet from those standing ahead watching the tape on the wall. Whenever there was some special news, usually about earnings or other business news, a bell within the machine would ring to gain the attention of those nearby.

I turned around to see what the special news was. It was a one-sentence bulletin stating that President Kennedy had been shot while visiting Texas with Mrs. Kennedy.

I yelled out the news to those standing in front me. I don't know if they heard me or were so engrossed in the action on the tape, which had stocks plummeting for no apparent reason, but nobody reacted. I repeated the news and this time it brought others over to the ticker-tape machine to read it for themselves. We waited for further news because the announcement was just one sentence. Normally the three of us would remain only a few minutes before walking back to the store. We decided to wait for further reports.

We left Putnam & Company after we learned of the President's death. On the walk back to the store, I said that the

145

store will be closed for the funeral. Both Karl and Jack disagreed. Mrs. A would not alter the store hours for any reason. They reminded me of the time during World War II, when President Roosevelt had called her to adjust store hours so those working third shift in factories could shop at the store. He wanted her to add more hours. Mrs. A refused, telling the President that customer service was key at G. Fox and she could not maintain its reputation with part-time employees hired to work the additional hours he was requesting. She was adamant on that subject.

During the Christmas season when stores, located in malls, remained open every evening, G. Fox was open one evening until 9 p.m. Mrs. A would not budge. Her attitude was simply that if people wanted to shop at G. Fox, then they could do so at its established schedule of hours. The other retail stores in downtown Hartford were not happy with her decision, because they knew that customers would not come to Hartford to shop if G. Fox was closed.

The next day we learned the store would be closed the day of the President's funeral. The Main Street windows were respectfully decorated with huge photos of the President, draped in black. Round-the-clock TV covered the sad event. When the President's casket was brought to the Capitol rotunda for the public viewing, the cameras were fixed on the casket as thousands filed past.

All night long, I watched the mourners pass by. There was very little traffic on the streets that entire weekend. People everywhere were glued to their television sets. I slept very little, sitting up in bed, emotionally drained.

I watched the killer, Lee Harvey Oswald, himself get shot by Jack Ruby. "No!" I screamed at the TV. Along with the world, I wanted to hear him tell us why he shot the President. Conspiracy theories were numerous. The rumor I heard most often was that he was shot to protect the others involved.

The Warren Commission was formed to investigate the President's murder and concluded Oswald was alone. It was one of those "where were you when" days, I will never forget.

• **Chapter 20** •

Just the Beginning

With Ann's "unexpected" victory on Election Day past, Ann's Army could now disband. Their work was over. For me, the work was just beginning. During the campaign period, I became aware of the voters' reaction to Ann's photo. Like me, they saw something in that photo that captured more than their vote.

I did not know then that I was beginning a journey that I would later refer to as a Fairy Tale of a life. I did not know then, and I still do not know now, why I was so preoccupied with Ann's new world. I have come to believe it to be some kind of calling. Why did my best ideas for the campaign always come while I was attending Mass? Whatever it was, I was totally absorbed in doing what I was doing. My very promising career at G. Fox was not nearly as interesting as her venture into politics.

The day after the election, my phone at work rang continuously with employees from all over the store calling to congratulate me and Mary on our unbelievable success. When later I went up to the Main office, the employees at their desks applauded when they saw me. Mr. Neisloss, upon hearing the commotion, came out of his office to see what was happening and invited me into his office. He went on and on about Ann's victory and my part in it. He joked that now I could go back to work and earn my salary. He was right; I did put Ann's venture into politics ahead of my work as the Budget Director.

I began attending the City Council meetings, which were held on Monday evenings, not to listen to the deliberations, but to gauge audience reaction to Ann if she would speak. I would position myself in the middle of the seating area and listen to anyone I could hear making comments. If people left after a matter was considered, I would walk out with them so I could hear them talking. I did this throughout the evening until the end of the meeting. I wanted to hear any reaction to whatever Ann might have said during the evening.

The comments, although few, were positive. "The new lady was the only one who made sense to me." "The new council-woman does not say very much, but when she speaks, I could understand what she was saying." "I like that council lady; she is very smart."

When she would raise her voice while debating an issue, to make a point, the audience applauded her remarks. She may have been a novelty on the voting machine, but she was beginning to hold her own with the men and the public recognized she was equal to the task.

The public was beginning to take notice, but not the media, who ignored her comments, not reporting them while covering the council news the next day. She was a member of the minority party and whatever she said would not change the vote by the majority.

However, I saw the potential in Ann, even if no one else did. A few months before the 1965 election, I approached Howard Kaufman, the Republican Registrar of Voters. He was the most influential Republican in the city. He had the advantage of holding his position for years, while candidates for office burst on the scene and later disappeared.

"Howard," I said, "I think Ann can go all the way this time. We can have a Republican Mayor and maybe a Republican majority on the council if only the party would get behind her and make her their leader.

His reaction was very negative. "A woman mayor, a Republican woman mayor in the city of Hartford? The men would never go for it."

I argued with him, trying to impress upon him what I had learned listening to the public at council meetings and other events that Ann had attended the previous months. It was obvious he was too close to the forest to see the trees.

Howard must have informed the Town Committee chairman of my conversation with him because a few days later, Ann told me that the chairman had ordered that there would not be any "private effort" in the next election. I laughed at that "order" telling Ann that I lived in Wethersfield and Mary lived in West Hartford, jurisdictions over which he had no control. I told her to work with her party members and Mary and I would do our thing.

"In the future," I added, "I will not keep you informed of our plans so you can say honestly when questioned that you do not have any knowledge of what we are doing." I also told Ann that if her chairman had any brains, he would encourage the other candidates to form their own "army."

I updated the phone card, changing the color of the card so it would look different than the one they had in their wallets. We would repeat our successful plan of the past. Another letter went out to the "Army," which now had grown well beyond the 100 or so that we had in 1963. The volunteers were looking forward to the next election and were just waiting for orders to go to work. When the new card was distributed, people took the old one out of their wallets and replaced it with the new one. The difference this time, the residents added favorable comments about Ann. Over and over again we heard how useful the card had been and that people associated it with Ann.

The pressure began building on Ann to disband the "Army." She told the chairman she did not have any idea what we were doing and since he ordered the "private effort" disbanded, I did not communicate with her.

"I have no control over George. He volunteers his time and ideas. I have not paid him one red cent. I do not have a paid staff," she said. I believed it was just impossible for the men to even consider having a woman as their leader. It must be a blow to their masculinity, I thought.

I refused to accept the chairman's decision. After all, what was the "private effort" doing? Some of Ann's friends were informing the public that she was a candidate for the City Council. It was that we were doing it so well that really bothered him. Did the other candidates not have the same opportunity to ask friends for support? Of course, they did. I believed most candidates for public office do receive some kind of help from family, friends and associates. The only difference was that we were more organized in our support for Ann.

When the voters had six votes, it was no big deal to ask for one for Ann. Most voters did not know six candidates. That was our campaign. Give one of your six votes to Ann. Simple and effective.

While I did refuse to accept the chairman's decision, I did give it a lot of thought. How would it affect Ann's relationship

151

with her colleagues and the party leadership? After some thought on the matter, I was still comfortable with my decision because the party was so weak in the city, what we were doing was promoting the party indirectly by promoting Ann's candidacy.

And most of all, I was driven to do what I was doing.

My relations with the Republican Party, which were never very good, began to decline noticeably. I thought that the best way to combat their distrust was to keep a low profile. I took pains not to be photographed with Ann. Most politicians do not make a decision without first considering its implications on their careers. I cannot count the times I had been asked, "What's in it for you, or specifically, what is it that you want?" I never wanted anything for myself, and I never asked for anything. The first time I was asked one of those questions, I replied, "What is there?"

Not wanting something made me a suspicious character, because in their minds everybody wants something. When you know what someone wants, then you can deal with that person. How do you deal with someone who does not want anything? Until they would find the answer, I could not be trusted. They never found the answer.

In the fall of 1965, we contacted the members of Ann's Army, only this time we had many more joining their ranks. I decided to repeat the 1963 effort, why mess with success? There was a major difference: Mary Barry, who worked with me from the beginning of this effort, was seriously injured in an auto accident and was unable to participate. She would be in the hospital for an extended period.

Her absence would not materially affect the operation, because we were repeating what we did two years ago, but I did miss having her around.

I had given some thought to resigning from G. Fox. I was not earning my salary and my superiors knew it. But if I thought leaving Sears was difficult, leaving G. Fox would be difficult on many levels. G. Fox was a part of my life. Friends would greet me, "here comes Mr. G. Fox." I really enjoyed my job, and I was very capable in performing this latest position. I was now so identified with the store that I would need a special reason for leaving. If I said I was accepting another position somewhere, they would offer me a raise.

I did not want a raise. I wanted to spend all my time on political campaigns. Here I was, 35 years old and finally had found the career I wanted. When I was a child and people asked me what I wanted to be when I grew up, I told them that I had no idea, but I would be good at whatever it was. Up until this time, I just took whatever came and did the best job I could.

Now I knew what I wanted. Political campaigns used many of my skills, marketing, public relations and business experience. I knew if I had a choice, I would rather be devoting my time as a volunteer in the upcoming campaign, but leaving would be too emotional for me.

When a most unexpected and unpleasant situation occurred, you might say the decision was made for me. I would have to face resigning and leave the position as Budget Director. For the next few days I thought about ways to leave that would make sense. I finally came up with my plan to exit the store in a way that would not raise any questions. I knew if I asked for a transfer to another division within the store, Mr. Katzen would never agree. I could hear him saying, "You are too valuable where you are."

I suppose I could tell him the real reason. No, I could not do that. That would never do. It would open a can of worms. Someone would have to be fired. There would be gossip all over the store. Mr. Katzen would want to keep it a secret, but he would have to answer the question, "How could he let George leave the store?" Once he told the truth, it would spread, one person at a time. I did not want to be the subject of that kind of gossip. I always avoided office gossip.

I had heard of an opening in a merchandise manager's office that would be perfect for me. I could speak to the merchandise manager about the opening. I believed he would jump at the opportunity to have in his office someone of my experience in the store. I knew also that Mr. Katzen would never allow the transfer. I would resign. He would offer me a raise that I would refuse. Sometime later, he would then agree to the transfer. Better to have me somewhere in the store, than not. I would answer that I had fallen in love with leaving. That would end the discussion. I hoped.

I put my plan into action. I spoke to the merchandise manager and as I expected, he was very agreeable to having me in his office, but – and there was the big but – "you know the rules in this store, you must have Mr. Katzen's approval to transfer out of his division." At least he had agreed to have me transfer.

Now onto the next step. I made an appointment to see Mr. Katzen. I was expecting to be put off for a day or two, but his secretary told me to "Go right in. He can see you now." I wasn't expecting an appointment so soon. I wasn't ready to make my case, but I could not refuse the appointment I had just requested.

The meeting, very cordial, was just as I had thought it would be. He told me how much I had meant to the store in all the positions I had held, and that as Budget Director I was doing so well that he was planning an increase in salary two months down the road, but he would now put it through immediately. I now knew he would reject my request. (So far, everything was going as I expected, even the offer of a raise.) I thanked him for his complimentary remarks and the generous increase in salary but told him I had wanted a position in merchandising for some time and I could not let this opportunity pass.

Mr. Katzen was very guarded in his response. He did not lose his temper like he did the last time we disagreed on a matter. This time, he said what I thought he would say, but the tone was softer. It was as if he were apologizing for having to refuse my transfer. He ended by leaving me some hope, that "maybe someday in the future, but not now." I closed the discussion by adding that if I could not be transferred, I would resign but remain in the position until he had named a replacement for me.

He did not expect my response. "Give me some time to think about your request and to name a possible replacement," he said rather dejectedly. (Everything is going as planned.) I hoped he would look for a replacement, but not too soon. (I needed time to fall in love with leaving.) Unless they hired outside the store, which was unlikely, finding a replacement for me was not going to be a simple matter. He had told me, when he offered me the position, that I was uniquely qualified for that position. He could not remember a Budget Director who had the experience in the store that I did.

Mr. Neisloss came down to my office to see me. He said Mr. Katzen had just told him of my request and possible resignation if he refused me. "I told him to approve the transfer, that it would be great for the store to have someone with your past experience, now in the merchandising end of the business. He can be a positive influence on merchandise managers who do not understand the responsibilities of the Control division. I hoped he would reconsider. When I hired you, I knew you would make me proud and you have." I was close to tears as I thanked him for his support.

The weeks went by and no news about my replacement. I was ready to end it. I asked to see Mr. Katzen, but this time I had to wait a few minutes because he was on the phone. I wanted to be firm, not angry and not disrespectful.

"Mr. Katzen," I started, "weeks have gone by without any news of my replacement. Did you think I was negotiating with you for a raise? I was not. Did you think I would forget that I wanted to resign? I think I made a mistake in saying I would wait until you found a replacement. So let me make it very clear. I will leave G. Fox at the end of next week."

For my part, it was over. I waited for his statement that he agreed to allow me to transfer to the merchandising department. He did not disappoint me. Then I added with a smile, "I'm so sorry sir, but while you have been stalling, hoping that I would change my mind, I have fallen in love with leaving. My last day at G. Fox will be Saturday of next week." I then left the office.

When the news that I was leaving became public, everyone was curious where I was going. I knew that I would not seek another position. I would volunteer my time as a silent campaign manager for Ann Uccello. I could now not only attend Council meetings, but also as her chauffeur, all the functions to which Ann was invited. I could not believe my plan proved successful, down to every detail. I guess it proved that I knew Mr. Katzen very well.

I was particularly pleased that I would leave without telling him the truth behind the reason I had to resign. I did wonder if it was a mistake not to make it public. I would pray that what happened to me would never happen to another employee. It is time to tell you the real reason I had to resign.

❀ ❀ ❀

One day as I was returning to my office, I met another employee, with a newspaper under his arm, going in the same direction. I could see the executive washroom up ahead and assumed that was where he was headed. I had never been inside the washroom. The memory of the incident at the Allyn Theatre, although more than 20 years ago, flashed through my mind every time I saw a restroom sign. There wasn't a sign on this particular door, but nevertheless I relived that day when I was 12 years old whenever I walked within sight of that particular door.

As we approached the door, I would be taking a right turn to my office. The employee asked me to enter the washroom with him so we could continue our conversation. I said I would wait outside and continue the conversation after he came out of the washroom. We were in full view of the office staff, and I was concerned that his repeated requests to enter the washroom would draw the attention of the employees within earshot.

I hesitatingly entered the washroom, shut the door and stood with my back to the door.

Once in, he came at me and we struggled while he said, "I have had my eyes on you for some time." We were about the same weight, and hearing that sentence, a burst of energy came over me and I pushed him aside and he fell to the floor. I opened the door and as calmly as I could, I walked to my office, looking straight ahead as if nothing had happened.

Once there, I sat down trying to make some sense of what had just occurred. I was dazed. My mind was looking for answers. My body was warm and somewhat unsteady.

There wasn't time to think when the phone rang. In an eerie, Bela Lugosi bass voice I heard "I will have you yet." I slammed the phone down. I was breathing heavily and fearful of his inevitable plan to do whatever. The other two times, those guys had seen what they wanted, but this time that wasn't true. Why is this happening to me again?

There was a mirror in the office, and I stood up to look at myself in the mirror. What was it that caused this kind of behavior? Unlike in Snow White, the mirror did not answer.

I wanted to leave the store. I knew I was in a weakened condition. My office had a large window, and I was concerned that anyone passing by would see me and know something was wrong. I sat with my back to the window and tried to compose myself. I wasn't a teenager anymore, yet I might as well have been, as the effect was the same.

I was planning on attending a "Grads" meeting later that evening, but now I wondered if that was a good idea. I didn't think I wanted to be around people. I knew I was not myself and anyone observing me would come to the same conclusion. If I remained home, something I almost never did, Mom would wonder if I was ill. That was a white lie I could manage.

That evening, I realized I would have to leave G. Fox. I could not go to work constantly looking over my shoulder expecting him to be lurking behind me. I now felt he might begin stalking me. I had to resign, I just had to, difficult or not. The only alternative was making his behavior public. He would undoubtedly deny my accusation and what would I do then? There wasn't any reasonable alternative to resignation. And now you have the rest of the story.

To this day, whenever I walk into a men's room, if no one, or two or three people are in there, I walk out. The same is true of public showers. My years at the University of Connecticut, when

I was living in a fraternity house, I waited until late evening when everyone had gone to bed to take a shower. The same was true in the Air Force, living with 59 other men. I took my shower when I could see everyone in bed.

There are some things one never forgets. Try as I did, and I did try, the sight of a men's room or public shower brings back the horror of another time. I happily report that nothing like that has occurred in the past 50 years.

❅ ❅ ❅

The news that I was leaving caused someone to suggest planning a going-away party for me. This was most unusual. In the past, employee parties were planned for employees who were retiring after long service. Under the circumstances, I wanted to leave quietly and definitely did not look forward to saying "goodbye." Usually, the retirement parties were rather small affairs attended by the people in the department of the retiree. My party turned out a throng, probably due to the fact that I had known so many of the employees through my high-profile positions. My role in Ann Uccello's success made others think of me as some sort of celebrity.

Mr. Katzen was the emcee. In his extremely complimentary remarks, he noted that the audience that evening was by far the largest he could remember, a testimony to the respect others had for me. That remark brought cheers from the audience and tears from my eyes. That evening was probably the most emotional one I had ever experienced. Those in attendance came up to me one at a time, hugging me and shaking my hand, some even with tears in their eyes. That was difficult enough, but it was their complimentary remarks about my work and relationships with them that had me holding back tears. This evening was something

159

I had not expected. When people tell me how much they hate "goodbyes" I understand what they mean.

I look back on my G. Fox years, so proud to be identified as an employee for nine years of the largest privately owned department store in the country. Today, when anyone mentions G. Fox I still get somewhat emotional thinking of my time with that incredible store and the dedicated employees I came to know and respect.

It was over. I had left G.Fox and was now a happy camper. I could now devote all my waking hours to the next election. My goal was to have Ann improve her standing on Election Day.

The 1965 campaign period went along as planned. We covered the city with the latest edition of our phone card. With Mary still in the hospital, Ann decided to hear the election results with her there. I notified the media that Ann would not be receiving the results at her home but would be with her friend in the hospital. This was a human-interest story and the media covered it well. Coming a few days before the election, media coverage was free publicity, and it would add to Ann's already positive image and remind voters of our campaign slogan to, "Give Ann one of your 6 votes."

On election night, there wasn't the excitement generated two years ago. At that time, no one knew for sure how voters would react to a woman on the ballot. This time, even the Democrats believed that Ann would be reelected. When the results were finalized, Ann was the fourth highest vote-getter. Normally a politician who came from nowhere to fourth highest vote-getter in two years would be a subject of much conversation and media buzz. Not so, this time. Although by this time everyone knew that Ann was well-liked, no one seriously considered her a threat to a leadership role. I was more convinced than ever that her growing reputation as a straight-talker and an honest person would someday catapult her into the mayor's office, and once there, who knew where it would lead.

The more I thought about it, the more I believed it was going to happen in 1967, the next election. Ann Uccello would become the first woman mayor in the city's 300-plus-year history. It would be international news, since Hartford was known all over the world because of companies like Aetna, Travelers, United Aircraft, Colts and so many others who now were doing business worldwide. She would be the first Republican mayor in 23 years in a city in which the Democrat Party registrations exceeded the Republicans by 4 or 5 to 1.

This was my dream and I kept it to myself.

Chapter 21

Making History

The year was 1966, a year in which voters would elect a governor. Clayton Gengras, a wealthy and generous humanitarian, had received the Republican nomination. I did not know him personally, only by reputation. He was someone I wanted to get to know. If Ann's political career continued its upward path, Mr. Gengras would be someone who could be very helpful in the future.

I called his headquarters and offered to volunteer for the campaign ahead. I was accepted and assigned to East Hartford as the Campaign Coordinator. I think each of the 169 towns had one. Because all the coordinators were being paid, I was not allowed to volunteer. I had to be paid $75 a week for the duration of the campaign.

The coordinator was to maintain the headquarters where residents could get information about the candidate and his positions on various matters of interest. I also had to develop a relationship with any news media in town and hope to get Mr. Gengras' positions covered for their audiences. The Town Committee and other volunteers would be asked to visit the residents, distributing door-to-door whatever campaign material was made available to us.

The most important item for me was to produce a reception for Mr. Gengras when he made an appearance in town. That entailed having a large crowd to greet Mr. Gengras, the news media present and refreshments for all attending. I would be given a few weeks' notice to plan for the event.

The evening affair turned out quite well. Our headquarters faced Burnside Avenue, one of the town's major streets, and a crowd on the street in front of the headquarters would be seen by many driving by. Mr. G's bus arrived with music blaring to attract attention. When he stepped off the bus, it was evident he was pleased with the size of the crowd and the hoopla we had created. When the event ended, he whispered to me as he boarded his bus, "Nice job, Georgie." His visit naturally made the front page of the local paper.

Mr. Gengras, as expected, did not carry East Hartford or the state on Election Day though East Hartford's vote for him was larger than the campaign expected in this heavily registered-Democrat town. I was pleased with our vote turnout, but I didn't think I had made a lasting impression on Mr. G. I had to do something to ensure he remembered me.

As I was cleaning out my desk and preparing to close the headquarters, I came across about $35 which was unspent money given to towns for Election Day expenses. I was able to get donations for refreshments and did not need all the money we were given for that purpose. I thought I should return the money to the campaign office. It was an insignificant amount to be sure, which should make returning it all the more memorable. When the check and my note were received, Mr. G. phoned me to thank me for my performance and for being the only coordinator to return funds. I now believed he would remember me and whenever our paths did cross in the future, he always did.

***

In the spring of 1967, I read in the Courant an ad in the amusement section promoting the summer schedule for the Oakdale Theatre, one of the state's landmarks. The campaign for 1967 would not begin for months and I had time on my hands. I drove to the theatre in Wallingford looking for a job to occupy the summer. I was hired as the Group Sales Director, a one-person operation, who visited large employers' cafeterias selling tickets for the current week's attraction. I enjoyed that summer at Oakdale because in addition to my work, I was able to see the shows on the schedule.

In September, the season ended and I left the theatre telling the owner I was going back to Hartford to elect a mayor. I am sure he did not understand what I meant.

We ordered the third edition of the phone card, contacted the volunteers and planned the schedule for door-to-door, factory-to-factory etc. The reception to the third edition was wonderful. The volunteers were having fun because the residents were so friendly and receptive.

It was time to make my dream public, at least to Ann. She laughed out loud when I told her she was going to be the next Mayor of Hartford.

"You are dreaming," she said, "that will never happen. The voters would never elect a Republican woman mayor, especially in this Democrat-dominated city. I am surprised at how naïve you are after all this time working campaigns." She continued laughing. I said that I was going to have the last laugh.

Ann repeated some of her comments. I then told her the public would not know they were going to make her the top vote-getter in the primary. She gave me a quizzical look, which required an explanation.

I answered, almost whispering, "If we ask the voters to give you one of their six votes, why would they object? You have done a good job for four years, and you are respected and thought to be an honest person, a characterization not usually accorded to politicians." I continued explaining my reasoning. "The appeal would be made to Democrats, 'You have six votes, give five to your party and one to Ann.'"

"It is too simplistic," was Ann's response.

"And that is why it will work," I quickly answered back. "Ann," I said, "I have never asked you for anything, have I? I know you trust me to put your interests first. Now I ask you to believe in yourself as I believe in you. Everywhere you go during this campaign period, after whatever statements you make, ask the voters listening to you, to give you one of their six votes. That is all you have to do. That is all I am asking you to do. You will campaign as you always have with no mention of the mayor to anyone, not even to your mother or sisters."

"Don't worry, I wouldn't think of mentioning that to anyone," she replied. I was positive I had found the formula for success. Not only would Ann make the appeal, but all the volunteers in "Ann's Army" who would be distributing the third edition of the phone card would be told to do the same.

Finally, it was Primary Day 1967. All our volunteers were at their polling places shouting to the voters to "give Ann one of your six votes." I was so confident, I felt as though I had won the lottery before the winner was announced.

Could I be overconfident? Many a candidate had lost an election by being overconfident. Not a chance. Not this time. Ann was going to be the top vote-getter and for the next three weeks, the media would do the rest.

That evening we listened to the results at Ann's home. As usual, Ann's sisters were there with other family members. No one mentioned the possibility that Ann might be the top vote-getter. They were among the majority who had convinced themselves that a woman could not win more votes than a man. They were there to support their sister. No tension here; she was almost assured of being reelected.

As the returns started coming in, Ann was near the top with each succeeding report. The family was exchanging glances. You could tell that they were just beginning to think of the impossible but didn't dare to say it out loud. I felt everyone was looking to me for a reaction, but I had none. I would celebrate when the last vote was announced, and she had won the primary. Still no doubt whatsoever in my mind.

The returns were complete: Ann had finished first. The room was a scene of jubilation. The family was screaming with joy, jumping up and down, hugging each other like long lost relatives, going over to Ann and hugging her.

Ann was surprised but not jubilant. She yelled to the others to calm down. "This is just the primary," she said. "There is still another election and now that the voters know I could be mayor, they will think twice before voting for me."

I had the opposite view. I believed once the voters realized that a woman could actually win the primary, it put an end to the belief that a woman could not take it all.

When the media realizes what has happened, they will have a story so captivating they will run with it. Ann was going to be a household name all over the state in a few hours. Who is she?

How could this be? And I believed they would be asking the questions with smiles on their faces. I began feeling emotional, so I left the room and went into the pantry in the kitchen and the tears started to flow. Suddenly it occurred to me that I had changed Ann's life. She would never be the same. Did I have the right to do that? After all this was my dream, not hers.

Nellie, Ann's youngest sister, came into the kitchen and when she saw me sobbing, she turned around and walked back into the living room. I don't remember how long I stayed in the pantry. No one else came into the kitchen. I thought Nellie must have told them what she saw, and they all decided to let me have my moment. They probably thought I was overcome with emotion because I was so happy with the results.

Until that moment in the pantry, I had never given a thought to what victory would mean for Ann.

When I thought I was in control of myself, I went back into the living room and now it was my turn to be celebrated. There were shouts of, "You did it! You did it! You have made history; it never would have happened without you!"

Ann just looked at me and smiled. I thought she must be recalling our conversation when I predicted what would happen. I thought this must be what a ballplayer feels, after he hits a grand slam home run with two out in the 9th inning to win the game and the whole team has left the dugout to express their joy by jumping all over him.

The next day was real fun. First, the huge headline across the top of the Courant's front page – "Uccello wins Primary." Everywhere people were smiling, all except the Democratic candidates. They did not see the results as a victory for Ann, but as a loss for their party. How did they lose in a city they owned?

The media could not explain it, they just capitalized on the story. And what a story and a photogenic star to boot! Could a woman actually be elected mayor of this capital city? The thought was intriguing, and the media had a field day which lasted for the weeks leading up to Election Day.

A new subject of conversation was emerging, especially among Democrats. How did this happen? The Hartford Republican party had not changed so much that it was capable of victory in Democratic Hartford. Who was behind this historic political achievement? Up to this time, my name or position as campaign manager had not gone beyond the local leadership of the Republican Party. The "private effort" never was noticed by the political pundits. I wanted it that way so as not to antagonize the men in the party even further. They thought I was arrogant and abrasive. I looked those words up in the dictionary and thought, they are right, I was arrogant and abrasive. I had to be under the circumstances. It is the squeaky wheel that gets the grease, I said to myself.

The next three weeks had to be fun for Ann. Wherever she went campaigning, she was greeted enthusiastically. It was as if the city took her into its arms and hugged her. The Democratic Party was divided. Should they unite, sheer numbers would guarantee a victory for the mayor. Human nature, envy and jealousy among themselves went to work. The candidates refused to unite behind one of their own and a victory for Ann could now be possible. The truth was that each Democratic candidate would rather see Ann in the mayor's chair, if each one could not win it for himself. I thought, isn't human nature wonderful?

Now that the Democrat battle was public news, I took a back seat for the next three weeks, satisfied that the media and the public's reaction to the primary results would give the victory that I had begun dreaming about after she won in 1963. The volunteers were ecstatic during this period, and I did not have to remind them of what was expected of them. The "Army" had grown as more women joined the effort. Ann's victory became their cause célèbre.

There was a new excitement in the air this Election Day. Would history be made? It had been a long time since Hartford politics had captured the imagination of political types, not only in the city, but also all over the state. As we had done in the past, Ann and I visited all 45 polling places, chatting with the volunteers, and for the first time, hearing voters wishing her "Good Luck." I felt the optimism in the air. Thanks primarily to the Democratic in-fighting, we did have a real chance. Would large numbers of Democrats turn out ensuring a victory for one of their own, or would the animosity among them keep them home on this Election Day? The Democrats had the numbers for victory, but would they come out and vote, that was the big question as the day wore on.

Ann and I spent the day visiting the 45 voting districts. About 7 p.m. we headed for Ann's home to get ready for what I believed would be "good news." Everyone was there before 8 p.m. chimed on the grandfather clock in the hallway. One could sense the tension in the living room where everyone had gathered, some sitting on the floor because all the seating was occupied. Ann seemed the calmest of the group. She expected to be reelected for the City Council, but still did not believe in what I felt was her destiny. No one talked about the top spot, not wanting to add to the tension. As in the primary, the vote was close for number 1, but when the final vote was tallied, Ann would be the Mayor of Hartford – the first woman mayor in the city's long history.

A police cruiser arrived at 207 Branford Street to escort the "Mayor" to City Hall. I felt like a proud parent watching his daughter graduate as valedictorian of her class. I did not have the same reaction I did following the primary results. No emotion whatsoever. I think had she not been elected Mayor, I would have reacted differently. When you convince yourself something is going to happen, it is not a surprise when it does.

While I was also convinced that she would win the primary, I had to allow for the fact that I was biased. I thoroughly enjoyed the festive atmosphere in the Uccello home, happy for those who were there to witness history. I could not imagine the feelings of immigrant Italians witnessing their daughter and their niece achieve such a personal triumph.

I left this joyous scene to go to City Hall and be present when Ann would meet the media there. A large crowd had gathered to observe history. It was a surprise to most. Yes, she had won the primary, but in the final election the less informed turned out and usually voted their party line. The Democratic registration dampened what enthusiasm Ann's supporters might have because most knowledgeable people had to admit the odds were against Ann being the highest vote-getter again.

When the press conference ended, I drove Ann home. I took a roundabout route through North Main Street, inhabited mostly by Black residents. As I drove up one street and down another, Ann for the first time saw this blighted area that I thought was a disgrace. I said to her, "THIS is your city also. No one should have to live like this. You are now in a position to do something about it." She did not respond, obviously lost in her thoughts of what she had just seen.

The next day Ann walked Main Street in downtown Hartford during the lunch hour. She greeted residents and thanked them for their support and good wishes. I watched the people's faces as they recognized her. Wide smiles and handshakes and even hugs followed. One very large Black lady approached Ann and gave her a lengthy bear hug. I was facing Ann and could see her mystified expression saying, "What do I do now?" After what seemed an eternity for Ann, the lady backed away and looking at Ann's expression of wonderment, exclaimed, "You don't remember me, do you?" I waited for Ann's response, knowing she did not have a clue as to the lady's identity.

"Well, you do look familiar," she said, giving a reply any politician would under the circumstance.

There was a pause, and then the lady happily shouted, "I voted for you!"

Later that same day, Howard Kaufman called to invite me to meet him at, of all places, the Parma restaurant, a Democrat hangout. Poor Howard, transparent as always, wanting to take me to this particular restaurant on this particular day. I assumed I was no longer arrogant and abrasive.

We walked into the Parma crowded with Democrats discussing the election results. Howard directed me to a table, one where we could be seen by the other diners. People were friendly as they came over to congratulate him on Ann's victory.

He introduced me as the one who engineered the victory. I could not believe my ears. Was he actually admitting my contribution to the cause? That would be a first.

What I Remember …

A little while later, a middle-aged woman walked into the restaurant. I had to notice her because she was greeted so warmly as she passed each booth and table. She wore an oversized sweatshirt (I thought, without a bra), a skirt, bobby socks and flat shoes. She really was a sight to behold. "Who the hell is that?" I asked Howard.

He roared with laughter and said, "You really don't know who that is?"

"No, I do not, who is she?" I replied. Before he could answer, we could see that she was headed for our table, and I expected the introduction to take place soon.

When she did arrive, we stood to greet her as Howard said, "Ella, I want you to meet George Ducharme. He was the architect of Ann Uccello's victory." I was flabbergasted. This is Ella Grasso? This is the Secretary of the State of Connecticut? This is the woman who is the highest vote-getter every four years in the gubernatorial elections?

She ignored Howard's introduction and said, "I know all about him, he made a fortune in the stock market." I do not know what kept me from bursting out laughing at that remark.

I thought it uncharacteristic of a politician to ignore my role in Ann's victory. For years, she had been the only woman in a high position in politics. Was she so upset at another woman taking the spotlight away from her that she could not even acknowledge me with a simple "Congratulations?"

I mentioned it to Howard after she had left the table. He was too much a politician to admit that she behaved rather unprofessionally, to say the least. Later that day, I told Ann what happened with Ella. We both enjoyed the moment.

Ella's comment that I had made a fortune intrigued me. How people can add two and two and get five. I drove a car that was, at that time, 18 years old and I appeared to be unemployed. I must be wealthy or eccentric or both. I was neither.

The Democrats had seen me around City Hall for a couple of years and wondered why a man in his 30s did not have a job. Ella was partially correct. I was single, earning a good salary when I was employed and had made about $50,000 in the stock market. When I left G. Fox two years earlier, I knew that I could maintain my lifestyle for several years without incurring any financial problems. I did not think $50,000 qualified me to be considered wealthy. I may have been unconventional, but I certainly was not eccentric.

The Parma diners were dwindling by this time, and I wondered when Howard would get down to the reason we were there. Surely, he did not invite me to that restaurant just to show that he knew me. Between interruptions, he was most generous in his recap of what had happened the day before. I did not think he invited me just to praise me. Something was up. He had something on his mind, and I anxiously waited to hear what it was.

Up to this time, our conversation was pleasant and innocuous. Then he suddenly got serious. "I have something I want to discuss with you," he said. He paused, seemingly searching for the proper words to say what he wanted to say. Evidently, he did not find them.

In a matter-of-fact tone, he said, "I think you should avoid being seen with Ann, now that she is the mayor of the city. You are both single and people will talk. They are already talking. The mayor's personal reputation should not be questioned in any way. It could diminish her popularity with the voters, and I don't think you would want that to happen after you have worked so hard to elect her."

I had always believed that the Republican Party leadership wanted me to be removed from the scene, and what a clever approach to the matter they had discovered. I should get out of the way to protect Ann's image that I had built. That was a brilliant approach to their problem. How could I ignore such a reasonable suggestion? I thought Howard was just being the spokesman for the party. He was hand-picked because he was the least outspoken about me in the party.

I, too, was concerned about the public's perception of us, after all, we were living at a time when two single people seen together often were deemed to be having an affair. I suppose I added to the gossip because I was a volunteer. The gossip could answer the question often asked of me: What's in it for you? Howard did have a point when he said it could reflect negatively upon her. And knowing Ann, she probably was already thinking the same thing.

We both knew that there was gossiping about the two of us, and why not? We were the newest item for discussion. I knew what was being said. That is why I always made a point in discussing our relationship, to make it clear that I was "a friend of the family of long standing."

Not all the gossip was negative, some was positive. We were a good-looking couple in the eyes of some people, who thought someday we would become one, as in marriage. That subject was not on my mind. I had come to look unfavorably toward politicians as untrustworthy, double-dealing, egotistical, and I could go on. That Ann did not fit that mold was what attracted me to her, that is professionally attracted me to her.

174

The Republican Party planned a gigantic victory dinner at the Hilton Hotel. There were so many "dignitaries," that it required two head tables to accommodate them all. Republicans from all over the state would descend on Hartford to fill the ballroom to its 800 capacity. A few days before the dinner, the Town Chairman asked me to lunch. This would be another first, Howard Kaufman and now the Town Chairman. There was no doubt he had something up his sleeve.

He was very pleasant, even acknowledged my "considerable contribution" to Ann's success at the polls. However, he had a problem with the dinner. There wasn't any room for Ann's Campaign Manager at the head tables. I hope I didn't smile too broadly at that remark because I was amused beyond words. He quickly added that the party wanted me to sit with Ann's family and at the appropriate time, introduce them to the audience.

My first reaction was negative. When I met with Ann later that day and informed her of this decision to publicly ignore my role, she was furious. "If you're not there, neither will I be, they can hold my victory dinner without me," she said in anger. By this time I had recovered from my initial reaction. I saw this insulting move as an extraordinary opportunity.

"Ann," I said, "they are going to give me a microphone. How stupid is that?" We both laughed knowing I would make the most of my time, which by the way, would be unlimited. If they were trying to ignore me that evening, they once again underestimated me.

Had they put me at one of the head tables, I would have been introduced, stood up and sat down, maybe 10 seconds at most in the spotlight. Now I would have as much time as I wanted to introduce seven family members, Ann's four sisters, one brother-in-law and Ann's parents.

I no longer was that frightened student who refused to stand at his desk when called upon to participate in class. I was not the nervous President of the Student Council with ink on the palms of my sweaty hands. This was Ann's night, but I would have my moment, too.

I carefully crafted an introduction of each family member and would end with Mom and Pop. If I do this right, I said to myself, the audience should be on its feet before I get to Mr. and Mrs. Uccello. Sixteen minutes, with the audience in the palm of my hands. You could hear a pin drop, it was so quiet. By the time I got to the parents, the audience was made aware of an immigrant couple who, on income earned as a shoe repairman, raised five daughters, four who graduated college, each earning their own place in society.

As I reached the climax of the introductions and began to speak, "Mr. and …" the audience was already standing, cheering this tiny couple who many could not see from their vantage point. I turned around to look at Ann. I was beaming and so very pleased that I had respectfully and with dignity honored her family. It was a night to remember. Russ, Ann's brother-in-law, was tongue-tied. He looked at me but could not find the words to say what he was thinking. He just looked at me and shook his head. The next morning, he called to tell me what he could not say the night before.

Sometime later, I came to the conclusion that Howard might be right. Maybe I should be seen less with Ann, but not for his reasons. I had my own reasons.

Those who live, eat, and breathe politics could not explain and refused to accept Ann's victory. It was a fluke. She would not win reelection. The political pundits analyzed it correctly. The division among Democrats was what made her victory possible.

However, the pundits overlooked the large vote this Republican had received. She obviously had won over many Democrats. The general consensus was that a male had to be behind this historic event because "everyone knew a woman could not be an effective mayor." Who was the most identified male with her? He would be a stealth mayor. Anyone who knew either of us would know how ridiculous that conclusion was.

While I did concede that Howard had a point, I did not take his advice. On the contrary, I continued attending council meetings, and when asked, was her chauffeur. I noticed that audiences were larger than in other years. I concluded the public was curious about a lady mayor and wanted to see her in action. Some meetings she put on quite a show. Hartford at that time had a city manager-council form of government. The mayor's position was ceremonial.

She conducted the council meetings and could express her opinion. There were times when her outbursts, especially when directed at the Democratic majority, drew applause. The public enjoyed watching her challenge the men on the council when she thought they were out of line. If she ruled at all, it would be through the strength of her personality. Ann was not some dumb brunette. She had energy and passion and brains and used them to express herself. She was proving that she could hold her own.

Ann did not need a stealth mayor. That she was photogenic was apparent, especially to television personnel who covered her as if she were a movie star.

177

• Chapter 22 •

Entering the Entertainment World

I did not spend all day on politics. The "Grads" club was another outlet for my time. I attended a social function at which the Al Jarvis Band performed. They were one of Hartford's most popular bands at that time and Sam Pasco was the band leader. During one of the band's intermissions, he called me aside and asked what I would be doing now that Ann was elected mayor. His band had performed regularly at the club's functions, and he was aware of my work on her behalf. I told him I would be looking for a job but had not begun to do so.

Without hesitation, he asked if I would like to go to Palm Springs, California and work as Al Jarvis' Business and Personal Manager. I knew Al because we were in the same class at Weaver High. Sam told me Al was recovering from a heart attack he suffered while performing (piano) at Caesar's Palace in Las Vegas. His family wanted to explore the possibility that he could rise to national fame. They believed he had the talent but needed someone to manage his career.

I would be living with Al in his home in the hills of Palm Springs and have all my expenses paid. Moving to California, some 3,000 miles from Hartford, would certainly put an end to the stealth mayor conversations. There was something very exciting about being involved in the entertainment world. Sam, like Mr.

178

Katzen, had ignored salary. There was a major difference this time. I did not care about the money. I just wanted to prove that Ann could do her job without any guidance from me. I began to really believe that someone was watching over me. Sam's offer, coming at this particular time, was not a coincidence.

Here was a new challenge and I really needed one. My new "office" was a beautiful single home in the Palm Spring mountains. Sam told me that there was an outdoor swimming pool and a new Cadillac in the garage. Look at me, I am going to be living at a resort where the elite of Hollywood relaxes. I would be working in a new business about which I had absolutely no knowledge or experience. A fairy tale of a life was about to begin.

My new client was Al Jarvis who did not know the value of money. He was the youngest son in a Jewish family, who had a medical history for the ages, polio and a weak heart, just to name a few of his major medical concerns. He also had a disease which I labeled, "friendshipitis" – the need to have people around him whom he called friends, who were not his friends. I called them something else, much less complimentary.

Al spent every dime he earned and then some. He was playing piano at the Lounge of Caesar's Palace in Las Vegas when he suffered his heart attack and was now recuperating at his home in Palm Springs. He was well enough when I arrived to be working in the lounge of the resort's most exclusive hotel. I think it was called the Canyon Club or something like that.

He really was a talented pianist, and his family was justified in thinking he could rise to the top in the music world, a young Roger Williams, if you will. He was appearing at the club five or six nights a week. There was a table set for six in front of his piano, reserved for his "friends." He was earning big money and

179

spending every dollar on the liquor bill for that table of friends. I asked him, "Why are you paying for their drinks? Why don't they pay for their own?"

He answered, "They would not come to hear me play if they had to pay for their own drinks."

"So what?" I said. "Who needs them? You already have a capacity audience every evening who is paying to hear you. The room is full of appreciative fans, you don't have to pay anyone to listen to you. That table could be sold to other paying customers, and you could be spending your salary on your own needs instead of having to call home for money."

Al repeated that they were his friends. I answered, "You do not need those kinds of friends, nobody does. I have been here for over two months now, and I am waiting to see even one of your friends at the front door with a bottle in hand." That subject was off limits from then on.

I called Sam and told him that I did not come here to babysit a spoiled child. I must get him away from Palm Springs and his freeloader friends. There was little doubt Al had talent. I coined the phrase, "Al Jarvis makes love to the Piano." San Diego was a major city south of Palm Springs; I would look there for a booking to get him out of town and those people he called friends.

There was a morning television program that showcased local talent. It was called the Regis Philbin Show. I was able to arrange a guest appearance. Al could tell his story, which was powerful in that in spite of all his medical problems, he still manages to entertain. It would make for a sympathetic conversation with Mr. Philbin before he was asked to play the piano.

That appearance led to a booking at one of the local "hot spots." It was a four-week booking and we were treated like royalty by the management. Word of mouth about Al's talent had attendance at the lounge increasing steadily. The management was pleased with the risk they took by booking an unknown pianist. About two weeks into the booking, the management informed us that a busload of Palm Spring fans was coming to San Diego to hear him play. I asked Al if he knew who was coming. He had a phone call a few days before and just forgot to tell me who was coming, he said.

He forgot to tell me because the bus would be filled with his favorite freeloaders. We argued over who was going to foot the bar bill during their stay. Thankfully it was an overnight jaunt. The bus would leave a short time after Al's performance, allowing time for a visit.

It probably won't surprise you that Al paid the bar bill. "They were coming to my new home to hear me play, how could I not be hospitable to them?" was Al's defense.

I began thinking, this fairy tale is over. I called Sam again to ask him to talk to his mother and tell her not to send him any more money; he is just throwing it away. That call was a waste of time. As with Al, that subject was off limits.

One evening, a tall Texan came up to Al during one of his breaks and asked him if he would consider travelling to Midland, Texas for a four-day event where he would be the principal entertainer. He offered Al $4,000, plus expenses. We jumped at the opportunity to spread his reputation beyond Southern California. That four-day booking resulted in a two-week booking in another city in Texas. I doubted we would have "guests" at this venue. Although his career seemed to be headed upward, Al did not enjoy living out of a suitcase. He wanted to return home and live his "normal life" again.

181

He had talent and a personal story that I thought could get him to the top. There was just one major problem. He had a fan base in Palm Springs, and he was satisfied with his Palm Springs booking, which he apparently could have as long as he wished. I could not get him to add to his repertoire or even practice his familiar music or be interviewed any more. I began to believe that I and his family wanted success for him more than he wanted it for himself. He was not willing to do the work it takes to make it in the entertainment world.

Al and I began arguing about everything, especially his refusal to appear at interviews I had arranged. His friends became more and more a test of my patience. I may not have learned much about the business, but one thing I did learn was that entertainers had to keep their names in front of the public. That is why most of them have public relations personnel to do just that – keep their names in front of the public.

Then to add to my concern, his public was beginning to notice that his piano playing was lacking. To paraphrase what customers in the lounge were telling me, "What is wrong with Al tonight, he is not performing up to the standard we have come to expect from him?" I knew that was because he would not practice. When I told him what the customers were telling me, he accused me of lying.

His finances were in a disastrous state, and he seemed totally unconcerned. When I need money, I will call home and my mother will send it to me, he said. He was right. Mom was always there with her checkbook. This fairy tale was not going to have a happy ending. I called Sam for the third time to inform him that I had had enough; I was coming home. Sam was sympathetic. He knew Al better than anyone.

When I told Al I was leaving, he was shocked. He promised he would do whatever I asked. I knew he did need someone, but that someone was not me. He liked his life the way it was. I was not going to wait around until he realized he could not continue as he had been. Our parting was not cordial.

• Chapter 23 •

A Run for Congress

The year was 1968, most notable for the assassinations of Bobby Kennedy and Dr. Martin Luther King Jr. and the riots that followed Dr. King's death. Major cities in the country were on fire. Black people took to the streets destroying and looting property in their neighborhoods, setting businesses on fire, even those owned and operated by Black people. Hartford, a small city, was one of the worst affected by Dr. King's death. Some estimates were that a third of the city was affected by the gangs of rioters, burning and looting neighborhoods where mostly Black people lived and worked.

Ann Uccello was, of course, Mayor of Hartford and was credited with cooling down the rioters by her courageous decision to go out into the streets and meet with the rioters. She told me, "There has been a death in their family, and they are holding the wake in the streets and I am attending the wake."

When she explained to the city officials, meeting in a "war room" atmosphere, what she was going to do, the Police Chief tried to persuade her that her idea was not a wise one, but Ann was firm in her decision. "Well, at least wear this," he said as he handed her his helmet. Ann stared at the helmet and said, "I'm not going to wear that, I just had my hair done," and off she went out into the streets.

184

The media was there to capture the scene and overnight Ann was seen as the gallant mayor facing the rioters. The Courant took a photo of her being surrounded by young Black people shouting at her. A woman showed the city how to lead. With all this happening, I wished I had been there to support her. In our phone conversations, Ann had expressed doubt about seeking a second term. I believed that she would be reelected. The rude treatment at council meetings made her a sympathetic figure and the incredible coverage of her every move and statement made her a great ambassador of the city. What more could one ask of a ceremonial mayor?

I returned to Hartford and the political scene. First order of business was to persuade Ann she should seek reelection. The Democrats on the council planned to change the form of government in the city to one of a strong mayor with a salary. One would have to campaign for the office of mayor, separate from the council. No longer would the top vote-getter be automatically elected mayor. Now the public would get to vote for the office itself. I did admit to Ann that this new system would make it more difficult for her to win because she could no longer ask for one of six votes. This time, it would be a one-on-one race and the Democratic registrations were significantly in their favor.

There was less chance she could win over a Democrat. However, now that this would be a salaried office, the Democrats were at it again. They did what they did best, disagree. There were rumors of some Democrats thinking of running as Independents, challenging the party's nominee. Some said there might be more than one challenger to the nominee. Once again, human nature might give Ann another victory. The media finally had a story to cover, most of the interest would be in the Democrat's battle for the nominee.

Ann was the obvious choice and the only choice for the Republicans. This time, the party leadership recognized her power at the polls and the Republican Party went all out to win this election. The belief was that Ann, at the top of the ticket, might carry the others to victory in the council.

While the men recognized it was Ann who would energize the voters, they insisted on equal treatment in the campaign. Money was spent just to satisfy the egos of the council candidates. To give a full-page ad to Ann was expected; this would be the first time in years that voters would be voting for the Office of Mayor. However, the council candidates also insisted on a full-page ad in the Courant on the same day. Imagine, reading the paper that morning and turning seven pages of the paper, featuring the photo of each of the Republican candidates. What a waste of money and some of the public reacted negatively to the extravagance.

"Ann's Army" went to work, doing what they do best, spreading the word to vote for Ann. The women in the group were ecstatic over the possibility of their candidate winning this kind of an election. The party would be providing candidates with 200, four-color posters, each featuring a photo of the candidate. Ann's poster was powerful. Ann was seen in the inaugural dress she wore at the swearing-in ceremony two years before. Wearing a blue dress, Ann was standing with one hand on a Bible and the other hand raised as she was sworn in as mayor.

It was the photo the Courant featured on the front page the next morning. It made one smile just to look at it. It was irresistible. I felt Ann's poster was dynamite. How could we take advantage of its power?

It happened again. I was at Mass that Sunday morning and as usual had difficulty concentrating with thoughts of the campaign swirling around in my head. How and where would we distribute that poster? It was key. It said everything I wanted it to say. It was a reminder of the way she conducted herself as a ceremonial mayor. But it had to be seen to be a reminder.

And there it was – the answer. Have Ann distribute the poster in person. Have Ann visit every street-level business in the city and ask the owner or the one in charge if she could put her photo in their window.

For most of the owners or managers, usually Democrats, it would be the first time they would have met the lady mayor. Who could refuse this attractive city official her simple request? I was well aware that most of their customers were probably Democrats also and the poster in the window of a Republican would definitely create a conversation.

We traveled the city, street by street. I would double-park the car and wait for Ann to do her thing. I cannot describe the rush that went through me when I saw the first store owner place the poster in his window for all to see. Whenever customers were in the store, she would take time to introduce herself and make her pitch.

In addition to the poster in the window, the owner or the one in charge, would most likely have to defend his decision to allow that poster to be placed in the window. Bingo, a new campaign worker and again, the best advertising a candidate could hope for – word of mouth. Ann had made a new friend. We ran out of posters and had to reorder. What she heard over and over were words of appreciation for cooling down the rioters after Dr. King's murder. "My store could have been next."

What I Remember …

When we completed the tour of the city there was about a week until Election Day, so we decided to make a second round of the stores. We were curious to see if the posters were still in the windows. There they were in full view of anyone passing by on foot or auto. Ann went into each store to express her appreciation for keeping the photo in the window. She learned that many of the store personnel had words with their customers when they had to explain why a Republican's poster was in a Democrat's store window.

The voter had four choices for mayor: the Democratic Party nominee, two Independents and Ann. Wilbur Smith, a highly regarded Black man, threw his hat into the ring. In a conversation I had with him before the election, he told me that he was unhappy with the two Democrats and that he would prefer to have Ann win again. Ann was victorious! Wilbur Smith's votes had made the difference. Hartford's lady mayor had won again.

Ann was on her way politically. The first election as mayor was seen by many as a fluke, but there was no denying this time that she had established herself as a politician on the rise. The next year the voters would be asked to select a governor, senator and six congressmen. Ann was sure to figure in there somewhere.

I had my eyes on the Senate because elections were held every six years. I had worked four elections in seven years, and I saw the Senate elections as a decent break from the grueling work of a campaign.

The party leadership, bless their hearts, wanted Ann to seek the First Congressional District seat. They were correct in seeing Ann as the strongest candidate in the heavily Democratic First District, but I saw it as a way to put an end to her political career. The last Republican Congressman, Ed May, was elected in 1956 when Eisenhower won the state by more than 300,000 votes and carried Ed May to victory. Two years later, despite rave reviews for his first term, he was soundly beaten. One cannot overstate the high Democratic vote in the First District. A candidate for governor or senator could lose the First District and still easily win the election statewide.

According to Howard Kaufman, a poll taken by the Republicans showed Ann to be the most popular office holder in the state. For some reason, the results of that poll were given very little publicity. Tom Meskill was the party choice for governor and Lowell Weicker, the choice for the Senate seat. Mr. Meskill was no General Eisenhower and was not likely to win by a large plurality, if he won at all.

Ann saw herself as an administrator and not a legislator and thought about seeking the governor's spot on the ticket. Mrs. Uccello, very astute in politics, reminded Ann that the Democratic candidate was likely to be Mim Daddario, a five-term congressman from the First District. She did not think the Italian population in the state would look kindly at an Italian woman challenging an Italian man in an election, especially when that man was a five-term congressman, and she was a new name on the scene.

Mrs. Uccello commented that in most Italian homes the male was the head of the family and most Italian women accepted that position. While many Italians did vote for Ann in the city elections, would they now vote for her when the opposition was an Italian male? Mrs. Uccello thought not. Her position was a valid one and Ann agreed. I tried to explain that Daddario could easily win the First District but lose in the state and, incidentally, that's just what happened.

The State Republican chairman met with Ann and me to discuss her place on the state ticket in November. He offered her the First District congressman nomination. I joined the conversation, reminding him how difficult it would be for a Republican to win in the First District, especially with Daddario running for governor. I was telling him something he already knew. I reminded him of the Ed May situation. Ann would definitely be the strongest candidate in the district for the Republicans and would likely help the entire ticket. Without an Eisenhower at the top of the ticket, Ann would suffer the same fate as Ed May when he sought reelection.

I said Ann would need considerable financial assistance. Where would it come from? Would the National Party be a source? I asked if we could get the President and Vice President to personally ask her to run? I saw front page headlines and the lead story on the television evening news in the event that happened. It would be news that would be covered all over the state and help introduce her to voters already not familiar with her. Publicity the campaign would not have to pay for.

The chairman said everything I suggested was doable. If Ann received funds from Washington, then she would agree to run. Vice President Agnew telephoned to ask Ann to run. The news coverage was statewide. President Nixon called to ask her to run. Again, big news all over the state. The National Party offered $50,000. We were building support for Ann and the possibility for success was increasing.

Ann announced for Congress and the campaign began. In previous elections, campaign funds were not a consideration; the local party spent what little they had, and we spent next to nothing for what we did. However, in a Congressional election when the candidate had to become known in thirteen towns, money was a major factor. Ann refused to make any calls or seek personal support from the so-called "heavy givers." There wasn't even a discussion on that subject. Ann would not campaign personally asking for money. She said it would taint her reputation and she would be like all the other politicians who were criticized for their involvement in seeking campaign funds.

We learned of a man in Greenwich who wanted to contribute $5,000, but he wanted to meet Ann and give her the check in person. Ann refused to meet with him. No amount of pleading would change her mind. As time went on, we were being outspent two to one in a campaign where the opposition had a huge lead in registrations. Where was the money from Washington? I repeatedly asked Ann to phone the President and report that the promised funds had not been received. She would not make the call and further, I was not to make the call.

Clayton Gengras, for whom I had worked in his 1966 campaign for governor, entered the picture. I asked to meet with him to discuss our financial concerns. We had many get-togethers at his office on 1000 Asylum Avenue. I asked him to sponsor a fundraising event for Ann and he agreed to do so. He planned a luncheon at the Hartford Club, and Ann thought we should invite Tom Meskill and Lowell Weicker. Ann said that the exposure in the First District would benefit their efforts to win state-wide. The event raised $39,000, money we badly needed. Meskill and Weicker insisted that the money be divided equally among the three of them. I objected. This event was for Ann, and the other two were invited as a courtesy. Once again, Ann refused to get involved in anything having to do with money.

As it happened, Ann's biggest hurdle in the campaign was to convince voters in the other 12 towns that she was running for Congress and not Mayor of Hartford. As we visited the other towns, again and again, voters were very happy to meet her. She was so identified as the Mayor of Hartford, voters wondered what she was doing in their town. What we were failing to get across to them was that this time, they could vote for her. She wanted to be their Congresswoman.

I created a television ad with Ann sitting in front of a map with the 13 towns and Ann saying, "If you live in one of these towns, you can vote for me to be your Congresswoman." The ads were expensive, and we ran out of money.

On the Friday before Election Day, I received a call from the Washington campaign headquarters. It was Charles Colson, a Nixon operative. Their polling had indicated Ann was in a very close race. Previously, Washington had counted our seat in the victory column, and that is why they did not send us any money; they sent it where it would do the most good.

Mr. Colson asked me if I could use $5,000. I was angry. "Where have you been all these weeks?" I answered. "What do you expect me to do with money now, would you have me hand it out at the polls?" All the television space was now sold out. The "map ad" was working, but we did not have money to buy time when it was available. Now that the Democrats knew that the race was close, they bought up what time was available. We had to hope that the voters would remember to look to the second line on the voting machine to find Ann's name. Most voters were voting for Daddario for Governor and his name was first on the line above. We needed some of those voters to split their ballot in order to vote for Ann. That we had worked so hard in this very

Democratic district, and we were likely to lose the election because voters did not know they could vote for Ann on the second line was painful, to say the least.

On the Saturday prior to the election, the Courant front-paged an article reminding Hartford voters that George Athanson would be mayor, should Ann win the Congressional seat.

Mr. Athanson was very unpopular with some Democrats, and while normally they would vote for Ann to give the mayoral seat to a Democrat, this time they would not, if it meant he would be the mayor.

Another negative involved an Italian Hartford policeman who had shot a Black man. The father appealed to Ann to publicly support his son in this matter, but she refused to get involved. The father, a long-time resident of Hartford, then went door-to-door visiting Italians, castigating her for not supporting "one of her own." For some Italians, this was enough reason not to support her candidacy for Congresswoman. Since this election was very close, every vote could mean victory or defeat.

Ann won 11 of the 13 towns, some by huge margins, but it was not enough to outweigh the votes in Hartford and East Hartford, where Daddario won big, carrying every Democrat on the ticket with him. Ann lost by 1,200 votes in a district that Daddario, as a candidate for Congress, had won five times with margins of 50,000, 60,000 and more. A poll taken after Ann left Hartford, gave her an 81 percent approval rating.

While examining the results the following morning, I noticed some very unusual numbers in some of the districts where minority voting was dominant. I called John Mastrandrea, a friend who worked on Ann's campaign, and asked him to help investigate these questionable totals. In a one-party city like

Hartford, fraudulent voting was easy to accomplish. The procedure for voting required two checkers, one from each party to verify the eligibility of the voter. There were some districts in the city where a Republican could not be found to be a checker, leaving that voting place without anyone from the Republican Party to challenge a voter. That is a situation guaranteed to lead to fraudulent voting.

John and I went to the area involved to canvass the neighborhood and verify the previous day's voting. I took one side of the street and John, the other. We knocked on doors and asked whether the resident voted yesterday. On that one short street we found 12 voters crossed off the voting list as having voted, who did not vote.

I wanted the Registrar of Voters to investigate further. We took our information to Howard Kaufman, who dismissed it. He told us the election was over. I went to Ann to tell her what we found, and she was so upset that she had lost in her own city, she refused to discuss the matter. I told her I would go to the Courant with my findings and she angrily said, "Drop it."

"Let me make it public so you would have an issue should you choose to seek that seat two years from now," I said.

She repeated, "I said, drop it."

President Nixon was so upset that Ann had lost the election that he created a position for her in Washington. He most likely blamed himself for not sending the $50,000 he had promised. The new position was called Director of Consumer Affairs for the Transportation Department. Ann accepted the position and resigned as mayor.

When the news was made public that Ann was going to Washington, many people suggested I would be going with her, that was the way of politics. I did not want to go to Washington and would refuse the offer if Ann made one. I had worked in Washington, D.C. for over three months when I was employed by Sears and did not like most of the people I met. Most everyone was interested in knowing the "power" in the city. Too many phonies for me.

I did not discuss the matter with Ann, but I knew that if I had found a job I would have reason to refuse any offer, if she made one. I had to find a job very soon. I can look back at that time and see it as the beginning of my "fairy tale" of a life that followed. I found a job, one that I, or anyone I knew, would ever have guessed possible.

When Jimmy Carter was elected in 1976, all the Nixon appointees had to offer their resignations. Mr. Carter would make his own appointments. Ann had performed so well in her position that Mr. Carter did not accept her resignation until April of 1977. She was told that she was second to last of the Nixon appointees to be replaced, such was her reputation in that town. Ann returned home and joined brother-in-law Russ in his insurance and real estate business.

Her reputation as a hard-working, honest politician was now indelibly stamped in the minds of those old enough to remember the 1960s in Hartford. I have been present at events since then when her presence evoked smiles. To put a smile on someone's face, now that is a legacy we should all seek.

Chapter 24

From Politics to Football

The next chapter in my life could not have been predicted. At home one evening, I passed by the TV as the local news was broadcast. The newscaster was saying something about the Hartford Knights Football Team and that its Public Relations Director had resigned.

For the four years I attended the University of Connecticut, I never had the slightest interest in attending a football game. In fact, for my junior and senior years on campus, my residence was only a few hundred yards from the football stadium. I could hear the roar of the crowd from my room.

My lack of interest in football could be traced back to my childhood. In gym class during the fall the class played football outside. My body was not built for football. The football itself was too large for me to hold. Now, I did not want to be a player – I wanted a job.

My stockbroker at the time was Samuel Blumenthal. During our many conversations we sometimes talked about sports, and I learned that Sam was a prep schoolmate of Peter Savin, President of the Hartford Knights Football Team. Peter's family was prominent in the area, owning several successful businesses. The Hartford Knights was just one of them.

196

There was a time when Peter wanted to upgrade Dillon Stadium, the home of the Knights. Peter was first-class all the way and felt that the stadium was not suitable for his team, and he offered to renovate it at cost, about $250,000, a very low price indeed for the work needed. The usual criticism followed from those who aren't interested in sports and had other ideas of how that much money should be spent. Why didn't the wealthy Savin family pay for the renovation? The criticism became personal and vicious and one day I told Sam that I wished I wasn't so busy with politics, I would like to work at improving his image. Now with this opening in the team's office, I saw the position as an opportunity to do so.

I telephoned Sam, who already knew of the opening, and asked him to arrange an appointment for me with his good friend, Peter Savin. He said he would, and he did. A few days later, I was sitting in Mr. Savin's office as an applicant for the position. I opened the conversation by telling Mr. Savin that I did not know a thing about football and did not like the sport, but I thought I could help him restore his "good name."

He said he was pleased to talk with someone who did not want to tell him how to manage his football business. "I already have a Coach and a General Manager." We talked for a few minutes, and he explained what the position involved and then the interview ended. He would inform me of his decision after he had interviewed others who had applied.

I left his office, thinking the interview went well, but there wasn't a chance I would be hired for that position that required, among other things, being the spokesman for the team. I was not qualified for that role, by experience or education.

197

What I Remember ...

Sam surprised me when he said that Peter wanted to meet me. Peter was a prominent Democrat, and he must have been aware of my role with Ann Uccello. Democrats paid close attention to the political scene, and I had a better reputation with many of them than I did with Republicans. Even so, I thought my chances were slim to none.

On the morning of the third day after the interview, the phone rang. It was 7 a.m. and I was awakened by the call.

"This is Pete, you have the job," said the voice at the other end. I was still half-asleep and did not associate "Pete" with Peter Savin. I replied, "Who is this calling?"

The voice answered, "Peter Savin, to tell you that you have the job." I was stunned. He wanted to hire me for a position for which I was totally unqualified.

"Mr. Savin," I said, "I have thought about the position since we met, and I think the news media would think your decision was not a wise one. You want me to represent the team with the sports media? I think I would embarrass you and the organization."

He responded in a very serious tone. "Anyone who can beat the Democrats in the city of Hartford, not once but twice, can handle this job." That would be the first of several times in my life when my association with Ann Uccello would open a door for me.

He offered me $15,000 and a new car. I told him I already owned a car. He insisted I have a company car. He would buy my car from me.

The very next day I was on the job. I met Mr. Savin in his office and he again explained what was expected of me. I would be responsible for the weekly game program, a 50-to-60-page production. I would sell advertising and be the editor of the program. I would plan and invite the radio and TV media to a weekly luncheon in our conference room at which I would update the attendees of any newsworthy items that had occurred since the previous luncheon. I would create news releases as needed, attend all home and away games, after which I would communicate with radio and TV sports departments, who would record my statement regarding the game that evening, giving the score and any pertinent facts leading to the scoring.

I would plan a sales campaign for season tickets and promote a group sales plan. I would visit the area's largest employers offering discounts to their employees. The position seemed more like that of a marketing director and not public relations.

Our meeting ended with his statement that I would report directly to him. I liked that very much. His last words were, "From now on please call me Peter or Pete." I felt instantly that we would get along very well.

Peter then escorted me downstairs to the team's offices. I was introduced to the Coach, General Manager and Secretary. It was clear to me from the start that they all questioned Peter's hiring of me for the PR position. I definitely had to prove myself to them. I was up-front with each of them, telling them how little I knew of football and asking them for their help in my new role.

Our offices in the basement of the Savin Corporate Offices were more than adequate. Each of the four of us had a private office with the usual furniture. I went to work immediately, familiarizing myself with whatever material had been left by the previous person holding that job. We were months away from the opening of the football season, so I had time to become acclimated to a routine.

The first day was fun. Every once in a while, one of the staff would come into my office and sit down to chat. I realized that at 40 years old, I was the senior of the group. They wanted to know why I was offered a position that I was totally unqualified for, but could not bring themselves to ask the question. They all danced around the subject, and I left them still in a quandary when our little get-together was over.

With the exception of my having to meet with the media and the reporting of the results following the games, I was confident I could do the job and prove it to all of them in time.

A few days later, I went up to Peter's office to ask for a list of the firms that did business with the Savin companies. "What do you want with them?" he asked.

"I'm going to approach them for tickets, advertising and group sales," I replied.

"I cannot ask those people for money when I know I have more than they do, I would be embarrassed," Peter said.

"You are not doing the asking, I am," I said. We conversed for a few minutes while I worked at persuading him there was no cause for embarrassment. I could tell he was amused by my energy while discussing the matter. He walked me out to another office where I met his assistant, an efficient and obviously loyal employee, who looked somewhat astonished at Peter's request, but he provided what I needed and I returned to my office to go to work doing some selling.

Peter was a generous man and very involved in community affairs. I had little trouble with my sales pitch. I don't think a single company denied my request for their involvement in Peter's football team.

During the preseason, we met with the media several times to update them on personnel. I was really nervous before the first luncheon. I suspected the members of the media would be taking the measure of me and I wanted to make a good impression. I did not have anything to worry about. I had ordered a hot meal of pasta, chicken and salad. I did not realize that heretofore they had eaten only sandwiches. When the meal was served, I could tell that I had won them over even before the meeting took place.

Before the first game of the season, I asked the Coach to spend time with me explaining the game as he would to a person attending his first game. After each game, I would visit him with a list of questions I had made during the game. When he was in his office, he spent most of his time looking at game films. The Secretary answered the phone and prepared correspondence for the three of us, when requested. I never could figure out what the GM did, other than visit with the Coach and Secretary.

A few weeks after the season had begun, a stunning woman walked into my office. "I am Elaine Savin, Peter's wife and I have come here to thank you," she said.

Thank me, what for? I wondered, since I had not met her before today. What could she be thanking me for?

She continued, "Peter is a different person since you came to work for him, he is a different husband and a different father. Last evening at dinner he told the family that for the first time, he felt he had someone working in the football office who was as interested in making the business a success as he was. That someone is you and I want to thank you for what you are doing for my husband."

I was speechless. How does one respond to a statement like that from the boss' wife? Naturally, I thanked her. I could not think of anything else to say, I was stunned to say the least. Nothing like that had ever happened to me. No one had ever said anything like that to me. Nothing said to me had ever caused that kind of impression on me. We shook hands again and she left.

I don't know how long I remained standing. I was frozen in place by her visit and comments. I relived her words over and over, not believing I really heard them. Peter never mentioned her visit. I do not know if she ever told him that she visited me in my office. Months later, when thinking about it for the umpteenth time, I asked myself why I didn't follow up her statement, sometime later, with a request for an increase in salary.

I was never about money. I accepted whatever was offered. I did question the $10 increase by Mr. Katzen, but that wasn't as much about the money as it was about treating me like an equal. I saw that $10 as an indication that I was still a young employee with much to prove. That is what I really resented in that offer. In returning to Bryant & Chapman, I did ask when I would be eligible for increases in salary, but I never challenged their answers. When I was happy doing whatever I was doing, money wasn't important to me. Even the changes of responsibility when I was employed by G. Fox were not about moving up the ladder. All I wanted was something more challenging to do. I got bored as soon as I conquered the work.

Peter Savin spoiled me for every employer I had later on in my career. We had a wonderful and respectful relationship. He clearly defined my role and left me to my own devices to accomplish it. He was a wealthy and powerful individual, but he was a soft touch for anyone with a hard-luck story. He treated his players like family.

One day I walked into his office while a player was walking out. "How much did that conversation cost you?" I said with a smile.

He answered, "I guess I will get that back in the next world."

Some weeks later, he walked into my office. He seemed in a more serious mood than usual. He made a few complimentary remarks about my performance and then added that he had considered for some time changing my title of Public Relations Director to one which more accurately described my role with the team. He had come to the conclusion that I was a particularly important part of the management team and he said he rarely made a business decision about the team without consulting me first. Without any fanfare, he said that he was giving me the title of Assistant to the President, shook my hand and left. I looked at my watch to check the time.

Of course, I was pleased by the recognition. Who wouldn't be? A few minutes later Peter returned with the news I had expected. "I cannot name you my assistant," he said, "because Ross (who was his assistant in all of the Savin enterprises) told me it would be confusing to the public." I smiled and he said, "You knew all the time, didn't you, that I would be back."

I was smiling as I answered. "Peter, believe me, I understand clearly."

There wasn't any doubt that Ross was much more valuable to Peter than I was. The football operation was insignificant in the big picture of the Savin operations. I could tell Peter did not want to upset Ross and therefore agreed with his reaction to my new title. I gave Peter a knowing look that said what we both knew was the real reason. In spite of his lofty position, Ross was very insecure and my relationship with his boss intimidated him.

What I Remember …

There were times when Peter would call me to his office just to talk, not about football, just anything that came into his mind, current events, politics, sports, you name it. After a while I would say that I had to get back to work and that would end the conversation. When I left the office, Ross would be outside waiting to learn what our conversation was about. I would simply answer as I continued walking away, that we just talked, nothing significant to report. I believed that kind of statement irritated him to no end. After Peter left my office, I thought my promotion must have set a record for shortest time in existence. Peter did change my title to Assistant General Manager.

The following year gave indications that the league was in trouble. We had a home game coming up and a few days before the game the owner of the visiting team called to say he did not have the funds for transportation. Peter offered to wire the funds so the team could play the scheduled home game.

At the 8 p.m. start, only a handful of players had arrived. Instead of hiring a bus, the players decided to travel by personal auto and lost their way to Dillon stadium. The players had not been paid and saw Peter's money as a way to get some of their salary, which was due them.

The game was delayed while the fans waited for more players to arrive by auto. Peter was so embarrassed. He kept pacing back and forth in the Press Box. Sometime later, cars arrived with the remainder of the team. Upon seeing them enter the stadium, the 8,000 or so fans gave them a standing ovation.

At half-time Peter took the microphone from the public address announcer and apologized to the fans for the dismal performance they were witnessing. He offered to return the price of their ticket. The fans appreciated the offer, but not a single ticket holder asked for a refund. It was clear that team would not return the following year and it was a harbinger of further deterioration in the league.

The next year was a special one. Early in the spring, Peter called me to his office to inform me that the future of the league was in doubt. Only four owners from the previous year had agreed to field a team for the next season. Football is a very expensive operation and owners of minor league teams, like the Hartford Knights, usually balanced the books out of their own pockets. Their love of the game motivated them to purchase a franchise, but after a few years of mounting deficits, some had to call it quits.

During our conversation, Peter said, "Whoever heard of a four-team league?" He did not think the public or the media would support such a radical idea. I asked him who the four teams were and learned that they were the four strongest teams on and off the field the previous year. In my ignorance about such things, I commented, "If I were a football fan, I don't know why I would object to witnessing a competitive football game every week. Why not schedule each team twice at home and away and give the fans an entertaining evening? Wasn't that what the public expects of sports events … to witness two competitive teams with the home team victorious in the end?" Peter stared at me.

I was thinking like a fan. Peter was thinking like a businessman. We discussed the matter at length while I kept notes. I suggested we operate as a four-team league and leave it to Peter to sell the idea to the other owners. He was the leader of the pack anyway and I believed the others would follow his lead.

I prepared a summary of the meeting and gave it to Peter to study in preparation for his phone calls to the other owners. As expected, they all went along with their leader. I called an emergency news conference at which Peter introduced this radical idea.

If Peter could win them over, then we would leave it to them to sell the idea to the public. Peter was a talented salesman and even though I knew he was not 100 percent behind the idea, I trusted his ability to win the day. The news conference was lengthy, made so by the numerous questions from reporters. In the end, we hoped they would buy into our position.

We anxiously awaited the evening sports programs on radio and TV. The reports were positive. The reporters had agreed that a four-team league was better than no league at all. Next would come the morning papers. So far, so good. Everyone was promoting the four-team league. Now we had to wait for the public's reaction.

Of course, the football purists, as expected, would laugh at the idea. Luckily, they represented only a small fraction of the audience and our appeal was not to them, but to the audience that came out on a Saturday night to be entertained. The phone rang all day long, with pros and cons by fans. Some thought it idiotic. Others just wanted to see Saturday night football.

In our first game program of the year, I wrote a double-paged editorial and placed it in the centerfold usually reserved for team information. The title of the piece was WHOEVER HEARD OF A FOUR TEAM LEAGUE? It was a full discussion of all sides of the question that left it to the reader to decide the validity of the decision to operate this year. The positive conclusion by the readers was seen in the attendance figures which were within a few hundred of the best year.

During the winter meetings, the four owners met to discuss the league's future. They sought to enlist others as franchise owners and increase the total number of teams. They not only failed to add teams, but also when the discussions ended there was only one team standing, the Hartford Knights. The Atlantic Coast Football League would cease operation in 1973.

For six years Peter Savin had offered the community a quality and competitive football team to call its own.

For the next few days, all the media highlighted Peter's involvement with superlatives for his effort. His image had been restored in the community that only a few years before was condemning him for wanting the city to underwrite the cost of updating Dillon Stadium. My main reason for accepting Mr. Savin's offer of employment was to restore his good name and I believed that had been accomplished.

We held one last news conference, not to make news, but to say goodbye to all those who had been such a big part of the Knights' history. In addition to the demise of the football league, most of the local sports news now centered around a WHA hockey team that was coming to Hartford as the major tenant in the city's new 10,500-seat Civic Center.

I paid very little attention to that news. I knew less about hockey than I knew about football. Practically every reporter in attendance that day made comments that concluded I would next be working for the hockey team. That was unlikely because I wanted a new challenge in a different world.

After the news conference ended, Peter invited the employees to his office where he expressed his disappointment at the demise of the league. He told us that he would continue to pay our salary until we were able to find a new job. When the meeting ended, I remained to tell him how much I had enjoyed working for him. We exchanged compliments and I added that I would be leaving as soon as I had stored the history of the team, wherever one stores such things.

When he asked me if I had already found a new job, I told him I had not, but that I was satisfied I would find one soon. We shook hands and we hugged. I think I was to the point of tears as I headed for the door.

I believed that wherever life would take me, it was unlikely that I would ever be employed by the likes of Peter Savin.

I looked to the future with optimism wondering what I would be doing next. I had been successful in the political world and been successful in sports administration, worlds completely unknown to me. I was confident that the energy and passion I brought to everything I did would take me somewhere where there was yet a new world for me to conquer.

Chapter 25

The Whalers Years

I started scanning the want ads and came across one seeking applicants willing to travel out of the country. Why not, I thought to myself, why not investigate that ad? The company was located south near the shoreline. I drove there the next day for information. While sitting in a waiting room filled with other job-seeking individuals, I was uncomfortable and felt I did not belong there. I left the office without seeing anyone.

Driving back to Hartford, I passed a construction site where a dinner theater was opening soon. While working for the Knights, I had been approached by Mr. and Mrs. Belkin, owners of the soon-to-open Coachlight Dinner Theater in East Windsor. They had heard about me and wanted to pick my brain concerning marketing and public relations for their theater. Before they could offer me a position, I told them I was very happy working for the football team, but that I would be willing to help them quietly in any way I could.

I don't know why I did not discuss it with Peter Savin. I did not think I could divide my loyalties by working for two companies at the same time. For some moronic reason, I still cannot explain, I refused to be paid for my services. Over a period of about three months, I produced a Playbill for the first two shows and encouraged the owners to hire my sister Estelle as a

Group Sales Director. I convinced them that group sales were the key to their success in their new venture. Most people do their entertaining on the weekends. An active program of discounted ticket prices with large employers and organizations could help maintain an audience during the week. My experience with the Oakdale Theater during the summer of 1967 showed me how important group sales could be for their new theater.

After the theater opened, I attended performances regularly and offered advice on matters of marketing and public relations. Estelle accepted the offer to direct group sales and did a fabulous job over several years. When I completed the second Playbill, I told the Belkins that I could no longer be available because I would be preoccupied with the Knights.

But on this day, I was looking for a paid position and believed my experience with the Coachlight would be valuable to this new venture. I parked my car on the yet-to-be-landscaped grounds and went into the building looking for someone in authority. Luckily, the owners were on the site. They were two young men in their 20s. My experience with Coachlight impressed them, because by this time Coachlight had established itself in the dinner theater industry.

They hired me on the spot for a marketing and public relations position yet to be developed. The opening was a few weeks away and I did what I could to help out.

I soon learned that the young owners did not have any knowledge of, or experience in, theater management and thought they could succeed working at it part-time. Therefore, I did not think the venture would succeed and I would soon be looking for another place of employment. These owners would soon learn that the entertainment business is a most difficult one. I felt I should begin my search for new employment.

One evening, after I had arrived home from the theater, I had a phone message from someone named Baldwin having to do with hockey. Since it mentioned hockey, I thought I would call my friend, Bruce Berlet at the Hartford Courant. Bruce was the Courant's staff writer who covered the Hartford Knights at home and away. We had become good friends over the three years and I believed he would know something about this Mr. Baldwin.

"Bruce," I said, "Someone named Baldwin had called me. Do you know who he is? He has something to do with hockey."

Bruce screamed. "I told you that you were going to work for the Whalers! He is only the President and Managing General Partner of the Whalers." We chatted for a while with Bruce giving me some background information on the Whalers coming to Hartford.

I put down the phone, looking at the phone number to call Mr. Baldwin. I was not interested in a position in hockey. Should I just ignore the call? He is the head man, so I do owe him the courtesy of a reply. I decided to return the call, only because he was the President of the Whalers.

"This is George Ducharme, I am returning Mr. Baldwin's call. Is he available to take this call?"

The voice on the other end said, "This is Howard." I thought I was calling an office, but this was Mr. Baldwin's home number. "George, I have heard nothing but good things about you wherever I go in this city. I would like to offer you a position with the New England Whalers." I asked him what he would have me do. "I want you to sell advertising in our game program." That

211

did not make sense to me. There were at least a dozen firms in the city that exist to sell advertising, why would he want me?

I let him go on with his praise for me, becoming more suspicious of his offer. Bruce had just told me that 16 major firms under the leadership of the Aetna had purchased the franchise. I thought to myself, that's 16 full pages in the program before I make a call. I can earn a year's salary in a few weeks, and then look for another position somewhere. We talked for a few minutes, and I agreed to meet with him the next day to further discuss the offer. The Whalers' front office was located across the street from the Civic Center complex, which was still under construction. The office was a makeshift one with desks all over the place in one large room. The office would be moved to the Civic Center when completed and ready for occupancy.

Mr. Baldwin was a cheerful sort of fellow, very informal in manner and attire. I had worn a suit and looked out of place. He was pleased to meet me and immediately offered me $20,000 to sell out the program book. This would be a temporary position, but if another opening became available after I sold out the book, for which I was qualified, I would be considered for it. I accepted the offer and left to notify the boys at the theater. I told them of my offer and that I would have to begin immediately in order to sell out the program in time for the opening of the season. They agreed to let me go without the usual two-week notice.

I went to work for the Whalers the very next day. This sales job was money in the bank. The entire business community was excited about having a major league team all its own. The Whalers had recently completed its first year in Boston and had won the AVCO Cup as the champion in the league. I thought it strange that a successful team would be leaving Boston for Hartford. It sounded like a great deal for Hartford and the 16 owners of the franchise.

A couple of weeks later Kevin Walsh, the PR director, was named Assistant to the President. Howard was living in the Boston area and expected to be an absentee executive. He would call in every day to speak to various employees. Once in a while he would ask to speak to me for an update on my progress. It did not take much time to sell out the book. I knew most every top executive in and near Hartford, having had high-profile positions in politics and football. All it took was one phone call to make the sale. I informed Howard that the book would be sold out in a few days. I would take my $20,000 and say "adios."

The next day Howard was already in the office when I arrived for the day. He asked me to come to his office. I could not believe my ears when he asked me to be his assistant. "You are going to need two assistants?" I asked. He said he had returned Kevin to the PR department, and I would be his only assistant. I reminded him that I knew nothing about hockey, and he jumped in with "And you knew nothing about football, and you knew nothing about politics."

Once again, I would be working in a business about which I knew absolutely nothing. With my track record, that seemed like a good omen. When I asked for a job description, he said to watch over the front office operation and make any changes I thought would improve it. Rather open-ended I thought.

Howard said my salary would be $20,000, the same $20,000 I had already earned selling out the game program. My mind was somewhere else because I did not question that statement. I already had earned the $20,000. He must have thought I was a small-town jerk to have accepted that offer. I was overwhelmed by the offer. Me, Assistant to the President of a Major League franchise. What would Papa say now? I had better accept the position before he realizes what a ridiculous offer he has made me and rejects it.

I was in a fog the rest of the day. One moment angry that I had accepted such a stupid offer. The next, proud of myself to be the Assistant to the President of the Whalers. I kept saying over and over: What was I doing here? I don't belong here. I kept reminding myself that Kevin Walsh had the position just three weeks ago. Where would I be three weeks from today? I wondered what I was getting myself in for with this impulsive head of the company.

How would Kevin react to the news? It is one thing to be returned to a former position, but another to have the position filled by someone like me. I heard rumors among the staff that I must be a spy, put here by the 16 owners. That made sense, having one of their own keeping an eye on their newest investment. What did not make sense, was me with the title of Assistant to the President of a Major League Hockey Team. My duties were undefined except that I was to apply my marketing and public relations skills to already established policies and procedures and make suggestions I felt could improve them.

Months later, my concerns about Howard were magnified. He phoned me from Boston. He was very excited about something. "I am about to make a deal to buy the Boston Bruins Hockey Team," he said.

"You are what?" I said in a voice too loud for this conversation. In a much softer tone, I said, "Howard, the ink is not yet dry on the Hartford deal and you are planning to move on to another franchise in a different league?" He said he always

214

wanted to own the Bruins, a storied NHL franchise, and that he thought that he left Boston a failure because he could not compete with the Bruins for hockey fans' support.

"I want to go back and prove I can succeed in this business. But do not worry, your position is not in jeopardy, I plan to take you with me," he added.

"Mr. Baldwin, I do not want to move to Boston or any other city," I responded. He continued talking about his life-long dream. I hardly heard a word. I was thinking that as Howard's assistant, I would be the first one replaced should Aetna have to find another president to operate the Hartford franchise. I wanted protection from that possibility and especially from Mr. Impulsive on the other end of the phone. I would have to think about that.

One day while discussing player contracts, I suggested some key office personnel should also have contracts. I was told that such contracts did not exist for staff personnel.

This subject was not open for debate. I need not worry about this matter at this time, because the Bruins deal did not materialize, and I never heard another word about it. Every once in a while, I would bring up the subject of employee contracts with Howard and on September 19, 1975, I probably made sports history when we signed a three-year contract for my employment with the Whalers.

In my earliest days, I was intrigued by the fact that the entire Boston staff was willing to move to Hartford. Who does that? Sports people leaving a city with four major league teams to go to Hartford? I thought they must know something I didn't.

What was it about Howard that made all of them so loyal? It did not take too long to figure out the answer. Howard paid well and I came to the conclusion that jobs were not available in

Boston at the salaries they were making. I believed they would leave, one at a time, just as soon as a position in Boston did become available, and that's just what happened, except for the highest-level executives.

Some of the Boston staff repeatedly degraded Hartford, calling its residents "hicks" and the city a "hick town." One evening at closing time, an employee walked by my desk with a bag full of office supplies. I asked where he was going with them, and he answered, "home." I reminded him that those supplies were the property of the company and should not be removed from the premises.

"Get off it," he said, "You had better get yours, while the getting is good. We won't be here in a couple of years. We will move on to another gullible town." I wondered if the other Boston people felt the same way. If so, not the sort we should have building a franchise here. Later I came to the conclusion that he was the exception.

One day I was handed a registered letter from a Boston attorney, threatening legal action to recover the cost of last year's playoff tickets not needed when the team lost in the first round and played only three games at home. The Boston fans were asked to purchase 10 tickets, one for each of the possible home games that year. Normally any refund would be credited to next year's purchase, but with the team playing in Hartford, fans could not be expected to travel to another city the following year. The refund check should have been mailed some time ago.

With the letter in hand, I walked over to the team accountant, Mr. Green, and said, "Look what I have here." He glanced at the letter and said, "Oh, that's nothing," as he opened a desk drawer stuffed with correspondence and then another drawer with more correspondence.

"What are those?" I asked.

"They are refund requests for last year's unplayed playoff games in Boston."

"What are they doing in those drawers, why haven't the refunds been mailed by this time?" I asked.

"We are not in Boston anymore, fuck them," he replied.

My blood pressure started rising as I asked, "Who made that decision?" He did not respond. I walked over to my desk as the phone was ringing. It was Howard. Good, we will settle this matter right now.

"Howard," I said, "I was about to phone you. I have just learned that we have several hundred requests for refunds for last year's unplayed playoff games. I was told these requests were not responded to because the team was no longer in Boston. Howard, I have a reputation in this city for being a person of integrity. I believe that is one of the reasons why you hired me to be your assistant. Your assistant will not tolerate this kind of behavior toward its fans."

In the most serious tone I could muster, I continued, "Howard, if these refunds are not mailed by the end of the week, I will resign my position and make public the reason for doing so." I hung up the phone. A few seconds later, Mr. Green's phone rang. He listened, said nothing, hung up the phone and opened the two drawers. The refunds were mailed.

The next day Howard came to town and asked me to join him in his office. He was very apologetic about the refunds. Someone had misunderstood that discussion. He thought he was making a joke and should not have been taken seriously. He did not want me to resign. He went on about my being the kind of assistant he needed. Although I accepted his explanation, I left his office more unsettled than ever. I would have to watch him closely in the future.

The construction of our new arena was well underway but would not be completed in time for the first home game. It meant that we had to find another arena to play our home games until the Hartford arena was ready. Howard negotiated an agreement with a Springfield arena and our team travelled there for its early home games. We did play an exhibition game in Middletown. Most of the staff attended. It was my first opportunity to actually see a hockey game and I was not impressed, at least not for the first half-hour or so.

"This will never sell," I said to the staff sitting near me. Then a player, Nick Fotiu, came on the ice and bodies started flying. "This will sell," I said.

The next few months were routine as we prepared for the January Hartford opening. Tickets were selling well and we expected a full house for Opening Night. The community's population was divided on whether this new venture would succeed. Businesspeople were unanimous in the hope the team would succeed, but many of the residents had doubts. There had been so much publicity about crime in the city, many wondered whether suburbanites would return to the city to watch a hockey game.

The Whalers were an immediate success. Night after night, the team filled the arena to capacity or near capacity. The restaurants nearby were packed before and after games. Optimism for the future of the city soared. I worried that our success was due to the novelty of it all and once that wore off, would people continue to come to the games? We would have to wait and see.

I was asked to seek an auto dealer who would accept tickets and advertising in exchange for six autos for some staff people, of which I was one. In addition to looking for autos for the management, one of my projects as Howard's assistant involved furnishing Howard's and Jack Kelley's offices when we would move to the Civic Center. Jack was the General Manager. Howard wanted the best office furniture money could buy and Jack insisted on having exactly what Howard had.

I went to Barney's, a prominent office furniture business. I told the salesman that whatever item I would purchase, I would need two of them. As for the autos, I was able to arrange for six autos from Mitchell Pontiac after meeting the owner, and that meant I could have one for myself.

I attended every home game but was concerned by the audiences' lack of spontaneity and enthusiasm for the entertainment on the ice. Much of that was due to the unfamiliarity of the game on the part of so many in the arena. I also believed that many in the arena were not hockey fans but wanted to see this one-of-a-kind facility.

One morning I went into Howard's office and said, "What would you think of a theme song for the team?"

His answer, "What the fuck are you talking about?" made it clear a theme song was not something I should waste my time on, but he did not say "no," so I left the office with the theme song on my mind. I wanted a piece of music that was spirited, a piece of music that would be played whenever the team entered the rink, every time the team scored, and whenever we won a game. I saw it as an identifying sound that would immediately say "Whalers" when heard. The music could also be used on radio and TV for ticket promotions.

Howard did not say no, so I began my search for the music that would be the Whalers' theme song. I met with the area's band leaders and asked them to write a piece of original music for the team. I was vague on what I wanted, except it had to be a sound that brought fans out of their seats. I explained how I planned to use it and pretty much left it up to the musicians to write it. When pressed further, I simply said, "it's like pornography, you know it when you see it. I will know it when I hear it."

Months passed and I was not satisfied with anything submitted to me. I finally had to admit that maybe it wasn't such a good idea after all. I put it out of my mind. In its place, a new idea had emerged. What about a retail outlet where fans could buy souvenirs of items with a team logo? I wanted to reach those in the community who did not know the game. I wanted to broaden the base of support for the Whalers beyond the hockey fan. I wanted to make fans of children, women and grandparents, aunts and uncles. Hockey was new to most of the population at this time. If the franchise was to succeed, it would have to increase its fan base beyond the knowledgeable hockey fan.

I brought the idea to Howard. I want to open a gift shop with merchandise featuring our team logo. His reaction was the same as with a theme song. I told him I could open a gift shop for about $50,000. Again, he did not say "no." He just walked away from me. That was all the encouragement I needed. I contacted the real estate department at the Aetna that was leasing space in the Civic Center for what was to be known as the Civic Center Shops. I informed them that the Whalers wanted the space nearest the Box

Office. We were the prime tenant in the arena, and we should have a prime location for our gift shop.

The Aetna regularly publicized the signing of leases of stores coming to the Civic Center Shops. I waited to hear about the space for our gift shop. When more time passed and I still had not heard from the real estate department, I called to ask why it was taking so long for a confirmation of space. I was told that they had searched the country for a shop like the one I wanted to open but could not find a single retail store selling what I wanted to sell.

"So, the Whalers will be the first to own a retail store, someone has to be first, why not us?" I answered. I got the feeling that since no other team had a store, who was I to think it would succeed. In other words, if no other team had a store, why would someone like me, with no knowledge of the sport, come up with an idea more experienced sports people had not yet considered? I now believed the gift shop would go the way of the theme song, but I was not giving up ... just yet.

Here I am, on the phone again with the Aetna real estate department. No, they did not have space for me. That was not as much of a surprise as the reason. I was told that I was the only one in the Whalers organization that wanted space for a shop and that someone in the Whalers' office had told them to sit on my request. When I asked who that someone was, they refused to tell me. It could only have been one of two people, Howard or David Andrews. Howard would not be interested in such details, so I believed it must be David.

I was so angry that I was ready to resign, contract notwithstanding. Howard was in Hollywood so I would wait until he returned. It was pointless to confront David, he would just deny it. We hardly ever agreed on company policy or procedure.

221

He was a graduate of a prestigious business college with little experience in the business world, while I previously had success in the retail and marketing worlds. I was working to ensure a future for the franchise, while he, in my opinion, was strictly status quo and not willing to make waves regardless of the merit of the suggestion.

I never brought the subject up with Howard, because before he returned, I received another call from the real estate office. This time, offering me 600 square feet on the second floor overlooking the courtyard on the main floor. Someone had reneged on a lease and they did not want to have that space unoccupied, in such a prominent area, on opening day, which now was three weeks away.

I asked if the space had been approved by management and they replied, "No, we just learned of the cancellation and we thought of you." I accepted the offer. While I wanted more than 600 square feet, it was better than no store at all.

I had three weeks to design a store, fixture it, order merchandise and hire and train personnel. I would call the store, the Whalers Gift Shop. The Aetna had emphasized that its mall would have tenants with national images. I thought calling it a "gift shop" rather than "store" sounded more sophisticated and fit the image Aetna wanted to convey to its shoppers.

The entrance had to be unique. I wanted a showstopper that created curiosity and would compel traffic walking by to stop and notice the shop. I contracted with a designer to build an entrance that was a cutout of a whale I had seen in our office. Virginia Phillipps, the mother of Ron Ryan, a team coach, had been asked by her son to design a patch to be placed on players' uniforms. She designed a caricature of a baby whale that was as cute as cute could be. The entrance cutout in the shape of a whale would definitely stop traffic. Most of all, it would appeal to children and parents, the market I was aiming for to be future Whaler fans.

The hockey department approved the baby whale patch, probably because Mr. Ryan suggested it, but was not keen on having it represent the team as a second logo.

It was too cute a symbol for hockey, which was a rough and tough sport, but perfect to attract the population I wanted to see in the stands. The team logo was a "W" with a harpoon through it. I did not think it conveyed the image parents would want on their children's clothes.

A few days before we opened in Hartford, I hired several Volkswagen Beetles to travel the downtown area during lunch hour. We added "ers" to a paper cutout of the baby whale and placed one on each side of the vehicle so it could be seen by lunch hour traffic. This vehicle said "Whalers Hockey." To gauge public opinion, I left my office and stood on Trumbull Street across from the Civic Center. There were lots of folks on the street at this time and I wanted to watch for their reaction to the car as it passed by. There were smiles as people pointed to the vehicle. When the game program was published, it was especially gratifying to see so many ads in the book that featured the baby whale and not the "W." Marketing people knew that the whale symbol was the logo the public would be drawn to.

The three weeks flew by, but we managed to have our shop ready for the "opening" of the mall. The entrance of our shop was a magnet for shoppers. Many had brought cameras and took pictures standing by the entrance. With so little time, I was unable to stock the store with many logoed items. Screen printers needed more time to process our order. The total sales for the day was $378. We sold out everything in the store.

I pleaded with vendors to rush my orders, even partial shipments. I spent the next few days with representatives of companies that sold novelty items. I wanted to put a "whale" on anything that would sell: T-shirts, sweatshirts, pucks, bumper stickers, hats, patches, ash trays, glasses, mugs, pennants, you name it. I walked through my home looking for items that I could order with a whale on it. Customers brought in hand-knitted sweaters, gloves and hats. I accepted anything that had a "whale" on it. The sales staff and I were having too much fun to call it work.

To publicize the gift shop, I wanted commercials to be heard in the arena during the game and between periods. The PR department refused this request. I went to Howard who approved my request for 30-second spots in the arena. The franchise had an investment in the shop, and it should be seen as a part of the fans' hockey experience. The commercials also invited the fans to visit the shop after the game.

Radio station WTIC, a 50,000-watt station that covered most of the state, broadcast our games and our commercials were heard during breaks in the action on the ice.

We remained open until every last customer had left the store. On game nights, it became routine to have as many as 1,000 fans "walk through the whale." I stood at the entrance directing traffic. We designed the shop so customers had to walk the only path available. If you wanted to return to something you had seen, you had to make a second trip. I adopted policies considered by some as unfriendly to customers. Food or drink was not permitted in the shop. I insisted that our shop would always look its best. Customers walking around the mall with an ice cream cone or any cup of liquid were not permitted to "walk through the whale." My most controversial policy was the absence of a telephone. No one could reach the store by phone. Because our shop was unique, I refused to spend time on the phone describing merchandise customers had never seen anywhere.

Not only were customers angry, but the receptionist in the Whaler front office was spending most of her time telling callers that the shop did not have a phone. At first callers thought it was only a temporary delay until one was installed.

As we approached the Christmas selling season, the telephone company was dealing with callers from all over the state inquiring about our phone number. The Information operators were having arguments with callers who insisted there had to be a phone in the shop because all retail businesses had a phone. All except the Whalers Gift Shop.

I always resented having to wait while a salesperson not only answered the phone, but also completed a transaction while I waited. I believed that customers in any store should have preference over the phone customer and I was now in a position to put that policy into effect. I had a number of other reasons for my no-phone policy. I strongly believed that our merchandise could not be described over the phone because our shop featured items not seen anywhere. Most importantly, over the phone the customer would usually be inquiring about a specific item, whereas when they visited the shop they might be purchasing several items.

I did not want to deal with returns when the customer was dissatisfied with the item delivered. I also believed that ours would be a high-traffic operation and whatever sales force I had, should be devoted to those customers in the shop. Another policy restricted smokers in the shop. That policy usually met with approval from the customers. The mall management kept records of transactions in each of their retail operations and the Whalers Gift Shop, month after month, was second only to the ice cream shop on the main floor in total number of transactions.

Most game nights, I would position myself outside the entrance, to hold back the traffic and check for people, smoking or eating. After the second period, regardless of the score in the game, there were long lines waiting to enter the shop. If there were children at the game, then "A Walk Through the Whale" was mandatory. To the surprise of many in the front office, sales did not depend on the team's winning or losing. Real fans supported their team win or lose and visiting the gift shop became a part of the Whaler experience.

At the end of the first season, the communication department produced an LP record of the year's highlights. Every member of the staff received a copy. The LP was added to items available in the gift shop. Since I had lived through the first year, I wasn't in any rush to hear it. I placed the LP on the living room coffee table and forgot about it.

One Sunday afternoon when the family had gathered, someone spotted the LP and asked what it was. I told them and left the room. Minutes later I heard a sound that caused me to scream, "That's it, that's it! That is the sound I was looking for! That is going to be the Whalers theme song." I rushed into the living room asking what radio station was playing that music. The sound did not emanate from the radio – it was coming from the LP.

I could not control myself. The kids thought their uncle was going crazy because he was going crazy. I had not mentioned the theme song to anyone, so they did not understand my excitement.

There was a lot of dialogue on the LP and a few bars of music were used to bridge the dialogue. What I had heard was one of the pieces of music on the LP. I replayed it over and over and realized in just three notes I could identify our product, "Whalers hockey." That is a marketing person's dream.

I did not sleep well that night. I had found my theme song and it was spectacular. I could not wait until morning to learn more about the music. I had to control myself. I could not make my purpose known. I had to play it cool. I was early as I waited for Bill Rasmussen and Bob Neumeier to arrive. They had collaborated on the production of the LP. I wanted to know more about the music, who wrote it and who owned it.

Somehow, I had to find a way to secure the rights to that music if Bill and Bob had not already done so.

When they arrived, as calmly as I could, I told them I had listened to their LP and congratulated them on a job well done. I wanted to bring up the subject of the music, but in a casual manner, not making it a big deal. I learned that they found the music at D & K Sound Services, in Wethersfield. I ended our conversation and nonchalantly left the office for a trip to D & K Sound where I met the owner, Ron DeLisa. The music I was interested in was named "Brass Bonanza." It was written by Jack Say, who had sold his entire library to Sam Fox Publishing, which DeLisa later purchased. Mr. Say had left the country for Austria.

I told Mr. DeLisa of my plan to make that music the theme song of the Whalers. At that time, I think every businessperson in the community was rooting for the hockey team to be successful. Mr. DeLisa offered me the music without any fee. I could not contain myself. I was convinced that "Brass Bonanza" was going to be a bonanza for the Whalers. It would add a new dimension to the entertainment of our hockey games. I kept telling myself that those first three musical notes were going to be famous. I believed that the hockey department would object on the grounds that ice hockey did not need any assistance to be exciting. Hockey was exciting. I also remembered Howard's four-letter word remark when I suggested music be added to the game. I expected he would side with the hockey department in any dispute with me. I had to have the Whalers so invested in the music that he could not reject it. I ordered 5,000 45 rpm records on the spot from Mr. Delisa.

The team was playing on the road. I wanted to introduce it at a hockey game, so I put the 5,000 records in the stock room to await the next home game. The first time anyone would hear "Brass Bonanza" would be when the team was introduced on the ice. It was late afternoon on the day of the next home game. I took a copy of the record, put it in a bag and headed for the sound engineer. As Assistant to the President, my title carried some weight, and he did not question my request to play the record. I told him to play it just as the team was introduced, until the puck was dropped; should the Whalers score a goal, play the record until they dropped the puck to resume play. If we win the game, play the music until every last fan has left the arena. The fans and the staff would hear it for the first time, and I waited for the reaction to the music. It was more than I could hope for.

When the public address announcer said, "Here are your New England Whalers," the music blared out and the reaction was instantaneous.

At the sound of "Brass Bonanza" the fans stood up and cheered their team skating on the ice. They started clapping to the music. I left the game to go to the gift shop and get ready to sell the record that evening. I had written a script for the 30-second spot which announced that the music was available in the gift shop. Even though they had absolutely nothing to do with this music being named the Whalers Theme Song, I thought it would make it more palatable to the staff if the names of Bill Rasmussen and Bob Neumeier were included on the record label. I felt it would receive a fair hearing if it looked like others were behind it.

I don't remember any reaction to the music the next day. I think the team only scored once, so the music played only four times over the entire game. I had purchased a 45 rpm recorder and placed it at the entrance to the gift shop for all to hear. From that day on, the music was played continually during store hours. From 10 a.m. until closing at 9 p.m., the music would be heard by anyone passing by. I wanted to give my theme song the full treatment in order to establish it before any opposition to it would develop in the front office and the hockey department.

The fans took to the music the first time they heard it. That evening we sold hundreds of records. I assigned one employee to do nothing but open boxes. It was an exciting night for gift shop employees and fans. A few games later, the Whalers scored eight goals and "Brass Bonanza" was played twelve times during the game. The fans were out of their seats cheering their team louder with each goal scored.

They were having a good time, but Jack Kelley wasn't enjoying the music. The next morning he came storming into the office, looking for Howard. He screamed at Howard as he entered his office, "This is not a concert, it's a hockey game! Do we have to hear that fucking music all night long?"

Here it comes, an attempt to limit the use of the theme song in the arena. I jumped up from my desk and ran into Howard's office. I looked at Jack and said, "You had better hope you hear that music in your sleep, because every time you hear it something good is happening to your team." Jack and I were now facing Howard who was sitting behind his desk. We looked like two lawyers at the bench waiting for the judge to give his ruling. I had no idea what Howard would say.

He looked at me, then at Jack, and said, "Well, Jack, I think you lost this one." After Jack left the office, muttering to himself, I said to Howard, "It is a good thing that you sided with me, because I purchased 5,000 records for sale in the gift shop." They would have to be sold to recoup our investment and it would be impossible to do that without playing it in the arena.

He smiled as he said, "You son of a bitch."

Now I had two major marketing products to sell the franchise to people beyond the hockey fan. The music and the cute whale. The gift shop was becoming a smashing success. Whenever Howard had hockey brass from other teams visiting, a trip to the gift shop was always on the agenda. Howard seemed to enjoy the praise from his guests. After they left, my staff noted that he failed to introduce me to his guests as the one who was responsible for the shop's existence. The Whalers had something no other team had, a gift shop and a theme song, yet the public relations department failed to take note of either in its news releases or game program. Kevin Walsh had control of the team's publicity and must have had negative feelings for me, since I replaced him as Assistant to the President. I do not think he ever mentioned my name during the four years I was employed.

The gift shop was taking up a great deal of my time. I had hired a manager, but he soon proved unsatisfactory. He did not have the marketing instinct or passion that is necessary to survive in retailing. I found myself spending more and more time in the gift shop and less time in the office as Assistant to the President. I made a decision most people would think stupid. I told Howard that I wanted to give up my title as his assistant and become the Marketing and Gift Shop Manager.

He reacted in disbelief that I would want to make a move to a lesser role, but I persuaded him that I would be much more valuable to the franchise in a role for which I had enthusiasm and considerable passion. I also wanted to guarantee that the shop would succeed. He reluctantly accepted my change in titles. Oddly enough, he did not name a new assistant.

In changing titles, I asked Howard to separate gift shop income from other franchise income and insisted that shop income be reserved exclusively for shop expenses. I also asked that all shop invoices be paid promptly. I explained how important it was to have good relations with our vendors so I could ask for and receive special attention to my orders whenever I needed to do so. Howard approved my requests.

The time I spent in the gift shop was the most satisfying and enjoyable of all the time with the Whalers. Howard treated me as though I were a contractor and not an employee. I had complete control of the gift shop operation. I purchased whatever I wanted, priced the merchandise as I chose, developed shop policies without comment from above and was treating the shop as if it were my own. The staff in the front office regularly referred to the shop as "George's store," expecting it to fail and did not want the team to be identified with it. I had believed for some time that I had managerial skills, contrary to what Mr. Winters at Sears thought, and the shop gave me an opportunity to prove it.

Sales continued a steady rise. I publicly promoted the fact that the shop would feature a new item on every game day. I did not want previous customers to think they had seen everything there was to purchase. I planned a contest to name the whale and received over 14,000 entries. The winning choice I selected was "Puckie." The name fit the cute whale to a T. I wanted a name that children and adults would find appealing. In selecting "Puckie," I knew that hockey purists, other adult males and the hockey department personnel would not approve of the name. I could hear them now. "It is too cute for the rough and tumble game that is hockey."

To further publicize the whale for the children, I asked two friends of mine, Charlene Ryan and Meredith Barker, to collaborate with me in creating a coloring book about Puckie. We entitled it, "The Whale Who Likes Hockey." I kept the publication of the book a secret, but I promoted for weeks a special new item available in time for Christmas. It would be a subject of much conversation. I could have added the word controversy. In early December, my 30-second spot featured the announcement that the surprise item would be available after the game.

The fans flocked to the gift shop and drew such a crowd that it required mall security to maintain some semblance of order, leaving walking space for other shoppers in the mall to continue their shopping elsewhere. Normally on game nights the shop remained open after the game for about 45 minutes to serve the fans. On Puckie night, we remained open for about an hour and a half. I had ordered 1,000 copies of the coloring book and when we closed the shop for the evening, we had sold almost every copy. Children and their parents were pleased with the book, but teenagers were vocal in their disapproval. The negative reaction to the book was expected and the male fans did not disappoint me. The staff and I had fun that evening.

Although I worked long hours, it was so satisfying that I left the store each evening energized by the growing approval of the shop and its merchandise. We were making new friends for the franchise, and I felt that someday they would be Whaler ticket buyers. I was especially pleased that the staff I had hired proved to be loyal and dedicated employees. We were a great team who enjoyed what we were doing and frequently customers remarked about the friendliness of the staff and how much they enjoyed the shopping experience at the gift shop. Once a while one would comment on the absence of a phone but agreed with the policy when I explained the rationale behind it.

The success of the gift shop was due in part to my good relationships with our vendors. Some of my vendors also did business with our front office. I heard from them that my invoices were always paid on time, but they were having some difficulty with delays in payment for front office purchases. I was happy when I could say I had nothing to do with that.

I learned that there was a policy of not mailing checks until a complaint was made. There was a stack of processed invoices sitting on the accountant's desk that had to have the business manager's approval to mail the check.

One day, I received a phone call from a vendor telling me that for the first time I was late with a payment. I called upstairs to investigate the situation and was told that the invoice had been processed for payment. A week or so later, the same vendor called again to tell me his invoice payment had not yet been received. I made another call upstairs and was told payment was awaiting signature on the check.

When I received a third call by that same vendor, this time I went upstairs to learn that checks had to be approved by the business manager in order to be mailed. I walked over to the BM's desk asking why that particular invoice was not paid, even though I was told it had been processed. The answer I received was a beaut. "You did not ask if it was mailed." I went to Howard to remind him that we had an agreement to have shop invoices paid promptly from shop income.

The story behind this sleazy tactic was that the franchise did not have the funds to make all the payments due. Shop income was no longer being separated from other franchise income, as we had agreed it would be. Whenever the franchise needed money, a "cash call" was made to the Aetna. Apparently at this time, a cash call had been made, received and spent. I assumed the BM felt he could not ask for funds again so soon after the previous call was made.

There was talk in the front office about the financial condition of the franchise and how long we could go on asking Aetna for money. The franchise spent money like it was going out of style. An example of the extravagance was a rumor that we had spent $3,000 for a team dinner following a West Coast game. Apparently $3,000 the franchise did not have. I never saw the invoice, but the dinner was the subject of much gossip in the front office.

This hockey venture by the owners was turning out to be a very expensive one. I think it was the Travelers that was the first to complain about costs and ask out of their involvement. Others soon followed and Aetna was almost alone in supporting the team.

It was just an office rumor, but in this case probably true. In a small office like ours, information like that spreads quickly. I was lucky not to be the Assistant to the President with this kind of talk becoming common knowledge. I worried about my vendor relations deteriorating in the future, but that was only the forerunner of more serious problems to come my way.

My relationship with Howard was beginning to concern me. Since I was downstairs in the gift shop, I was unaware that someone must have been at work trying to undermine our relationship. The first evidence came when I received my season tickets for the new year. In my contract with Howard, I had asked for six season tickets. It was early in our existence and our future was controversial in some quarters. I had a positive attitude about the future and asked for six tickets. The other employees received two tickets. Employees could, and did, ask for additional tickets for a specific game and received them.

I called the ticket manager to ask why I had received only two season tickets this year and was told that the BM had ordered him to send only two tickets to every staffer. Did Howard forget about our contract which was clear in giving me six tickets? I went upstairs to see Howard and remind him of our contractual agreement. I could tell it was an awkward moment for him. He told me that there was dissension among other staffers.

I interrupted him saying, "You mean one staffer, don't you? Doesn't your signature mean anything these days?" I explained that I gave my tickets to vendors and people who were helpful to me in the management of the gift shop. In a tone he did not appreciate, I said, "If you are going to restrict me to two season tickets, then I want you to pay me for the cost of four tickets so I can purchase them on my own and distribute them as I see fit." I left the office in a huff. A few minutes later, the ticket manager, Brian McLeod, personally delivered my four tickets. I wondered if the two-ticket policy had been cleared with him.

A couple of days later, Mark Mitchell, the son of the owner of Mitchell Pontiac with whom I had arranged for the six cars, was on the phone. Mark and I had become friends in the meantime. "George," he said, "they want your car to give it to another employee." I could tell he was embarrassed to have to make that call. I told him that I would look into the matter. The thought that Howard did not have the decency to tell me in person, ran through my mind as I left the shop for another unpleasant trip to his office.

He was behind his desk as I entered without knocking. In a loud and angry voice, I said, "What is going on here, first the tickets and now my car?" I waited. No response. "Don't you have anything to say?" I continued. He seemed to be caught off guard and lost in his thoughts. I stood there waiting for him to say something.

"I need your car for a new employee I have hired. You will get another one soon," he responded.

I answered in a furious manner, "No, Howard, I will keep my car as we have agreed by contract, you can get another one for your new hire whenever you wish." I thought he was about to come over the desk at me and I stepped backward to get out of range. I thought, "I will never get another car if I give this one back, contract or no contract." The shop was so successful, maybe he thinks he can operate without me and is intentionally annoying me so that I will resign. I decided right then to do just that. I did not want to work in this kind of atmosphere.

"Howard, my contract will expire shortly. You have my resignation today effective at the end of our arrangement," and I walked out of his office and returned to the gift shop. I informed my staff of my resignation. They were shocked, even though they

236

knew that my relationship with the front office was not going well. I think they thought Howard and I would work it out, but I had enough. Having worked gift shop hours since the opening, I told myself I had earned a rest.

❆ ❆ ❆

I decided to take a vacation. I had promised my assistant, Joan Hayes, that I would not call her while I was away. She did not believe me. All the employees knew I kept on top of everything, and it would be impossible for me to ignore the shop for a two-week period. They were correct.

I did not call back to the shop on Saturday or Sunday, but by Monday morning I just had to check in. The shop opened at 10 a.m. and I placed my call at 10:01 a.m. and no one answered. Everyone knew how I felt about the shop being open on time. A few minutes later, I called again, still no answer. A third call about 10 minutes later was not answered.

I called home to my mother to look for my assistant Joan's phone number so I could call her at her home. She interrupted my conversation by saying, "Don't you know what happened here? The roof fell in."

"What roof?" I answered.

"The roof of the Civic Center. Isn't it on the news down there?" she said.

I was in my room at Miami Beach and rushed to turn on the TV. There wasn't any word of the collapse of the roof. My mother gave me Joan's home phone, and I called her to get more details. There had been a heavy snowfall overnight and the weight of the snow collapsed the roof. No one was hurt because the collapse occurred just before dawn.

237

I tried to get a flight home, but the weather had closed down the entire East Coast to air travel. It took two days before I could purchase a return flight home to see what could have been a horror story had it happened that evening when there were 5,000 people in the arena watching a UConn basketball game. The shop was closed. A steel beam from the arena came right through the wall. What a mess to clean up. I never completed that vacation.

On my last day with the Whalers, I went to the front office to say goodbye to the staff. I walked into Howard's office and said I would be leaving today. He stood up from behind his desk. I reached over and extended my hand, not knowing whether he would extend his. We shook hands.

"No hard feelings," I said and left the office. That was a stupid thing to say, of course there are hard feelings. The gift shop was my baby, and I looked forward to it every day, but it was no longer fun having to work in a hostile environment. I was convinced I had made the right decision.

Out of a job, I could now take a vacation, but I did not. The scuttlebutt in the Whalers front office was that no one had ever quit on Howard. He ended the employment, not the other way around. He called daily, asking me to return. I kept telling him that I was not interested. The calls continued less frequently, but at least once a week, same conversation, same answer. Finally, during one of his calls, I said in a very firm tone, "Howard, I do not wish to work for YOU, why won't you understand that?" I kept thinking he wants to hire me back so he can fire me and have the last word.

The weeks went by and the calls continued. The latest conversations were not about me, but about the possibility of Hartford entering the National Hockey League, something Howard had dreamed about from the time he got involved with the business of hockey. I would wish him well as he negotiated that possibility. His regular calls now kept me up to date on the talks with the NHL and it began to appear that it was more than a possibility that Hartford would soon become an NHL team. What a coup it would be for the city to be home to a major league sports franchise.

Then it was official. Howard told me that the deal was made, and it would be announced in a couple of days. I congratulated him. I was happy for him to have achieved his dream. Our recent calls had been civil because he stopped asking me to come back to work for him. During the conversation, after telling the good news about the team, he said he had a position in mind for me.

Before I could respond, he said "Hear me out, before you say no, again. We will need a farm team once we enter the NHL and I want you to direct that operation." He was offering me the position of Director of Operations of the development team.

I was somewhat taken aback by the offer. The years I was with the team, I concentrated on administration and marketing. When I sat in the arena during a game, my mind was elsewhere, especially after the gift shop was opened. Most of the time, while supposedly watching the action on the ice, I was waiting to hear the gift shop commercial. Sometimes when I wasn't in the arena, the gift shop commercial would not be heard. I wanted to be sure it was. He told me I would not have to be involved with the team, that was the coach's responsibility. Lastly, he said the team would be located in West Springfield, Massachusetts, at the Big E arena.

If he thought the location was a plus, it was not. "You are asking me to drive Route 91 twice a day? That two-lane road is a parking lot most of the time. I would not have the patience for that every day. Thank you for the offer and thinking I could perform in that capacity." He kept on talking obliviously to what I had just said. Howard always ignored what he did not want to hear. He told me that I was perfect for the job, and I would not have to be in Hartford. That was a statement to remind me of my problems with someone on his staff. That comment had some appeal, but I was not convinced.

Then Howard dropped the bomb, he thought. The only negative was that I would have to operate the concession stands in the Big E arena on game nights and at any other event in the arena. There was a high school hockey league which played its games at that arena and there were horse shows scheduled throughout the year. He did not know that I disliked concession stands. I hate them. I did not like the quality of product, the lack of service and especially the outrageous prices that were charged. I wondered if I could operate concession stands with G. Fox and Sears standards. Now that would be a challenge I could accept. I told Howard that I would have to think about his offer.

The very next day Howard called pressing me for an answer. Had I thought it over, would I return to the Whalers? I told him that I would discuss the matter at a meeting in his office at his convenience. He was pleased and we agreed on a date to meet.

He then told me that he forgot to mention that my salary would be $30,000, plus a performance bonus based upon agreed conditions. All that was immaterial to me. Did I want to return to the Whalers? I kept thinking about the concession stands and my role in managing them. That was certainly appealing to me.

This would be a new challenge and I had thrived on challenges in the past, especially in positions where I had no previous experience. The opportunity to manage the concession stands was the reason I accepted the offer.

I need not have worried about commuter travel to Springfield because I would be on the highway about 9 a.m. when the commuter traffic had reached its destination and I would be returning home around midnight.

There was an established franchise in Springfield, which by the way, was the home of the American Hockey League. The team office was located at the Big E arena. A former Whaler goalie, Bruce Landon, was hired as the Public Relations Director. I knew of him when he was with the team, and he had a positive reputation among the players. When I met him there wasn't any doubt in my mind that we would work well together. On staff also was a secretary who sold tickets during the day.

It did not take long to discover that I was in a hostile community, hostile to anything having to do with the Whalers. Not only was this Boston Bruins territory, but also Howard Baldwin was Public Enemy No. 1 since he was so identified with the World Hockey Association. When that new league was formed, it took its players from those who were in the final days of their career, and those who were on the way up to a possible NHL career. These were the very players who previously would have been hired by the American Hockey League.

There was great concern that the League would disband and since the main office of the League was in Springfield, local hockey fans were privy to discussions about the serious possibility that AHL teams might not survive. Howard Baldwin was one of the faces of the WHA and Springfield hockey fans were eager to show their disapproval of him or any venture in which he had a major role. Thanks Howard, I thought, for the honor of being the Director of Operations in this city. It was going to be much more than I had bargained for.

Mike Reddy, Howard's brother-in-law, had been selected to operate the gift shop after I left the company. He was a friend and a good choice, I thought, and would do a good job. When it came time to reorder "Brass Bonanza" records, he changed the label and eliminated Rasmussen's and Neumeier's names as among those who had selected this music to be used as a theme song, leaving only my name on the label.

When I asked him why he had made the change on the label, he said he knew that they had nothing to do with the theme song. He knew it was my idea and that I was the only one thinking "theme song." He knew others were taking credit now that it was so popular. I thanked Mike for setting the record straight, once and for all.

The Springfield hockey fans' hostility toward the Whalers did not extend to the business community. They saw the obvious strengths in the arrangement with an NHL team that would keep the franchise in operation, and therefore a benefit to the city. Bruce and I were successful in selling them advertising and tickets and we were able to negotiate a car deal for Bruce and myself.

An unexpected concern developed with regard to the previous concessions' staff. A few weeks before the season opened, I asked my secretary to contact the workers who had staffed the concessions the previous season and schedule a meeting with them. I told her I would be available at any time for the meeting. When she returned only minutes later, I was surprised how quickly she had scheduled a meeting. "When are we meeting?" I asked.

She shocked me when she said, "There isn't going to be any meeting."

"Why not?" I asked. Those who had worked the previous season showed their anger toward the Whalers by refusing to work for anyone employed by Howard Baldwin. That was an unexpected problem that had to be solved quickly.

I decided to do what I had done in politics, call on my family for help. At that time, I had two married sisters, and six teenage nieces and nephews, making a total of ten, all of whom I thought had good work habits and wanted to help Uncle George. Now we had the staff we needed to get the job done. If someday they should read this book, I want them to know that I was proud of the manner in which they accepted my call for help. To Dan, James, Danielle, Karen, Darlene, Mary, Aly, Denise, John, Mark, Al and Marion, your Uncle George thanks you for performing above expectations, and I love you all for being there for me when I needed you.

We bought quality brand-name products, sold them at reasonable prices and were friendly and accommodating to the customers. The team lost its first game and remained in last place all season. We were drawing fair crowds and slowly the fans told us that they appreciated the change in prices and service at the concession stands.

As the season was coming to an end, rumors that the Whalers were leaving Springfield started to emerge. I visited Howard and told him we were beginning to build a following for the Whalers and its convenience to Hartford would create another base of support for the NHL team. At each of the remaining home games, I was repeatedly questioned by the fans concerning the future of the team in Springfield. They wanted us to return the next year. My conversations with Howard now were more frequent as I continually stressed the positives of remaining only twenty-six miles from Hartford.

Before the final home game, I met with him and he assured me that we would remain in Springfield for the next season. The rumors were flying high that we were not returning, and the fans filled the arena to near capacity to show their support. I went out on the ice after the first period and told the fans we were returning. Cheers, whistles and applause greeted the announcement and I believed next year's attendance would be substantially higher than this season's.

The next morning, I was still in my pajamas as I picked up the Hartford Courant, turned to the sports page to read that the Whalers development team would be moving to Binghamton, New York. I stared at the paper; it cannot be! There must be some mistake. Howard was very clear in telling me again and again that we would remain in Springfield. I dressed in a hurry and headed to Howard's office. I was getting angrier by the minute. Even now, after all these years, I cannot put into words my reaction to the news I had just read.

I stormed into Howard's office, almost screaming at him. I was told that I could be heard outside the office. "How could you do this?" I asked, as I threw the Courant at him. "You told me only a few days ago that we would remain in Springfield. Then you decide otherwise and don't tell me? Did you know that I went out on the ice and told them that you said we were remaining in town? That was the only time the entire year that your name was cheered."

Howard did not look at me. When I ended my tirade, he looked up at me and said he was sorry.

"Sorry?" I screamed at him. "You are sorry that you lied to me over and over?"

He said he did not make the decision; the BM had signed a contract with Binghamton without his knowledge.

"Then unsign it. This is a stupid business decision. Contracts are broken all the time. Why are we doing this? It does not make any sense. The fans are just beginning to come around. Why are we moving four hours away to a community that is New York Rangers territory? It makes no sense. How many Binghamton fans do you expect in Hartford next year? We have built a solid foundation and now we are throwing that away because your BM signed a piece of paper?"

Again, he said he was sorry. I was not interested in sorry. "Howard Baldwin," I rarely called him by his last name, "are you telling me that a financial arrangement of this magnitude was made official without the knowledge of the Managing General Partner? Pardon me sir, and I do not wish to sound disrespectful, but I do not believe you."

The decision was made; it would stand regardless of who made it. I turned to leave the office when Howard asked me to sit down, PLEASE. He informed me that in spite of the team's last place position, the franchise in Springfield broke even financially.

"You have made a miracle, I do not think that has ever happened in Minor League Sports," he said. I was not impressed, too angry about moving the franchise. I remarked that the fans came to eat. Normally I would have smiled while making that statement, but this morning I was not smiling. If that was meant to be a compliment, it was lost because of the anger I felt at being repeatedly lied to. Howard had a talent for ignoring what he did not want to hear. He told me that he wanted me to follow the team to Binghamton. At that moment, I would not have walked across the street for him.

245

Chapter 26

On to the Binghamton Whalers

Howard would be spending little time in Binghamton, and he wanted someone he could trust to look after the franchise's Farm Team. "Every decision you make, will be made in my name. You will in reality be the Managing General Partner of that team. I like your energy and especially your passion, (he paused) except when it is directed at me," he said with a smile. The job would be less stressful because I would not be responsible for the concessions operation.

He completely ignored the few minutes prior and spoke to me as though our meeting was an employee annual review. He asked me to think about it. I left without a comment.

That he wanted me to go to Binghamton was not a surprise. No one in the organization would have left Hartford for that position. I had the perfect opportunity to negotiate a good deal for myself, but I was still angry about the lies I had heard about moving the team. I did a good job in Springfield, even modestly I could say it was a great performance. I was reminded of the times in my early years when relatives would ask me what I wanted to be when I grew up. My answer was always the same. "I don't know, but whatever it is, I will be good at it." Almost 30 years later, that statement now seemed quite prophetic.

I had a decision to make. Would I accept Howard's offer to go to Binghamton, a four-hour drive from home? Would I want to remain with a firm that could not see the error of this move from Springfield? Would I want to continue to work for someone who could lie to me repeatedly? As much as I enjoyed the concession business, the new job would be less stressful without having that responsibility along with managing the operation. Howard had told me that the community was solidly behind the team, and I would not be working in a hostile town. There was some appeal to working four hours away from the front office.

The main negative had to do with trust. Yes, he would want someone he could trust to do this job; my concern was could I trust him? He would say anything to get me to agree. I remembered the aggravating situation regarding my season tickets and my car. How could I forget his 180-degree decision to go to Binghamton, when he said he would remain in Springfield? There was much to consider before I could make a decision.

I discussed the matter with my family, especially those who had worked the concession stands in Springfield. They knew what a good job I had done in Springfield. I had proved I could manage a front office and the concession stands. They all agreed being four hours away from Howard & company was a plus. They were unanimous in their belief that I should take the offer, even though they would see less of me. If only I could forget the anger I felt over his lies.

I decided to accept the offer, but first I had a few conditions that must be met, or I would refuse. Our meeting was cordial. I had put aside my emotional outburst of the last time we met. Two items had to be included in my contract: I would have complete control over front-office policy, and there would be no

247

interference from Hartford. I must be included in a pension plan. I was now 50 years old and the matter of retirement was just up the road a bit. The other employees were much younger and retirement was probably the last thing on their minds. I had felt from the beginning of my employment with the Whalers that the front office staff should be eligible for a retirement program. I was told that the company could not afford one. I remember answering that statement, "Give me 10 minutes and I will find you the funds; fewer $3,000 dinners would be a good start."

Suddenly there was a pension plan in existence. It was a non-contributing plan. The company would pay into it, and I would receive $800 a year for each year I was employed starting the day I became the Director of Operations in Binghamton. That $800 was in Canadian funds, which at the time was worth 70 cents on the dollar. My contract offered me $35,000 a year, plus performance bonuses of 10 percent of income over budget and 10 percent for expenses under budget. I could also negotiate a car deal for myself. I could have asked for more money, and received it, but I did not.

Now that I had agreed to go to Binghamton, Howard said he had left out one important fact. "There is one thing you should know. In Binghamton, you will be a prominent figure. You won't be able to go anywhere without being recognized." I think the reason Howard left that little item out was because he knew how much I disliked being photographed. I did not want my photo in the game program, but I had to consent to it. When I was involved in politics, I kept my involvement a secret for years, and always hid from the camera when others were being photographed.

The years I was active in political life, I saw how intrusive people could be. I could be sitting in a restaurant having a meal and people would interrupt to talk about politics. People would stop me on the street to talk politics. My life was not my own. One day a woman approached and said, "I know all about you." That remark alarmed me. I promised myself I would do anything I could to avoid being photographed. If people did not know what I looked like, I could move around without others interfering in my private life. After Ann had been elected, I received a call from a writer at the Hartford Times, then the city's afternoon newspaper. Judy Vik wanted to do a story about "the man behind the mayor." I accepted with two conditions. That the emphasis of the piece had to be about the mayor and not me, and I would refuse to be photographed for the article.

The next afternoon, on the front page of the city section, there it was – a large photo of a crowd with me in the background and a circle around my face as though I was a convict on the loose. Immediately I phoned Judy to express my displeasure at the photo when I was specific that no photo of me should be part of the piece she was writing.

She answered, "You said you did not want to be photographed. That photo was in our files and fit the title because it showed Ann in the forefront and you in the back row, the man behind the mayor." I had to agree, it did fit the title.

So now I was being warned that I would be a celebrity in Binghamton. I considered rejecting the offer to go there. It did not bother me to have my name well-known, but I wanted my face to myself. I had to do something to ensure my privacy in that town. While shaving the next morning an idea came to me. I had not shaved for a couple of days and I had the semblance of a mustache. I was not going to Binghamton for three weeks; I should be able to grow a substantial mustache in that length of time. Three weeks later, I looked God-awful, but it would accomplish my purpose.

I left for my new home and the introduction to the Binghamton community. A news conference had been scheduled to introduce the new coach, Larry Kish, and me to the population. The size of the audience reminded me that Howard had said the hockey team had wide support. There must have been 100 people in attendance. There I was, mustache and all, while the cameras snapped away. Later, I went home and shaved the mustache. Mission accomplished.

We were the number one story on the TV evening news and the morning papers the next day. In my new position, I was all over that community promoting their new hockey team. On game nights, I was at the entrance welcoming the fans. For the four years of my time in Binghamton, every time I was in the news, both TV and newspapers used the file photo with the mustache.

Four years later, when announcing my return to Hartford, the mustache photo was used again. There were times when I was referred to as the "Mustached Director of Operations." It always amused me that no one ever commented on the absence of my mustache.

Binghamton was the kind of community you dream about. I called it, "My Shangri La." The people were simply wonderful to me, and not just hockey fans. I was frequently invited to people's homes. When I would do my grocery shopping, usually buying only a couple of items, not once did I stand in line to pay for my purchases. When people in front of me saw that I had only a few items, I was asked to go to the front of the line. These people did not know who I was. It was an example of the friendliness of the people. I contrasted that with a similar situation at home. People would comment that I had only one or two items and then turn around to wait in line.

One evening after a game, I went to CVS for something. There were a number of cars in the lot, but I found one parking space. I left the store after having made a purchase and as I approached my car, I realized I did not have my keys in my pocket. I went back to the cashier's desk, thinking I might have left them on the counter. They were not there. I remembered that a fan had stopped to talk to me as I was locking my car door. I was thinking that in many cities my car would not be there now, but there it was, but no sign of the keys in the door. I tried the door, it was unlocked.

On the driver's seat was a note: "Not a good idea to leave keys in the door." The note was not signed. That was just one of the thoughtful and caring moments I had experienced in that wonderful town. I could go on for pages with other tidbits, but you get the idea how much I enjoyed my time in Binghamton.

The name of Binghamton's hockey team was "Broome Dusters." Binghamton was a part of Broome County in New York State. I could not possibly be Director of Operations of something called "Broome Dusters." That name had to be changed. But I was in a new town, and I had to respect customs. Fortunately, the major sportswriter covering the team did not like it either. We conspired to change the name. He would write an article suggesting to the fans that since the team was now owned by the Whalers, Binghamton's team should reflect that fact. Since this was beginning to be a controversial subject, why not have a contest to name the hockey team?

The paper conducted the contest and almost daily detailed names that were suggested. We both wanted the team to be called the "Binghamton Whalers." When I suggested we turn the "W" sideways, looking now like a "B", the paper showed the new look in its future articles. Surprise, surprise, the winning name was the Binghamton Whalers. There were, of course, some who did not want the new name. Tradition means a great deal in small towns.

I brought "Brass Bonanza" with me and used our front office entrance as a mini gift shop. The music proved to be as popular in its new home as it was in Hartford. So was the merchandise. Whereas the Springfield fans were loyal Boston Bruins supporters, Binghamton's hockey fans were loyal to the New York Rangers. Again and again, I was asked if the Whalers were going to play the Rangers in a preseason exhibition game. That was a great idea. What a way to ingratiate our new fans to their new team.

The previous owner was an absentee landlord from Canada who was rarely seen in town, therefore very unpopular with the fans. They liked the idea that I would be living in Binghamton and would be a part of that community. I talked with Howard about bringing the two NHL teams to Binghamton for an exhibition game. I kept after him to make it happen, and he arranged the game between the two teams. When we announced that the Rangers were coming, there were smiles all over town. For the first time, Rangers fans were going to see their heroes in person.

The game was a sellout, of course. The visiting Rangers received a hero's welcome, and each player was introduced to a loud ovation. When the Whalers, the unknown Whalers, were introduced there was only polite applause. In the first period of play, the fans cheered the Rangers every move, but by the middle of the third period, they were cheering the Whalers' attempt at scoring. The Rangers were the emotional favorites, but now they had a new team, and they owed their loyalty to it. It was as if someone had said over the sound system, "Okay hockey fans, you have seen your Rangers, but now it is time to root for the home team." Our team understood the situation and was prepared for the lukewarm welcome, but they were surprised by the almost sudden change in attitude late in the third period.

Public relations-wise we hit the jackpot. The fans were so grateful for the opportunity to cheer their Rangers that they could not say "thank you" enough times. From that day, the interest in ticket sales and advertising improved. I spent the next weeks canvassing the city, promoting our team and asking employers to order group tickets for their employees.

The season began. The news conference to introduce the new management was particularly memorable because the Whalers had promised a competitive team and one that would give a 100 percent effort on the ice, every game. As the season progressed, the team was not only losing most of its games, but it was also playing very poorly. Where was that 100 percent effort we had promised? The fans were getting restless. We had promised so much and raised expectations. The fans began booing the team not only as they left the ice, but also during the game.

I told Howard I thought the hockey department had underestimated the strength of the teams in the league. We had spent all of last year in last place and we were not doing any better this year. My retailing experience had taught me that when customers are justifiably unhappy, you replace the merchandise or give a refund. After we had lost a game 9-to-2 in what the media described as "abominable," I asked the public address announcer to make this statement. "Fans attending tonight's game need only show their ticket stub at the box office to get a free ticket to the next home game." The audience cheered as it left the arena. Howard and the hockey department were not cheering, but some of the players agreed with me that we needed reinforcements to be competitive and thanked me for making our need public.

In Hartford they believed that I, who had not only never played the game but also had never even seen a hockey game, had insulted the players in public. The press in Binghamton was on my side, even an editorial calling my decision a "gesture of class." I did not expect my decision to turn the team into a winning one, (although they did win the FREE home game); I made it to let the fans know that management also was not happy with the performance on the ice. I wanted to wake up Hartford, which up to this time had naturally ignored my pleas for help.

Howard had told me that I would be him in Binghamton and that he would back me up on every decision I made. He certainly did it in a strange way. The paper quoted him as saying, "I disagree with what he did, but I back him 100 percent." With that statement, he supported me and the Hartford hockey department at the same time. Our coach saw it the way I did and hoped Hartford would send some new talent, but he would not say so publicly for fear he would be replaced.

Now that I had the press and the fans on my side, attendance remained steady. A sellout crowd greeted the San Diego Chicken, who I brought to Binghamton to entertain during period breaks. After the game, the man who created the Chicken and who had traveled the entire country appearing at all sorts of venues that appealed to children, told me how impressed he was with our office operation. Coming from someone who had visited so many different venues, his comment was a compliment we appreciated.

From time to time in our regular conversations, Howard would ask me when I was coming back to Hartford. That was a strange question coming from the one who made such decisions. I was happy where I was, but I would listen to any offer he made, knowing it would take one hell of a position to get me back to Hartford.

During my time in Binghamton, Howard and his wife divorced. It was a particularly difficult time for him and he would call me, especially on weekends, just to talk. All I could do was listen, which I did. It seemed odd to me that of all the people he knew, he would want to share his personal situation with someone with whom he had a stormy relationship, to say the least.

Players moved back and forth from Hartford. Marty Howe, the youngest of Gordie Howe's sons, was sent down to Binghamton. At first he was very popular with the fans, who transferred their respect for his father to him. Unfortunately, Marty, who any parent would love to have for a son, did not have his father's hockey talent. If he had, he would have remained in Hartford. When his salary was revealed, the fans became more unhappy with his performance on the ice. Every mistake he made was greeted by loud boos. One could only feel sympathy for him. He was doing his best, but that was not good enough for the fans.

One evening, the fans were particularly cruel and Marty, in a moment of anger, made an insulting gesture that caused an uproar among the fans. While I was in attendance, I did not see what happened and only learned of it after the game when scores of fans approached me wanting to know what I was going to do about Marty's behavior. The next day after practice, I called Marty into my office to get his side of the story.

He admitted that he had lost his temper. He tried to rationalize his behavior at his reaction to fans, who thought he should be another Gordie Howe. It wasn't fair of them to expect him to be his father. I reminded him of the benefits of being a Howe, for example the salary he was earning, which was maybe five or six times what other players earned. I told him for what he was being paid, he should tolerate any kind of abuse from the fans. I also told him we could not let the incident pass without some form of punishment. At the time, I was told that the highest fine that was made public by the NHL was $500.

After our meeting, I called Howard and told him what had happened and that I was going to fine Marty $500 and that he should inform the hockey department of my decision. I also asked for their approval before I made it known to Marty. I did not want to be overruled after the fact. Howard told me I could levy the fine. There was a rumor that the Hartford office was amused by my plan.

I called Marty into my office and told him of my decision, which he accepted without comment. After practice, I went into the locker room to inform the players, some of whom gasped at the decision, until I told them the $500 would be added to their fund, which was used to underwrite the cost of their end-of- the-season party. I also told the players that the fine would not be made public. It was a family matter and should remain such. They were told not to speak of it outside the locker room.

When fans asked what action I took, I merely said that I took appropriate action. Had I chosen to make the fine public, I believed it would have been news throughout the hockey world. I had no intention of embarrassing Gordie or his family. The incident was over, and it served as a message to all the players that insulting fans would not be tolerated.

Gordie, who regularly came to visit his son, was curiously absent for some time. When he did appear, I greeted him with a comment asking why we had not seen him lately. He answered, "I couldn't afford to come here," an indirect and humorous response to Marty's fine. He looked straight at me as he shook my hand. I saw that gesture as approval of the disciplinary action I had taken. Later, when we were alone, he said there probably wasn't another person in hockey who would have fined his son. Later, I received a framed black-and-white photo on which he wrote, "Here's looking at a winner." The photo was a profile of him, out of uniform, lost in thought. It has a special place in my home.

He came to Binghamton one year, to play in a celebrity golf game, after which he sent me three photos of the event framed and inscribed, "to Big George, in friendship." Gordie was a regular visitor to the gift shop. He liked to walk around and see all the different items on which there was a team logo. I would have given him anything he wanted, but he always insisted on paying for anything he selected. He heard "Brass Bonanza" for the first time when he came to Hartford. He said he enjoyed hearing that tune because he liked what it did to the fans in the seats. Most people know him for his accomplishments on the ice. I knew him as a soft-spoken gentleman and a friend.

❈ ❈ ❈

While I remember fondly my time in Binghamton, there was one incident that I would rather not have experienced. One evening during pre-game warm-ups, a player shot a puck into the seats which hit a young woman on the side of her head. There were very few fans in the stands at that time. The young woman was with a girlfriend who persuaded her to go to the ladies room and from there to go to the hospital even though the woman said she was feeling okay. The woman was examined and released by the hospital. As the two of them were leaving, she fainted and was admitted.

When I heard of the accident, I rushed to the hospital to learn that she was in a coma. Her parents had just arrived and pleaded with me to keep the accident from the public. They thought it would hurt attendance at hockey games and they did not want the team to suffer any bad publicity. I stayed with the family until midnight when we all left together. I stopped at the desk and asked the person in charge to keep me informed of any change in her condition and to pass my request on to those working the next shift.

The next day, before practice, I went into the locker room to inform the players of the accident the night before. I told them of the victim's parents' wish to keep the news from the public and asked them not to speak of the incident in public. Luckily, the sportswriter who covered every game was on vacation and his replacement arrived just in time for the game. Had the regular sportswriter been in attendance, he was the type who would have learned of the incident. I informed Karen, my secretary, to find me, wherever I was, should I receive a call from the hospital. Every time my phone rang, I hesitated to answer thinking it would be the hospital calling. From then on, Karen would announce my calls so I could relax.

Every evening after work, I would stop at a restaurant and purchase hot meals for the family and spend the evening with them. The nurses had told us to talk to the patient, because she might be able to hear us. Actually, it was a good idea because it occupied our time and we thought we were helping in the healing process.

As the days passed, the pressure built inside of me. I slept very little and prayed a lot. I could not concentrate on my work. My thoughts were of the woman and the traumatic experience her family was enduring. I notified Howard of the accident and he called every day to inquire about any change in the woman's status. I could not get out of my mind that I was working in an entertainment business and one of our customers might die because of that entertainment.

In a small town, news travels fast. I don't know how the matter was kept from the news media, but it was. I worried just how long we could keep it a secret in such a small town, where everyone seemingly knew everyone. If the media had gotten word of the accident, it would have been major news not only in Binghamton, but probably throughout the world where hockey is played. The uniqueness of the accident would probably have been a major news story beyond the sports world. If that were to happen, the family would be involved in a circus-like atmosphere which would only have added to the pain they were now experiencing.

The days seemed to drag on, eight, nine, ten, eleven days and she was still in a coma. On the morning of the twelfth day, the hospital called. Karen walked to my door and said softly, "It's the hospital." She stood in the doorway, as I hesitated before picking up the phone. The patient was out of the coma and was speaking to her parents. She was expected to recover. I put down the phone, and through tears, announced the good news. For the next few minutes, the Kleenex box was passed around and around.

I rose from my seat planning to go to the hospital, when I had a guest. It was the reporter, returning from vacation. He was inquiring about rumors of someone in a coma as a result of an accident at one of our hockey games. I told him that it was true, someone had been hurt at a game, but she was not in a coma. "No story here," I said and after a few minutes of small talk he left and I left for the hospital. When I walked into the room, the family embraced me. We cried a little, then prayed a little, and then cried a little more. I now believed there was such a thing as "happy tears." Ours were tears of relief and thanksgiving.

At the end of each season, we had established a "fan of the year" award which I would present between periods of the last home game. The award this year was to be given to the entire family, but I was too emotional to make the presentation. I asked Phil Jacobs, the PR person, to do the honors, while I stood in the press box unsuccessfully trying to dry my eyes.

The next day, I asked the league office for a special meeting to discuss raising the glass barrier to avoid most pucks going into the stands. The president did agree to call a meeting after I had obtained the required three members who agreed. When we met, the members were sympathetic for the experience I had just lived through. But when it came time to discuss the issue, the members' attitude was incredulous. "When I played hockey, there wasn't any glass at all."

I jumped in to say, "and when you played hockey, there wasn't anyone who paid to watch you."

Another member spoke up. "When I played hockey, the goalie did not wear a mask." With comments like those, it was a short meeting. I have noticed that today the glass is higher than it was in the '80s. One person in hockey who agreed with me was

Gordie Howe. He sent me a letter. The first sentence was "I agree with you 100%." I wondered if Gordie had been at that meeting and spoke favorably would the members have voted differently. Sometimes it is more about who makes the presentation, rather than the merits of the situation.

In my second season at Binghamton, the team played well and we went to the finals in the playoffs. It was the best year for any hockey team that had played in that city. The mayor planned a "Day" for the team and in spite of the fact that we did not win it all, over 3,000 gathered at City Hall to cheer their heroes.

At the annual AHL meeting, attended by the management of all the member teams, it was customary to name the Team Executive of the Year. With our performance in the 1982 season, on and off the ice, the candidates to win that award were sure to include the Director of Operations of the Binghamton franchise. I had my doubts. Honors and recognition somehow manage to elude me. There was the Air Force screw up which denied my being named top student of the class. Then there was the victory dinner for Ann Uccello, where there wasn't a seat for the campaign manager although two head tables were necessary to accommodate the dignitaries from all over the state.

For this award, I could not overlook the fact that members of the AHL still harbored negative feelings for Howard Baldwin for his role in the WHA, and some still voiced their disbelief (I thought it was envy) that Hartford was home to an NHL team. Therefore, I was not surprised when I was not selected. The choice, however, had to raise a few eyebrows.

In the past, the Team Executive of the Year was naturally a team executive. That may seem obvious to most, but it evidently wasn't to those who voted this particular year. The person chosen

261

as the Team Executive of the Year was the president of the AHL. That decision told me there wasn't another team executive in competition with me and that I, as a representative of Howard Baldwin, was not to be honored in any way. They had to find a way to deny it to me, and did, ridiculous as it was.

The guilt on the part of the voting members in the room when the announcement was made, was evident by their behavior. I looked around the table after the announcement, and to a man, everyone had their head down. They could not face me. So now the league had some degree of revenge. I thought it curious that Howard never commented on the decision.

As my fourth season with Binghamton came to end, Howard informed me that he wanted me back in Hartford. He said he would discuss my new role when I arrived in Hartford. Naturally, I was eager to learn what that role would be. A news conference was held announcing my departure and introducing Larry Pleau as Coach and Director of Operations. It was no secret that the hockey department, under Emile Francis, preferred having one of its own at the head of the franchise, reinforcing its attitude that front office personnel contributed little to the success of any franchise. Whatever success there would be, would be due to the performance on the ice.

It was difficult saying goodbye to Binghamton. I had enjoyed my time there and would miss the warm and friendly residents of that community. I was pleased that I had conducted myself as a professional and would leave the franchise better off than when I arrived.

• Chapter 27 •

Return To Hartford

I returned to Hartford in April of 1984 and was anxious to learn of my new assignment. I was told I would meet with Howard the following Monday, time to be determined. I could not wait for Monday to come. The meeting was cancelled. Another date was set, then postponed, then cancelled. That went on for weeks. The excuses for not meeting began to pile up. The frustration of the numerous postponements and waiting for the phone to ring began to take its toll. Although my pay arrived at the beginning of each month, I wanted to go to work. I needed something to do.

April, May and June and still nothing. In one conversation with Howard, as he apologized again for delaying our meeting, I asked, "Howard, have I been fired?" In the sports business, that happens all the time, especially after a reorganization such as happened in Binghamton.

His answer, "How could I fire you with your performance record? I have been very busy. We will get together soon, I promise."

During these months, I would regularly hear from sportswriters in Binghamton, who were following up on my new assignment. Readers wanted to know what position I now had. When I would tell them that we had not met yet, I was asked if it wasn't unusual for so much time to have passed without a decision. "Not if you're dealing with Howard Baldwin," I would reply.

July passed, then August without any meeting. My check would arrive at the first of the month and I told myself something had to give soon. It was almost time for a new season and surely I would know prior to that date what I would be doing.

When September came and there wasn't a check in the mail, I called the accountant's office to inquire why. I was told that he was following the BM's orders. I asked to be transferred to Howard's office. "Howard, I did not receive a check this month," I said.

He interrupted me with an astonishing response. "How long did you think I was going to pay you?"

"What are you talking about? I have been waiting since April to be reassigned! Did I not ask you if I had been fired, and did you not say 'no' to that question? When did you change your mind? Was I supposed to make it easy for you and see the handwriting on the wall and just go away quietly? I am not going away quietly."

I am not sure which one of us ended the conversation, but it was over. I was bewildered. I was puzzled. Even for Howard, this was absurd. I was totally unprepared for what had just happened. How naive could I be? Did he not tell the Binghamton news conference that I would be given a position in Hartford? Was this his management style of firing me? Not only did I lose my job, but also my health insurance was cancelled. Is this the way I should be treated? This employee, that he called weekly following his divorce, just looking for a friend to talk to? I was blindsided by that call.

I knew I would not let it stand without some kind of action. In my various positions with the team, I had met several of the city's top lawyers and decided to get their legal opinion. All I received was sympathy. "You do have a case, but any legal action against the Whalers, is legal action against Aetna. Our firm does business with Aetna, and we cannot risk losing it because of your dispute with Baldwin." When I approached lawyers who did not do business with Aetna, my case was refused because they hoped one day they would.

Sometimes you can be too close to a situation to see the solution. Why did I not go to the state Labor Department? The threat of doing so would have been enough to cause them to settle out of court to avoid the publicity. I could have made it very uncomfortable for the Whalers. I guess it just wasn't my style. I never thought of it at the time.

What followed the next few weeks was confusion, depression, anger and revenge. The worst part for me was that I did not have anyone to counsel me. Whenever I would mention that I was looking for a job, I would be told, "With your record of accomplishments, you won't have any trouble." There were nights when I laid in bed, unable to sleep, short-winded one moment, breathing heavily the next. I had counseled others to never make a decision while angry. Emotional decisions almost always turn out to be the wrong ones.

I took a different approach. I would call Howard every day. I was going to nag him to death. I believed that his conscience would get the better of him and I would be rehired. Most of the time, his secretary would put me off, with the usual, "He is out of town, he is in a meeting. I will have him return your call." I kept calling every day. I would tell whoever answered that I would keep calling until he talks to me. That got results. He called; he had a job for me. I was right, he had a conscience.

What was my new position? He wanted me to visit the other team offices in the league and analyze their operations as compared to the Whalers. He hoped I would find ways to improve the day-to-day operations of the franchise. That sounded like a reasonable project that I could do. I suggested that he would have to call ahead and get approval of the CEO of each team and a time that would be convenient for me to arrive there. I did not think that I could just waltz into an office without some kind of introduction from Howard.

Fine. He would have his secretary make the contacts and travel arrangements. I was on the payroll again. I did not expect his secretary to give my request a top priority and drop everything else she was doing to arrange my schedule. I let a week go by before calling her to discuss her progress on the matter. Now it was her turn to be out ill, in a meeting or on vacation and would return my call at a later date. Damn it, they could at least be creative enough to alter the routine.

I decided to go into the office and offer assistance to anyone who needed it. I was being paid; I wanted to earn my salary. I never followed through on my project. No calls were made by the secretary. The suggestion was just something to quiet me until they thought of something else.

About this time, it had been announced that Hartford would be the scene of the 1986 National Hockey League All-Star Weekend. It was a three-day event that showcased a member city to the hockey world. When I had returned to the Whalers to become the Director of Operations in Springfield, I told Howard that if and when Hartford was scheduled for the all-star event, that I wanted that project. I was a native of Hartford and wanted to prove we were a major league city.

Now I had another reason to want that project. For the five years I had spent in the minor leagues, I heard so many criticisms of Hartford. They added up to one conclusion: How did that city ever get an NHL franchise? I wanted the opportunity to tell them why. Who better than someone who has a motive to coordinate this event?

A young woman was hired for the position of coordinator of the event. She lasted three weeks and resigned. She must have thought she was in over her head. I spoke to Howard to remind him that I wanted that project. He did not give it to me; instead Howard gave the project to Vice President William Barnes, but he asked me to be his assistant. Bill had other duties as vp and would need someone to back him up. It was only a few days later that Bill Barnes suffered a serious heart attack and would be out of the office for an indefinite period. Fate now put me in charge of the event. It was not a coincidence. I would come to believe that someone was watching over me.

I was given an office away from the front office and with 15 months to prepare, I threw myself into this project. I wanted to prove to the other members that Hartford was a major league city. I remembered the comments from Canadian teams who considered New England "Pilgrim territory." I had been asked, "Are homes heated by wood? Do you have paved roads, indoor plumbing and electricity?" I thought they must be joking, but they were serious.

The three-day event included a dinner for about 1,500, special activities for women guests and, of course, the game on the final evening. The entire organization was involved in some aspect of the event. The most time-consuming item of the event for me was the assigning of the tickets to the game. Each team would order a large block of tickets and all the teams insisted that their CEO have seats in prime locations. There were 21 teams involved ordering large numbers of tickets. After I had assigned a team its tickets, there would be another request, this time for more tickets in the same area as the previous order. I was forever readjusting the seating to accommodate the requests. Finally, I made a decision. I would assign the additional tickets without regard to the previous order; each team could decide who gets what ticket.

I was left alone in my office with very little contact with the others. I desperately needed a clerical. I made my need known to Howard. Weeks later, he called me to his office. He had found a clerical for me. Jim Mulvihill, the head of the UConn Medical Center, wanted to help out with clerical duties. The proceeds of the all-star game, estimated at $100,000, was to be donated to the Whalers' charity, the Whalers Children's Cancer Fund, at the medical center. Dr. Mulvihill had a daughter who had just graduated college and was out of the country on a trip, a gift from her parents.

When she returns, he wanted to offer her to assist in clerical duties. He said that since his institution was benefiting from the event, he felt obliged to offer some assistance. I gave Howard a knowing glance before he asked what he was going to ask. We had several times over the years discussed hiring relatives and he knew how I opposed hiring unqualified people just because they were relatives. It is true that I had recruited my relatives to help me in politics, hockey and the MS Society, but they were volunteers and the need was temporary. I did put the concession workers on the payroll, but that was an unexpected emergency and I expected to hire others the following year.

I needed help, but someone who was experienced, not just a relative of Dr. Mulvihill. Howard asked, "Will you at least interview her before you reject her? I owe Jim that much." That did not seem to be an unreasonable request and I agreed to meet with her when she returned home. About a week later, Howard called me into his office where I met a very attractive young woman, Karen Mulvihill. After a few words of introduction, we left for my office and her interview.

I was really impressed with her. She seemed to have two feet on the ground and was willing to do whatever I asked of her. I think I had pre-formed an opinion that she would be a rich spoiled brat whose only interest was meeting the hockey players. I could not have been more wrong. I agreed to have her work with me, and we got along very well.

I was old enough to be her grandfather, so I warned her about getting involved with the players. Her absences from our office were few and I had no reason to think she was goofing off. One day, a few months later, she asked if she could speak to me about a personal issue. "There is something I want to tell you before you hear it from someone else," she said. I waited anxiously to hear what was so serious that she closed the office door, making sure no one could hear our conversation. She said it was a personal matter. Was I now to play the role of grandfather?

The next sentence was totally unexpected. Not in a million years could I have guessed what she was about to tell me. Karen looked toward the door, to make sure no one could hear. She whispered the next sentence and I thought I was having trouble with my hearing. Did she just say that she was dating Howard, and it was getting serious? Did I hear her correctly? I hoped I wasn't smiling, because I was thinking of the time I had told her not to get involved with the hockey players.

When I recovered, I hoped I said something in the form of good wishes. She seemed relieved, having shared that bombshell with me. What I did not know was that the entire front office was gossiping about the time she would spend in Howard's office with the door closed. Time she took away from our office. Time I thought she was at the copy machine or in the ladies room. It was not surprising that I would be unaware of the office gossip. I did not participate in that activity. Just do your job, I don't care about who is doing what to whom.

The gossip had to do with their difference in ages. Howard was 25 years older than Karen, and he was a divorced man. As far as I was concerned, that was their business. I reminded Karen that we had work to do and her relationship with Howard did not exempt her from her duties. She continued to perform at her usual high standard and nothing more was said about the matter.

The all-star event was now only a few weeks away. The regular weekly staff meetings suddenly became contentious. In the past, our discussions were very business-like. Differences in opinion were settled in a friendly manner. But now there was a decided difference in attitude. It seemed to me that now that everything was falling into place, I was no longer needed. I was being treated disrespectfully and at one point, when the insults became objectionable, I answered back, "You are wasting your time if you think I will leave this project at this point. You make a serious mistake if you think my strong personality, when I differ with you, will cause me to throw my hands in the air and walk out." The meeting ended on that note.

A couple of days before the big event, a PBS reporter with a camera crew came into the front office, wanting to talk to somebody about the preparations for the event and they were sent to my office. They planned a 30-minute program before the game. I answered what questions they asked, and they left. The questions were not thought-provoking or controversial. It would be what in the industry is called "a puff piece." I wondered if I had sounded intelligent in my responses. I did not want to embarrass the Whalers. When I remembered how unpleasant our staff meetings had become in recent weeks, I wondered how the brass would react to my being the spokesman for the event on TV.

The big dinner was a spectacular success and kudos to those who had worked on it. I sat at a table with other members of the staff. At the end of the dinner, Howard took the microphone to say a few words. He started with recognizing the governor and other political dignitaries, the hotel management and staff, the chef, the waiters and so many others that I quipped only a few in attendance were ignored. Those sitting with me, throughout his statements, kept saying to me, "Get ready, you are going to be next." My history at such times had prepared me to be ignored. Howard completed his endless list of appreciation messages and sat down. The others at the table looked at one another, seemingly puzzled that I had been overlooked.

After the dinner, local businesspeople I had dealt with during the years, and those who knew my role in this event, went up to Howard, one after the other, asking the same question in different forms. "Howard, you forgot George. Howard, how could you overlook Mr. Ducharme."

At first, Howard made some excuse but when the questions continued, he answered, "I don't have to thank George, I pay

271

him." Some of those who heard him, told me what he had said and apologized for his behavior. He lost a few supporters that evening and more later when the word spread.

On the evening of the game, PBS aired its half-hour special. I must have forgotten about it because I did not watch the broadcast. The top Whaler management had reserved rooms in the hotel to dress for the occasion and were in their rooms when the broadcast aired. Evidently, they did not approve of what they saw. When management lined up to greet the guests at the reception following the game, I was told that I was not invited to stand with them. I surmised that in the introduction to the broadcast, the reporter must have given too much credit to me for the event. I do not think it had anything to do with my responses to his questions. They could have been unhappy with the fact that I was being interviewed at all. Some of them had trouble with anyone but themselves taking credit for anything to do with the franchise.

❖❖❖

A few months before the game, Raymond Howell, who I had met while campaigning for Ann Uccello and now a friend of mine, awakened me late one evening with a telephone call. He was crying and it was difficult to understand him. He was saying something about the MS chapter in Hartford being rumored to be closed because of poor performance. Raymond was now living with MS and was a member of the board of directors of the MS Society chapter. Previously he had told me that the chapter did very little for its clients and I remarked, "Since they do very little, why do you care?" He answered that once a chapter is closed, it is unlikely to ever be reopened. He wanted me to leave the Whalers and become the MS executive director. I replied that I did not know anything about MS.

Ray was quick to remind me that I did not know anything about politics, football or hockey. He said that "I should use the gifts that God gave me to help mankind, and not make money for other people," and he hung up the phone in anger.

I sat up in bed thinking about what he had said. He was really angry. He had never talked to me in that way. Maybe he was right. Is this another challenge in a world where I was ignorant? Sounds like just the right place for me. I would think about it.

When things started deteriorating with the Whalers, I remembered Ray's comments and decided I would end my career with the Whalers after the all-star event had taken place.

I called Ray to tell him that I would be available on March 1, which was my birthday. I explained that I could not leave until after the all-star event. Ray was not happy with the delay but accepted my decision.

• Chapter 28 •

The MS Society Turnaround

The All-Star weekend was a fabulous success and I believed that the hockey world would now accept Hartford as a Major League city. I looked forward to my new challenge with MS and being away from the small minds I had known in professional sports. I spent the next few weeks cleaning up the details and storing records for the future. I had not heard a word from Howard.

Toward the end of the month, Howard asked me to join him for lunch at Chuck's Steak House in the Civic Center. At last, he mentioned my work with the All-Star event and suggested I probably needed a rest and should take a vacation and we would discuss my future assignment when I returned. I was so happy that I could tell him that I was leaving the Whalers at the end of the week. He almost seemed relieved.

I left the Whalers on a Friday and on Monday walked into the Multiple Sclerosis office, the executive director of the Greater Connecticut Chapter. It was a small office with four employees. After a few minutes of small talk, I said, "Will someone please tell me, in one sentence, what is Multiple Sclerosis? I am going to be asked that question repeatedly, and I want to answer it briefly."

"My second question is, how do you spell 'sclerosis'?" I walked toward my office with a wide smile on my face, wishing I could see the expressions on their faces. This person is supposed to save this chapter and he cannot spell the name of the illness?

It was March of 1986, and I was now 56 years old taking on a new challenge in a world in which I was completely unfamiliar. I took a cut in pay because of what Ray Howell had said to me in anger, that I should use the gifts God gave me to help mankind instead of making money for others. So here I was, in a business that might be shut down because of poor performance. I had no place to go but up.

In the large room with the three desks sat a middle-aged woman who was the Secretary of the chapter. One desk was not assigned. The other desk was the Marketing Director's. The chapter Services Director's office was down the hall. I could hear the phones ringing and the responses to the callers. "I'm sorry, we don't do that. I cannot help you because we do not do that."

After a few hours of listening to that, I walked into the main room and called the employees together to ask them what it was that we do here. "All I have heard for the last two hours is 'We don't do that.'"

The three of them answered as a chorus. "We do not have any money to do anything. Our board members pay for office supplies out of their own pockets." Without funds, very little could be done for the clients. Ray was probably correct in thinking the chapter would be closed. I wondered why he would want his friend trapped in a situation like this one. Later in the day, Ray paid us a visit and I asked him that question. He said that I could solve their problems and turn the chapter around.

One would think that in a small office there would be unity and cooperation among the employees. I learned that the two women employees did not speak to each other. They communicated through notes placed on the other's desk when that person was away from the desk. The young man, though willing, was not exactly my idea of a go-getter. He needed lots of direction. I had my doubts that anyone could turn this situation around.

I went back to my office to think about this money problem. We needed money and we needed it now. I was told that the chapter had 1,800 clients enrolled. That is a good base of support. I had to find a way to utilize that base. I asked myself what was the fastest way I could raise money and utilize that 1,800-client base of support. The answer was simple – a raffle. Have the clients sell raffle tickets.

With 1,800 clients selling tickets, I thought raising money would be an easy task. I needed a prize that would capture the imagination of the buyer and create a buzz around the raffle. At that time, the state of Connecticut had begun venturing into the lottery business. They now had a scheme called "Lotto," which awarded the winner one million dollars. Why not have the only prize, 1,000 Lotto tickets? One thousand chances to win a million dollars! That should indeed create the buzz I sought.

Bringing the three employees together, I told them of my plan. They wanted to know who was going to sell the tickets. I told them that we would divide the 1,800-client list and each one of us would take a quarter of the list and call the clients to ask them to sell the tickets. The staff did not think that was such a good idea. Why would clients sell tickets for us when we have done nothing for them? Good point. I told them to tell the clients that we have a new executive director, and he means to change our reputation. I told them that if a client refuses to sell tickets, refer that call to me.

We divided up the client list and started calling. I did not make many calls from my list of 450, because so many calls were referred to me. I listened to client complaints, which were mostly about having to pay a toll charge to call the office, to learn help was not available. I promised them that the first thing I would do with the proceeds was to install an 800 line. Some were satisfied with my promise, others were not. I pleaded with those to give me a chance to change things so that we could be helpful to them.

In a short time we had orders for 35,000 tickets and when the returns were in, we had raised over $30,000. Before the drawing for the winner, the 800 number was ordered and our monthly newsletter headlined its arrival. We began changing our image, slowly, very slowly.

Early on, I was informed by the Marketing Director that he had planned a meeting for the Bike Tour Committee. For several years a bike tour was the only fundraiser sponsored by the chapter. It was almost April and the bike tour was scheduled for June. I was asked if I wanted to attend, and I accepted the invitation.

I was pleased to see twenty-something men and women at the bike tour meeting. I told them that I did not have the slightest idea how to conduct a bike tour, having never owned one, or ridden one. The energy coming from that committee encouraged me and I went home with a very positive feeling. My spirits were dampened the next morning as I reviewed the report of last year's tour.

I was interested to learn the average amount raised by riders. As I scanned the lists, I saw that many bikers paid the registration fee of $15 and did not raise money for the cause. It was surprising to learn that most of the $15 riders were Bike Tour Committee members who I had met the night before. The Marketing Director did not seem concerned, "After all, they did most of the work," he said. I asked him to call an emergency meeting of the members. I believed that all the committee members would appear, believing the chapter was being closed and there would not be a bike tour this year.

When we met, and everyone did attend, I reminded them that the bike tour was a vehicle for raising funds to help people and their families who were living with a horrible illness. We were not sponsoring a social event for the community. I continued that I had expected those serving on the committee would be the most dedicated to the cause. I paused as I looked around the room. Then I stunned them with a shocker.

In as serious a tone as I could speak, I told them that if they did not believe in the cause and were not interested in helping our clients, then their service was no longer required. I asked for a show of hands of those who wanted to ride for the cause and only one hand went up. I thanked the others for their service and said they could leave now. They left all right, mumbling to themselves, suggesting the event could not be held without them. That was a challenge I welcomed.

When the Board of Directors heard what I had done, they were beside themselves with concern. This man they had hired, without even an interview but on his reputation and recommendation of Ray Howell, has fired the experienced committee of the bike tour. Mr. Howell attempted to calm their fears, for he had much confidence in me. Maybe too much, they thought.

This shocking development was not as serious as it seemed. The bike tour committee had completed most of the work at its first meeting. All the major decisions had been discussed and made. I was not starting from scratch. I did need volunteers to staff the rest areas, serve the meal, and at the end of the meal, clean up the premises. Where would I get these volunteers on such short notice? You guessed it, the same place I got them for my political campaigns and the concession stands – my family. In addition, I would ask the office staff and board members and their families to join us.

I did not have any problems soliciting the aid of my family, the office staff and board members. I could now concentrate on the last major detail, the food for the meal for hundreds of hungry bikers. In the past, the records showed considerable money spent for food. I planned to acquire whatever we needed through donations. I learned a long time ago to ask and you shall receive.

I must tell you of an amusing story regarding the food. When our family lived on Addison Street, a neighbor across the street, the Nardi family, owned and operated a bakery. A son, Charles, was my age and we became friends. Now it was years later, and Charles owned and operated the business which had moved to East Hartford and larger quarters. I went to see Charles to ask for home-made cookies for the bikers.

I would need hundreds of any variety he would offer to give me. Charles told me to return the day before the tour and he would give me as many cookies as I wanted and they would come right off the conveyor belt, ready to eat.

On the day before the tour, I went to Charles' bakery, this time to pick up the cookies. Charles stood at the end of the conveyor belt and began putting several varieties of cookies in a large plastic bag. When I thought there were enough cookies in the bag, I asked Charles to place it in the back seat of my car. I left, after thanking him for his most generous contribution to the cause.

The next day, the day of the bike tour, I along with some of the volunteers, prepared for the meal at the end of the ride. I asked one of the volunteers to take the bag of cookies out of my car and place each variety on a separate dish and place them throughout the several tables. A few minutes later, the volunteer came over to me and said, "I want to show you something."

He had placed the bag of cookies on one of the tables. He handed me a plate and said, "Put some cookies on this plate." I walked over to the table and put my hand in the bag to take out some cookies. The cookies had become a colossal ball of dough! They were hot when placed in the bag and continued cooking when the plastic bag was tied and placed in my car.

There was nothing wrong with the dough, except it wasn't cookies anymore. The volunteer kept asking, "What are we going to do?" A few minutes passed. Then I said, "Pull the bag cover away from the cookies, and let it serve as a centerpiece. Place small plates around the dough and have the guests grab a hunk of dough." At the end of day, only crumbs were on the table. The bikers thought it was a brilliant idea. They did not realize it was not planned that way. It was a humorous end to what we hoped would be a successful bike tour. We would know that in two weeks at the appreciation party.

It had been the custom to hold a pizza appreciation party for the bikers and make known the dollar amount raised through their efforts. I called clients and asked them to attend the party with their wheelchairs, crutches and any other aids needed to travel. I told them that I wanted them to circulate among the bikers, to tell the bikers what it meant to them, to meet people who were helping them cope. I believed the memory of those conversations would make a lasting impression and the following year they would work for the cause, motivated by what the clients had told them.

When it was time to announce the results of the money raised, the bikers gathered around the microphone. They knew that in the past, the tour had raised in the low $30,000s. I made the announcement. "We did not raise $30,000." There was a groan of disappointment. I paused and then added, "You raised $57,000!" I think that their response could be heard for blocks away from the building. I could see people reaching for handkerchiefs. Those were happy tears, very happy tears.

At the next board meeting, all the members were smiling. They apologized for their remarks following the firing of the committee earlier. Ray Howell was the happiest person in the room. Now we had some money. The successful raffle and now the bike tour. I told the members that next year's tour would raise $100,000. I don't think anyone believed me, but no one dared challenge my prediction.

Over the next few months, both the Chapter Services and Marketing Directors resigned. God was with me, and I had another situation where I believed someone was watching over me. Now I could build an office to my standards. I interviewed candidates for each position and struck gold when I hired Bob Smith as Marketing and Susan Raimondo as Chapter Services Directors. Susan was unmarried at the time, but I cannot remember her maiden name. Each was a recent college graduate, being hired for a position for the first time. Each willing to learn and most important, each one believing that we could make a difference in people's lives.

281

Bob had a winning smile and a million-dollar personality and Susan was a dream come true, the perfect person to meet clients in a troubling time in their lives. As a client, you would feel you had just met a friend who wanted to help you with your problems. With a team like that, the sky was the limit and we reached for it.

I told Susan to tell me what she needed to do her job and we would get it for her. She was an instant success with the clients, especially those who had been with the chapter for some time. The office personality changed drastically. Bob was a sponge, soaking up whatever I could teach him that I had learned over the previous twenty years. I was having the time of my life. We were helping people and loving it. We now were a friendly and accommodating operation. Rarely did a caller hear the words, "We don't do that."

Susan brought specialists to speak to the clients, informing them of the latest research being conducted. She planned a week at a camp, for clients only, with guest speakers who educated clients on how to live with their illness.

Our income from contributions began to rise. In obituaries, mourners were asked to contribute to the MS Society, in lieu of flowers. The clients were spreading the word that we were actively working to help them. People like to contribute to causes where they are assured their money is going to make a difference in peoples' lives, and not be spent for administration costs.

The board was reminded of my prediction that the next bike tour would raise $100,000. They listened, but I knew they still did not believe. Bob assumed the planning for the bike tour, and I went to work seeking community support.

My board members were special. One of the jewels of that board was Judith Gengras McDonough, the daughter of Clayton

282

Gengras, who ran for governor in 1966 and for whom I worked during that campaign period.

Although a woman of privilege, Judy did not hesitate to do whatever was necessary. I came in one morning and she was washing the floor on her hands and knees. One afternoon when she was in the office, I was at the copy machine having a difficult time and I screamed, "If I could lift it, I would throw this piece of junk out the window!"

The next day, a new copier arrived, paid for by Judy. She brought her children to the office to volunteer. Their parents had set a good example for them to follow, and nothing was beneath them. Whatever I asked of them, they did and did well. Their energy increased my passion for the job I was doing.

Thinking of Judy, I remember the time that I learned the chapter would be celebrating its twenty-fifth anniversary and suggested to her that we plan a fundraising dinner to celebrate the occasion. At that time, we had not yet seen the results of our endeavors. Judy asked, "What are we celebrating?"

I replied that we were celebrating that the chapter still exists. In a moment of jest, I suggested to Judy that she invite 400 of her closest friends to our celebration. She not only did that, but also she chaired the event.

She packed the ballroom of a local hotel and we celebrated our existence. By the time the event took place, we were living up to our mission, even earning awards for service to clients. The president of the national organization attended with the obligatory plaque, commemorating the event. In those days, the national organization believed that the Board of Directors of each chapter was considered the driving force for success. Staff merely did their bidding.

283

Following his complimentary remarks, the president of the national organization called our President, Judy McDonough, to the microphone to accept the plaque. Judy approached the president but refused to accept the plaque. She took the microphone and said that she "had nothing to do with our recent turnaround, that no one on the board did. The recent success of the chapter was due to our new executive director," and she called me to the microphone to receive the plaque from the president.

I was stunned, not expecting this generous gesture of recognition. Walking up to her, she turned away to allow the president to present the plaque to me. He sort of shoved it at me. I then expected I would say something to the audience, but the president, with the microphone in hand, moved away from me and began talking. I stood there, I suppose like a bump on a log, not knowing what to do, then finally returned to my seat. It was a very confusing time for me, at one moment, overwhelmed by Judy's generous comments, and the next moment, insulted by the president of the national organization in front of 400 people.

After the dinner, the board members came up to me to congratulate me. They commented that they had never seen me speechless. I told them that I was not speechless, that the president did not allow me to say anything because I was a staff member, and not a board member. To the audience, the president's slight was not seen as an insult. I am told that many of them thought I was too modest to say anything. If they really knew me, they would have known that modesty was not one of my strong points.

* * *

The following year's bike tour was memorable. We had a year of experience behind us. The bike tour committee was now made up of believers in the cause. We improved the prize structure, raised the registration fee and improved our publicity of the event throughout the community. The donations began pouring in.

The staff remembered my prediction of $100,000. Each day when the mail arrived, we were like little children in a candy store, anxious to get the envelopes opened so we could count the loot for the day. We passed the $50,000 mark, then $75,000 and on the day of the appreciation party, we had just over $80,000.

I was so disappointed, and the staff was disappointed for me. It appeared we had not reached my goal. As the bikers and our clients arrived, I played host visiting with our guests, while the staff was at the entrance, greeting them.

Later in the evening I spoke to the crowd, words of appreciation and was about to divulge the total dollars raised when Bob came toward me with a shoe box in his hands. It was filled with checks and cash. Some bikers had postponed collecting their donations until after the ride. They were making their returns this evening and when all the money was counted, we had not raised $100,000 – we had raised over $120,000. We had done it! One of the clients threw his crutches into the air while the audience roared its approval.

I was too emotional to make the announcement, Bob did it for me as tears covered my face. Recalling that evening, so many years ago, brings all that emotion back again.

The chapter was making a name for itself throughout the national organization. But I was not the fair-haired boy because I did not do it according to their procedures. I did it my way, the only way I knew how. I tried and failed to persuade them to follow my lead, but they would not. I suppose that would have suggested that someone in the chapters actually knew a better way. Susan, though, did receive special recognition for her work on behalf of the clients. I thought they should promote Bob to a marketing position in the national office. He could teach them a thing or two.

The third year was more of the same … larger individual contributions from the community. People are always generous when they see the fruits of their generosity. The bike tour that year raised almost $200,000. The chapter had over a quarter of a million dollars in the bank. That figure was net of the 40 percent of our income that went to national for research.

At the next board meeting I told the board that we should put stair lifts in homes of those clients who were prisoners in their bedrooms. I said, "The only time they left the bedroom was to go to the doctor, the hospital or the funeral parlor." I also wanted to purchase air conditioners for every family that did not already have one. The hot weather was especially difficult for MS clients.

Up until this time, I was the leader of the chapter; whatever I asked for was approved. Now that we had money in the bank, the board was acting like Depression parents who remembered paying for office supplies, and now that they had funds they would see to it that they never faced that situation again.

The board refused my requests. I pleaded with them and asked for a second vote. It, too, was a rejection of my proposals. I left the board meeting disappointed in myself. For the first time I was not able to sell my ideas. I had tried, without success, to persuade the board that with our growing positive image, as long as donors could see where their donations were being spent, we could raise all the money we needed. The board was apparently satisfied with our present status. I was never satisfied with the status quo, always wanting to do more. I did not accept their decision to put money in the bank and leave it there.

I lost the argument; the chapter lost its Executive Director.

Raymond was upset at my resignation. He cried as he pleaded with me not to leave. I reminded him that he had asked me to accept the position of Executive Director in order that I might save the chapter from bankruptcy. I told him that I had accomplished what he wanted, and now I wanted to leave. I repeated to him what I had told the board: "I did not accept this position to put money in the bank." He told me that I could have had that position for life. Security was never a factor for me, in fact, I always seemed to get bored with success. I needed a new challenge once I had met the old one.

I could leave the chapter knowing that it was, not only solvent, but also it had in Bob and Susan two very special employees who would continue to maintain the standards that had been set these past three years. I walked out that door proud that I had helped change peoples' lives for the better. It was a wonderful feeling, one I had not experienced in any other work I had done in the past. No matter where life would take me, my time with the MS Society would always be the one position that gave me the greatest sense of accomplishment. Raymond had told me that I should use my God-given talents to help mankind and I believed that I had done just that.

For many years that followed, Raymond would see that day as the day I had betrayed him. I was really sorry that he felt that way. I did what he wanted of me, and probably much more than he had expected. It was time for me to leave.

287

Chapter 29

Yet Another New Challenge

Time for that someone who was watching over me to come up with a new challenge. The afternoon of the day I left the MS Society, the phone rang. It was Enzo Dedominicis, the president and owner of radio station WRCH, one of the most popular in the state. I had met Enzo during my involvement with Ann Uccello and once again that involvement would prove beneficial. Enzo told me he was creating the position of Director of Community Relations at his radio station, and he wanted me to fill that position. Once again, out of nowhere, comes a new challenge.

I knew I would accept the position without knowing what it entailed. Working in the radio world sounded really exciting and I told Enzo that I had just resigned from the MS Society, and would welcome another challenge, especially because it was another challenge for which I believed I was totally unqualified. He laughed at that comment. I did not know anything about the radio business and in my life, that made it just right for me. It excited me just thinking about it.

I was now 60 years old with a new world ahead of me. WRCH was a very friendly place to work. Enzo would be the reason for that. He was the ideal boss, easy going, but firm. He allowed his employees to participate in decisions. They were a part of the business, not just employees receiving a paycheck. It was not surprising to learn that most of his staff had worked for him for some time. I enjoyed my new position, but fate would interfere and I would not remain at WRCH for long. The economy turned downward; real estate transactions declined. Clients reduced their spending on advertising, the life blood of any radio station.

Howard Baldwin reentered the picture. He had purchased a yogurt company and wanted me to come to California to work in his newest endeavor. It did not take long to refuse that offer. "I do not want to leave Connecticut," I said. With my stormy relationship with him, I was not about to travel 3,000 miles on a whim. There were a dozen other reasons not to want to work for him again. So, what does he do? A few months later he called to tell me that he had moved the business to Connecticut. Will I come to work for him now?

Enzo had created my position when business was good, and now the recession was reducing income at a time he had increased operating expenses. I met with him to discuss the fact that he could not afford to have me on staff at this time. I was saying what Enzo knew to be true but did not have the heart to tell me. To make it more difficult, we had become good friends over the years. I would make it easy for him by telling him that Howard had offered me a position in his yogurt business. He seemed relieved. I did not expect the new project to be a long lasting one, but it would do until I found something else to do with my life.

I began work with Malibu Magic, Howard's yogurt company. When I tasted the product, I was really impressed. We had a machine in the office and would sample different flavors of the yogurt. I liked it and yogurt was becoming the latest food fad. Howard had hired a person to manage the business but was not satisfied with the little progress being made. He wanted me to look over the operation and tell him what was wrong. Why wasn't the business making any money?

My title was Director of Food Services and it would be shared with a relative of Howard's, Taylor Baldwin. Our job was to promote our product in arenas and other mass market venues. We visited the major arenas in New York City and Connecticut but did not make a sale. In the meantime, I kept my eyes open as I tried to investigate the operation just by observing the day-to-day routine.

After a while, it became clear that the costs of operating the business were not balanced by the income. There wasn't any income. The president of the company was busy trying to sell franchises but had not yet been successful. As expected, money in a Baldwin operation was being spent as it was in the Whaler days. There also was another relative employed in the business. The two relatives and the president had maxed out on the company's American Express cards.

I reported my findings to Howard, who did not want to hear what I had to say. I told him it was time to end his role as head of the family's welfare department and that he should replace his relatives with other employees qualified for the positions. I learned that it is true, that blood is thicker than water. He did fire one of his employees … me.

For the first time in decades, I was without a job and no prospect of one. I could have told myself that I earned a vacation. Not since the Civic Center roof collapsed when employed by the Whalers had I taken a vacation. I wanted to go back into sports administration. I missed the excitement of working in the sports world.

• Chapter 30 •

The 1990s & Fate Intervenes

Although it was early December, we had a late fall and leaves were still on the trees. The gutters on my home were filled with leaves and I knew I had to remove them before the first snow arrived. On December 10, 1990, I awoke with two thoughts on my mind. One, I would clean the gutters, and two, I would place calls to friends and former associates, asking them to help me in my efforts to have Phil Esposito hire me for his planned NHL expansion team, somewhere in Florida. I believed I could generate enough positive referrals to persuade Phil to at least interview me. I filled a legal-size page with names and phone numbers and planned to make the calls after I had cleaned the gutters.

Our house was a small Cape Cod, whose gutters could be reached with a household ladder. I put a plastic bag on my left shoulder and started in the rear of the house to clean the gutters. They were filled with leaves, and it was necessary to empty out the bag every few feet. It was a slow process, but soon I was in the front of the house moving toward the garage. My mother had asked me to take her car out of the garage because she had planned to do some errands and I stopped with the leaves to do so. I forgot to put the garage door down.

When I reached the pavement in front of the garage door, I knew I had to be cautious with the ladder because there was a drop of about a foot at the extreme end of the garage. I wanted to be careful not to get the ladder too close to the end of the house where it might tip over onto the lawn below. I placed the ladder in the middle of the pavement and climbed up to complete my task. A few handfuls remained and I would be finished with leaves for this year.

Now I had just one more handful. I turned my body to the left to reach the last handful of leaves when the ladder turned on me and I fell the seven or eight feet to the pavement. The ladder had not been secured properly and with the garage door open, the ladder fell quickly to the pavement. I was wrapped around the ladder, bleeding from my head. My right shoulder was in severe pain, and I thought I had dislocated that shoulder, something I had done twice before. My legs were wrapped around the ladder, and I could not understand why I could not move either of them.

I lay there, not too concerned because there was a stop sign on the property, which was a corner lot. It was about noon, and I thought cars would be passing by and see me. I suppose seconds seem like minutes in times like these, but no one drove by. I was thinking that mom might be calling me for lunch, and I did not want her to see me in this condition. With the blood all over my face, I must have been a sight. She was 81 years old, with a complicated medical condition, having already experienced cancer, heart attacks and strokes. I was afraid the sight of her son might cause another stroke.

I tried again to free myself from the ladder but was unsuccessful. With no one driving by, I decided to call out for help, hoping a neighbor could hear me. I later learned that I could be heard, but not seen because mom's car blocked me from view. Later, two houses up the street, a woman holding an infant came out of her home. I yelled to her that I needed help. That was a

292

stupid thing to say, any idiot could see that. The woman went back into her home. I thought the sight of me had frightened her. Later, she returned without the infant and yelled to me, "Do you want me to call 9-1-1?"

I thought to myself, I would hope you would call someone, but I answered, "Yes, please."

In a few minutes, a police cruiser drove onto the driveway. I asked him to park his car around the corner so my mother would not see it. He did what I asked and returned to me. I could see the concern in his face as he told me an ambulance would be here shortly. We talked, but I don't remember any of the conversation. I learned he was attempting to keep me conscious.

When the ambulance did arrive, it was in the driveway, and I asked that it also be moved to the side of the house. I was fully conscious through the entire ordeal, giving me reason to think that my injuries were minor. The EMTs did not have to ask any questions, they could see the problem. Carefully, they untangled my feet and arms and removed the ladder from my body. Because of my head injury, they were concerned about my neck and after some time used a protective gizmo to hold my head in place.

With the police and the ambulance in the neighborhood, a crowd began to gather. I asked them to move so they would not be seen, should my mother look out the window. I kept insisting to the EMTs that my problem was my right shoulder, and would they please get me to a hospital where it could be reset. The longer it remained dislocated, the greater the pain.

The EMTs seemed to take their sweet time. I wanted to get to the hospital. They knew what I did not know. My problem was not just my right shoulder. As they were placing me on a stretcher to take me to the ambulance, my next-door neighbor, Pat, came out of her home and walked over to me. The fear in her eyes caused her to look away. I just assumed it was my bloody face. I asked Pat to knock on my front door, after we leave, and tell my mother that I had dislocated my shoulder and was being taken to the hospital to have it reset. I would be home in a few hours. Pat sometime later told me that after she had conveyed my message, she went home and vomited.

Once in the ambulance, I realized I felt a pain in my right leg and mentioned it to the personnel. One of them tore my pant leg and looked at my leg and said, "Oh, oh."

"What does that mean?" I asked.

"You will find out when we get to the hospital." I surmised that EMTs were not allowed to diagnose the patient's injuries. I asked the driver not to use the siren as we left the property.

When we arrived at the Hartford Hospital emergency area, there was a crowd of white-coat personnel outside waiting for me. I learned that they had been notified, in advance, of my arrival and told something of my injuries. I was taken inside and placed on a gurney. The medical personnel began taking X-rays. I kept asking to have my shoulder reset, but they ignored me. I could hear voices behind me looking over the X-rays and whispering, "We have to take more pictures, with what we know from these, there must be more damage."

The pain from my right shoulder was increasing and I pleaded loudly to have it reset. I remembered that I had several errands to run, one of which was to take Ray to the doctor. I asked a nurse to make some phone calls for me, to inform others not to expect me today. As the nurse walked away, she said to another nurse, "He thinks I am his secretary."

The other nurse answered, "And you are doing what he asked, aren't you?"

A few minutes later, they were now satisfied that they knew how to proceed. First, they reset my right shoulder and as soon as it was in place, the pain I had felt in that shoulder moved like a bolt of lightning to the other shoulder. I had not realized that it, too, had been dislocated. Then they reset my left shoulder and the pain shot down to my leg. I told them it was burning like hell. They ignored me.

Soon, a gentleman in a white coat came over to me to tell me he was going to treat my head wound. I assumed he was a doctor, but he was a nurse practitioner, a title unfamiliar to me. We chatted while he stitched my wound. I was not too happy to have someone sticking a needle in my head who was not a surgeon, but I must say, he did a damn good job. It is hardly noticeable, except to me.

Then a doctor came over to me and said they had done all they could at this time. The knee would require surgery, which would be done the next day. The pain from the knee injury intensified as time went on and I begged them to repair it today. "I have to go to work. Every day is important to me. I want that surgery done today," I said in a rather firm voice. I think I heard someone say, "Poor devil, he is not going to work any time soon." I was too preoccupied with the pain, and trying to persuade someone to operate today, to follow up on that statement.

My pleading was successful. A surgeon had been located who was willing to remain after he had completed his scheduled appointments for the day. I don't know where they put me for the rest of the day, but it was about 11 p.m. when I met Dr. Santoro, a youthful-looking man, who was the one who had agreed to operate at this late hour. After he had introduced himself, I asked him, "How tired are you?" He smiled and said that he was wide awake, and I should not worry about anything.

The next thing I remembered, it was morning. Dr. Santoro came into my room to see his patient. "You are a very lucky man. That fall could have been fatal." Wow, what was he talking about? It was true that I was now a quadriplegic lying in that bed, with both arms and legs immobile, but I was conscious through it all. How could it have been near fatal? He explained that had the head wound been higher, it would have caused serious brain damage, or lower, at least the loss of my right eye.

I had told the nurse to call Ray and inform him that I would be unable to transport him to his doctor's appointment. I forgot that Ray had been the head of the emergency room at St. Francis Hospital before his MS attack, and he knew everyone there was to know in the medical field in Hartford. All he had to do was make one phone call to learn the extent of my injuries. He then called my sister Estelle, telling her what I did not know and she passed the word on to the family.

After Dr. Santoro left me, my mother and two sisters arrived. They stood at the foot of my bed with painful expressions. I tried to convince them that I was okay, but I could tell they did not believe me. I was okay mentally, which masked the seriousness of my injuries. I think I was of a mind that if one is conscious, nothing else matters. Someone sent word to Howard, who phoned his concern.

For the six days that I was hospitalized the thought of death kept coming to my mind. My brother, James, had died instantly of a freak accident and here I was, a survivor of a freak accident. While in the hospital, a nurse attending to me told me again how lucky I was. She said that she had just heard of a similar fall which was fatal. Why had I been spared? That thought would not leave my mind.

I was released from the hospital on the morning of the seventh day. My arms were still in slings and my right leg was wrapped from my ankle to my hip. Whatever material it was made of, it was heavy and damned hot. Because my left leg now was just sore, I could walk up stairs, one at a time. The right leg remained covered until I was ready for therapy, some three months later.

The channel CNN had recently been introduced to television. The 24-hour worldwide news service was covering the Gulf War, which had just begun. Every 15 minutes, James Earl Jones, with his incredible bass voice, would break in with "This is CNN."

I laid on my back for the three months before therapy because the covering over my right leg was so cumbersome that I was less uncomfortable on my back than on my side. I slept very little with the TV on and James Earl Jones talking to me every 15 minutes. I thought it odd that I was never tired. I was taking very little medication and I was wide awake most of the time. My meals were not only brought to me, but also I had to be fed. Through it all, I maintained a very positive attitude. I wanted to get well and back to a normal life as soon as possible.

A neighbor across the street, Bob Beard, visited me early in my confinement and offered to take me to my therapy appointments when they were scheduled in the future. Later, I learned that the therapy sessions would take place three times a week, for three hours each day. That meant that Mr. Beard would have to drive me to Rocky Hill, about six miles each way, and return three hours later to take me home. The only way I could travel was to lay on my back in the back seat of a car with my right foot extended. Without Mr. Beard's generous offer, transporting me to and from my sessions would have created a very complicated situation.

297

What I Remember …

My therapy sessions in the beginning were hell. On the first
day, I could not move my right hand away from my body even
one inch. My arm was useless. I had to learn to walk all over
again, step by step, as a therapist held me. There were stretching
exercises that were extremely painful. I would lay on a table and
the therapist would take one arm and try to move it away from my
body. I would scream and he would stop. I told him not to pay
any attention to my screaming, just do what he had to do.

I learned that when other patients complained of the pain, the
therapist ended the session, thereby delaying their recovery. I
began looking forward to the pain because it meant I was making
progress. I approached these sessions seriously with the attitude,
"No pain, no gain."

I was told I was a star pupil. Maybe so, but I was exhausted
when I returned home after those sessions. I wanted to recover
and end the need for therapy. About three months into my
sessions, I was put on a new machine where I would press my feet
against pressure from the machine. On the second attempt to
press forward, I felt a burning in my right leg. It was similar to the
pain I had experienced before the surgery. I called for a therapist
and told him of the pain, and he had me end that exercise. I was
told to see my surgeon without delay.

During the original knee surgery, only the fragments of my
crushed kneecap were removed. I was told that it was practice not
to remove what appeared to be "good bone." In the months since
surgery, the remaining bone had either deteriorated or I had been
too aggressive on the new machine. In any case, the knee would
require further surgery to remove what remained of the kneecap.
This second surgery meant that I would have to repeat the leg
exercises I had completed in therapy. Dr. Santoro told me that he

would not replace the kneecap because he felt at that time replacements had a life of about five years and, at 61, I would have to look forward to repeated surgeries. He told me he would use the same cut for the surgery, meaning only one scar.

The second surgery on my knee was successful. However, my plan to return to normal so I could go back to work was dealt a severe blow when I learned that I would be unable to run or walk rapidly or stand for long periods. Howard called me the same day I received that unpleasant news and he wanted to know how I was progressing. He was planning to buy a minor league hockey team in San Diego and he wanted me to head the staff. When I told him that I was just beginning to recover from a second surgery on my knee, there was a rather long pause. A pause that told me if I had any future in hockey, it was now over.

Returning to therapy, I was less motivated than in the past. What was the hurry? I would be limited for the rest of my life. I was 61 years old, but with the energy of a much younger person. What do I do when I complete my therapy? Years before, I had purchased a long-term disability policy, with a provision that I must return to a similar occupation following any long-term disability. My injuries precluded my returning to normal, so the policy would now keep me solvent for at least 10 years.

With my income guaranteed for 10 years, I could delay any decision about employment. When I did test the waters of the employment world, I found that my broad experiences made me over-qualified for every responsible position in which I had interest. One personnel manager responded to my resume, "Sorry, we do not need another president."

I came to believe that my fall from the ladder was meant to keep me home, and not go to Florida. My mother's health was beginning to decline. She was becoming more and more dependent on me for what used to be her daily routines. After decades of not being permitted in the kitchen while she was cooking, I now found myself washing dishes and even cooking on days when she was not up to it.

Others in the family thought she should give up driving. I refused to force the issue. There is something about being behind the wheel of an auto that gives one a sense of freedom and independence. I did not want to take that away from her. When she wanted to drive, I would sit in the passenger seat and criticize every driving rule she failed to adhere to. I was hoping it would speed the day when she would no longer want to drive. My sisters thought I was twice stupid, once to allow her to drive, and second, to sit in the passenger seat while she drove.

One day while driving, she said she would not renew her license when it became due on her 90th birthday. That was years away, but at least she was talking about it. There were more immediate concerns. What would I do when she could no longer climb stairs? We had four steps at the entrance to our home. I disliked the wooden walkways I had seen on some properties. What would I do if her medical condition required her to live in a nursing home? She was opposed to nursing homes. They were not for her. She had seen too many of her friends alone, unattended and unhappy in such situations. She had only six teeth; they were just falling out one by one. What would I do when they were all gone? She had no bone structure to allow for implants. What would I do when her condition deteriorated to the level where I could not care for her? I had promised myself that she would never again be without her family, and I meant to keep that promise.

• Chapter 31 •

Party Time

The months seemed to fly by, and Mom would soon be celebrating her 85th birthday. I decided to plan a surprise party for the event. It would be a family reunion, inviting those one only sees at funerals and weddings. I also invited those friends she had not seen in years but had communicated with only by telephone. I had planned a similar party for her 75th birthday, which I think was the best party of all those I had given, maybe with the exception of Dan and Estelle's 25th wedding anniversary.

That party was a grand event for about 400 guests, and it would fall on Memorial Day weekend. I remember there was concern that guests would not forego the holiday weekend to attend a wedding anniversary party. I was not worried. I knew the reputation this couple had in their community. Theirs was a family known for its kindness to others, especially during emergencies. Dan and Estelle were always there to help out people in need.

A Whalers season ticket holder with whom I became friendly owned a restaurant in Manchester and I asked him to cater the event. He went all out for me. I had told Dan and Estelle that I wanted to take them out to dinner for their anniversary, just the three of us. In all the 25 years of their marriage we had not had dinner, just the three of us. I rented a limo and was driven to their home in Windsor Locks and went inside to get the happy couple.

Some minutes later, Estelle happened to look out a window and saw the limo and began to giggle. It turned into extended laughter that brought tears to her eyes. "Wasn't it stupid and very expensive to rent a limo to go to lunch?" she asked. I answered that it was only once in 25 years, and I had been saving up for 25 years. Of course, that was not true.

As we approached the restaurant in the limo, its marquee proclaimed, "Welcome, Dan and Estelle." "You are crazy," she said, as the limo traveled to the rear of the restaurant, which was the entrance to the banquet room. As we turned the corner the guests, who had come outside to greet them, cheered their arrival. It was a fantastic beginning to a memorable day for them.

Later that afternoon, I was checking out the bar to see if everything was going according to plan. The head bartender supervising four other bartenders, came up to me and said, "The strangest thing happened today, one minute they were five deep at the bar and the next minute, nobody at the bar."

"Oh," I said, "that must have been when the guests of honor arrived, and they went outside to greet them."

"You mean to tell me that people left the bar where the drinks were free, to go outside to see guests of honor arrive? That is a first. They must be a very special couple," he added.

"They certainly are," I said. Memorial Day weekend notwithstanding, with few exceptions all those invited attended. The highlight of the event was the announcement that we were sending them to Hawaii for a second honeymoon.

❈ ❈ ❈

Mom's 75th was special also. I was still working in Binghamton and had to plan it from a distance. A friend of our family, who was now a priest, Father Mayock, was pastor of the

302

Sacred Heart Church in Bloomfield. I contacted him and asked him if he would say a special mass for Mom on this day. His church had a hall which held 150 people. Father had made a point of the capacity; it was the law. When he asked me how many would be attending, I said 150 people.

The party room was decorated in shades of pink and maroon, the color of her birthstone. I had told Mom that we had promised Father we would one day attend Sunday Mass at his church. Because this was a surprise party, I wanted to be sure that all the guests had arrived before we did, so I drove from Wethersfield about 20 miles-an-hour with Mom regularly questioning why I was driving so slowly. Father had told me he would only say Mass, and not attend the event, because he had a busy day ahead of him.

When we arrived, he was at the entrance, saying, "I will take her from here," as he escorted her down the aisle to applause from the guests. Father had gotten caught up in the excitement of the day and forgot about his busy day ahead. Honoring Mom in church made it special for me as well as for her.

Another fun party was the one I planned for my sister Marion's 50th birthday. At the time, she was divorced, and it seemed unlikely that she would ever celebrate a 25th wedding anniversary, so I decided to celebrate her milestone birthday. Marion's birthday fell on February 11 and Mom's was February 8. Why not celebrate both birthdays at the same time? I told Marion the party was for Mom and told Mom the party was for Marion. I could now speak about the party in front of either of them and it made it easier to keep it a secret. Friends of mine had just about a week before opened a three-story "hot spot" called "The Russian Lady." I asked them if I could hold the party at their

new venue, which meant closing the business for that day, a
Sunday. They agreed. It pays to have good friends.

Mom and Marion coincidentally arrived for the party at the
same time, and each one tried to hold back so the other one would
go first. The party was planned on the second floor and as they
walked up the stairs, at the landing were two huge birthday cards.
It was a great day for both. I was working at the Civic Center
with the Whalers, who had only weeks before played their first
game at the Civic Center. I had previously told Howard of the
party and asked him, since there was a Whalers game that
evening, could I invite my guests to the game. He said I could.

A few minutes before the party was to end, I offered the
remaining guests tickets to the game. Most of them accepted the
offer, 124 to be exact. No one had seen the new arena or the
Whalers at this time, so it would be a double feature for them. We
had one section to ourselves. The next day when Howard received
the game report, he called the box office manager to inquire why
there were 124 complimentary tickets issued for the game and was
told that I had approved the number. He then called me to ask
about the number. I assumed he had forgotten about the party
and his approval for me to invite my guests. When I reminded
him, he said, "When you give a party, you give a party." I told him
the number could have been much higher had all the guests
attended the game. When I told him that the guests were told that
the tickets were a gift from him, the situation was calmed.

❈ ❈ ❈

Family reunion parties became my trademark. Now I was
planning Mom's 85th birthday party. Who knew if those attending
would ever gather together again? The guests, almost 200, arrived
from ten states. We began with Mass at Corpus Christi Church,

our parish church, and later convened to the hall on the lower level. This event was catered with dinner and a Venetian dessert table, ice carving etc. When it was time to sing "Happy Birthday," Mom's entire family, children, grandchildren and great-grandchildren entered the hall holding lit candles and made a circle around Mom, who was standing in the middle of the hall. Quite a scene, not likely to be forgotten by those in attendance.

Because I planned such huge affairs to celebrate family milestones, the guests thought I must be wealthy. I had high profile positions and they believed I was earning a fabulous income. The truth was, I rarely had much money in the bank, and when I did, I planned another party. The purchase of my first car, the 1949 Cadillac, even though it only cost me $750, probably gave the impression that I was either wealthy or eccentric; I was neither.

What I was, was someone who found more pleasure in spending my money on such events, than I did spending it on myself. Bringing the family together to celebrate an event, gave me much more pleasure than any purchase I could make for myself. I discovered that this false impression of wealth and my independent attitude was an asset in the business world.

One day at G. Fox, I had a difficult time with a department manager and walked past Mr. Neisloss' office muttering to myself. He apparently heard me and called me on the phone as I reached my office. He wanted to know why I was so upset, and I told him I did not know why I tolerated such abuse from other employees. I think I said something to the effect, that "I don't know why I put up with this crap." Mr. Neisloss made it worthwhile by telling me that he had authorized an increase of $25 a week in my salary and was waiting for the right moment to inform me. That was a huge increase at the time. I think he thought I might resign. I was single and a free spirit and he could not deal with me the way he did with those employees who would never leave the company because of family responsibilities.

Speaking of that, I am reminded of the time a fellow employee became a father and Mr. Neisloss told me he would raise his salary, now that he had another mouth to feed. I was incensed. I wanted to know how being a father would make him more valuable to the company. The explanation only increased my anger. I was told that being a father would make him a more reliable employee because he now had new responsibilities. At that time, I had been employed for several years, not having missed a day of work, and felt I could not have been more reliable than I was. I asked that I be given the same increase as the new father. I received it.

❖ ❖ ❖

Returning to the subject of parties, there was one party with which I had no part. It was January 1990 and Raymond called to ask that I help him with this year's income tax forms. Ray's MS condition was progressively deteriorating, and he frequently asked me to do errands or take him to the doctor. We settled on a Sunday, weeks ahead, and I marked it on my calendar as a reminder.

When that Sunday arrived, it was a miserable day, cold, wet, and windy. I came home from Mass and told Mom I would call Ray and postpone my visit. When I called Ray, he was adamant that his tax forms had to be prepared that particular day. I tried to persuade him that we had several weeks before the deadline and the weather was really awful, and I did not want to travel in it. Saying no to Raymond was very difficult, even when he was unreasonable, as he was being this day. I put down the phone and was thinking, only Raymond could get me out of the house on a day like this one.

The drive to his home, the Woodland House, near downtown Hartford, was frightening. All the sensible drivers were home. The wind was so strong that my car was all over the road and it was fortunate that there were few cars to deal with.

When I did arrive at Ray's home, he asked me to put away some items in his storage area on the mezzanine level. He lived on the 7th floor, and we took the elevator and his items to the mezzanine level. The storage area was a right turn off the elevator, but Ray wanted to go left. He said he had another item for storage in the community room.

He said it was just inside the door of the community room and he followed me in his wheelchair. As I entered the room, a roar went up, "Surprise!" The room was filled with family and friends who had come to celebrate my 60th birthday. I had forgotten it was my birthday, a day I never made a big deal about. I was overwhelmed, not that a party was planned, but that so many of the guests, some who were elderly, would go out on this miserable afternoon. It was clear I was surprised. When the noise quieted down, I think I said, "What are you crazy people doing out on a day like today?"

I received many wonderful comments about how much I did for others, and this was their way of thanking me. I felt real special that day, a feeling I remember even to this day. Ray was pleased that he had a part in planning the surprise party because it gave him an opportunity to also say "Thank you."

• Chapter 32 •

Glory Days at the Oakdale

O ne year after the ladder incident, I completed my therapy. I settled my long-term disability issue with the insurance company and took a lump sum payment in lieu of monthly payments for 10 years. The year was 1991 and I wondered how I would spend my time. I was over-qualified for any position I found interesting and was resigned to a life without employment.

I saw my almost fatal accident as a message that I should remain home. My mother's declining health situation found me spending more and more time looking after her. I was now preoccupied with chores around the house. I was cooking, cleaning and shopping and her chauffeur for doctor appointments and our many family events. It was a full-time position. I rarely left our home unless someone was available to stay with her.

The years passed uneventful. Sometime, in 1996, I read in the Courant that the Oakdale Theater, a summer theater in Wallingford, was to be converted to a year-round theater with seating for over 4,000. I had worked for the theater in the summer of 1967 as their sales manager. The campaign for mayor that year would not begin until September, so I had time on my hands to kill.

When I read about the conversion, I remembered that Ben Segal, the owner, had told me of his dream to one day convert the tent theater to a year-round operation. I wrote him a note congratulating him on the realization of his dream. A few days later, he phoned me to ask me to assist with the grand opening, about two months in the future. I told him I was now spending all my time looking after my mother, whose health was declining and could not commit to a full-time project at this time. She was my top priority.

Ben said I could do both. I could make my own hours, and he would accept whatever time I could give him. I made it very clear, that I would be unable to work, if for any reason my mother needed me. He accepted my conditions and I agreed to do what I could for the approximate two months and maybe a couple of weeks after the opening.

On my first day at Oakdale, Ben said he needed me in the box office, where ticket sales for the upcoming attractions were already on sale. He was not pleased with the operation and wanted me to help improve it. That he needed someone in the box office who could organize and develop procedures was obvious to me. Ben had hired his summer staff to continue as full-time employees, but they did not adjust to the hectic pace and the increased volume of business in a larger venue.

It was a situation where the left hand did not know what the right hand was doing. When an attraction was announced, the box office took phone orders at the same time they were selling tickets at the window, sometimes the same tickets. The new theater was an instant success with the public and the volume of ticket sales was overwhelming.

I soon determined that the box office was without an experienced manager. The current individual was a candidate for a nervous breakdown. He could not deal with the pace and the pressure. It did not surprise anyone when he resigned or was asked to leave. I became the go-to guy in the box office.

After weeks of utter chaos, things became routine. A new manager was hired, and I was asked to become the Broadway Subscription Manager. As G. Fox budget director, I was trained in working with others. I had no problem dealing with difficult patrons who insisted on seats, 5th row center.

Although I was not a permanent employee, I was invited by Mr. Segal to attend staff meetings of department heads and was treated like one of them. I was encouraged to participate in the discussions and my contributions were accepted as an equal. Mr. Segal had now brought together a professional staff who were eager to succeed in this new adventure.

Then it was opening night. A capacity crowd filled the new theater with enthusiasm. There was no doubt the public approved of the new theater. There were problems, of course, but patrons were understanding that it would take time to smooth out the rough edges. I planned to remain about two more weeks and then leave, as Mr. Segal and I had agreed upon earlier.

When I informed Mr. Segal of my exit date, he pleaded with me to stay. He said that he had received compliments from Broadway season ticket holders regarding my performance. He said that I was perfect for that role. He was the kind of employer for whom you wanted to give your best effort. He did not care that I would not keep a regular schedule or that I might have to leave without notice if Mom needed me. I loved the business, so how could I say no to such an open-ended offer?

I was permitted to give complimentary tickets to anyone I wished, and I treated members of my family to attractions they wished to attend. Mom saw many shows while I was working there, and the staff treated her like royalty whenever she appeared in the lobby. I remember a call from my nephew, Jason. "Uncle, if you can get me tickets to see Jewel (a new and popular female singer), I will owe you for the rest of my life." How could I not respond favorably to such a request?

I had a great time for almost two years and then I noticed a change in management style. Mr. Segal was not spending much time in the theater and his partner was making the decisions. He was a building contractor, I think, without much theater experience. It was not the same anymore. I slipped on ice one snowy night leaving the theater, injuring my shoulder. I did not return to work after that.

I had seen the end of two eras, G. Fox & Company and now Oakdale Theater. Both businesses had been family operations since inception. G. Fox was Mrs. Auerbach's life, not just a business. The same was true of the Segal family with Oakdale. It must be more than sad to witness a life's work change so drastically.

For me, I considered myself fortunate to have been a part of the glory days of both of those family businesses.

• Chapter 33 •

A Promise Kept

I returned home to my priority, looking after Mom. Her 90th birthday was coming up soon and I planned another family reunion. Guests from all over the East Coast attended. Mom looked fabulous in a maroon velvet gown that Marion had purchased for the occasion. It was the only time that she wore that gown.

I would keep in touch with Ray. I would inform him of changes I noticed in Mom's demeanor, and one time he told me she would not live more than six months. Previously, she had read the morning paper, especially the "Dear Abby" column and the obituaries. Now, I noticed that she did not ask for the paper. She would stare at the TV, but I felt she did not comprehend what she saw. We would stay up until about 11 p.m. every evening playing Uno. I would purposely make wrong moves so that she could win the game. How happy she was when she could win over me at Uno. She would laugh out loud, she was so pleased with herself. It was a joy just to hear her laugh.

❁ ❁ ❁

In the early part of the 2000 decade, Nancy Doyle, a dear friend for more than 50 years, persuaded me to accept a position on the Development Board of Directors of the Sisters of St. Joseph. The meetings were held monthly at 7:30 a.m. and lasted about an hour. The time was good for me because Mom was a late riser, and I would be back home in time to prepare her breakfast.

On the morning of September 11, 2001, I was driving home from a board meeting, listening to radio, WCBS news. The program was interrupted to report that a plane had flown into one of the Trade Center buildings in the city. I instantly remembered the time when a small plane had flown into the Empire State Building and there were pictures of the plane protruding from it. I had arrived at home just as the station reported that another plane had hit the other Trade Center building. I rushed into the house, fearing Mom might be awake with the TV on and she would see this horror story.

She was getting dressed and had not yet turned on the TV. I turned it to a station that was showing reruns of comedies. I did not want her to see any of the news. I prepared her breakfast and sat with her while she ate, thinking all the time about the planes in New York City. I was anxious to go upstairs to my TV and see what was happening. After breakfast, she laid down on the couch to rest and asked me to turn off the TV. I left the room to go upstairs. The news was so unsettling I would turn away from it from time to time. While I wished I could ignore it, I really could not take my eyes off the screen. Every few minutes I would go downstairs to see if Mom was still asleep.

For the next week, my main concern was keeping the news from her. On Sunday, my niece and nephew Denise and John Kana were celebrating their 25th wedding anniversary in Windsor Locks. We were planning to attend, but Mom did not feel well that morning and we did not go to church. I called Denise to tell her that we would not be attending their celebration. I sat in a chair keeping my eyes on Mom.

About noon, Mom suddenly awakened and sat at the edge of the couch. "I have to get dressed for Denise's party," she said.

I asked her if she was sure that she wanted to attend.

"I always attend family functions," she added, and I helped her to the bathroom. It took us almost an hour to get her dressed and then we left for the party. Her arrival caused the usual commotion, as one at a time everyone came up to greet and kiss her.

We remained only a short time and then she said that she wanted to go home. As I helped her into the car, she said she wanted to stop by and see Nathan, the youngest great-great-grandson, a child of great-granddaughter Jessica and great-grandson Tim. Nathan was two years old and the youngest member of our growing family. As we arrived at their home, Nathan was outside playing. Mom called to him and opened the passenger door. She hugged and kissed Nathan and then said, "Okay, we can go home now."

On the way home, she said that this was her last family visit. I did not see that statement for the prophetic comment it was. We had a quiet evening. About 10 p.m. she wanted to play Uno. We were still playing Uno at midnight. I was especially tired, but I would not end the game until she said that she had enough. We laughed a lot during the evening because she was winning every hand. Then suddenly she said that she was tired. I tucked her in, kissed her and said, "I love you." I put out the light and went to bed. By this time, I had been sleeping downstairs so I could hear her if she needed me.

The next morning, as I was preparing her breakfast, Danielle, the first grandchild, appeared. She said that she wanted to spend some time with her grandmother, and I could do other things with my time. I said that I would go grocery shopping at Shop Rite in

Manchester. It had been a long time since I was able to casually walk up and down aisles of a supermarket. Usually, I would run in, purchase what I wanted and leave. This day, I purchased several weeks' worth of supplies and food and returned home.

It was 12:30 p.m. and Mom was beginning to watch, "The Young and the Restless." I put away the purchases and spent time with Danielle, discussing the 9/11 disaster. Suddenly, I noticed it was 12:55 p.m., and the time in Mom's soap opera when the station breaks from the story to promote the news coming up later in the day. I went into the den and stood in front of the TV. I knew I could not turn off the set without questions being asked. I talked with Mom until I could hear that the story had returned. I then left the den and went back to the kitchen to continue the discussion of the planes' attack.

Just about 2 p.m. Danielle said she had to leave for home and get some sleep before she went to work. She was an LPN in a nursing home and worked the third shift. I left the kitchen to go to the den and tell Mom that Danielle was leaving. As I turned the corner of the living room, I saw Mom, face down on the floor, parallel to the couch.

I called to Danielle to come into the den. Turning Mom over so she was face up, I knelt down to hold her head in my lap and said to Danielle, "I should call 911." Danielle held my arm and said, "It's too late for 911, Gramma has left this world."

The next few minutes were difficult for both of us. When we were back in control of ourselves, I asked Danielle to use her cell phone and call the family members and I went out into the kitchen where there was another phone, to call Dr. Pope. Mom was his first patient when he opened his office in Wethersfield as a new doctor in town. They had a wonderful relationship for years, and he had seen her just yesterday for her regular checkup. During all those years, there were times when I thought we visited him when there wasn't a medical reason to do so except that she wanted to spend some time with her doctor.

Mom was popular with the doctor's staff, and the receptionist put me through without delay to Dr. Pope after I told her mom had died. The news must have been a shock. He said, "George," and then there was a long silence before he spoke. He expressed sorrow for himself and his staff. I asked him what I should do. He told me to call the funeral home, he would create the death certificate.

Mom's funeral Mass would be held at Corpus Christi Church, our parish for more than 45 years. We regularly sat in the third row. Although we had a large parish, the priests knew Mom because she never left Mass without saying a few words to the celebrant. At Easter and Christmas, Mom would bake individual cranberry breads for the priests. On her 90th birthday, Father Campion and Father Colton surprised Mom with a visit to our home with a gift for her, a framed painting of the "Madonna and Child," which now hangs on my bedroom wall.

Before Mom's funeral Mass, I spoke with Father Campion about times in her life that I would find difficult to recall during my eulogy and asked him to do so. We were a five-generation family at this time, and I wanted someone from each generation to speak at the Mass. Mom was 92 years old.

Father Campion opened his remarks by saying funeral Masses for someone her age usually were attended by few people because most of the deceased's family and friends had passed on by that time. He said it was a tribute to Minnie that so many were present at this time. He spoke at length and included those moments I found difficult to express.

As the Mass ended, the priests came down from the altar to escort the casket from the church. Sitting in the front row I stood up, surprised that Father Campion had overlooked the family eulogies. He said it was too late now, we could deliver them at the cemetery. Great-granddaughter Gianna, grandson James and I did just that. He later told me that he misunderstood.

He thought I had told him that I was too emotional to deliver a eulogy. I had doubts; it was common knowledge that he didn't approve of the practice of family members giving eulogies, and he had limited them to three minutes. It would be impossible for me to recall Mom's 92 years in three minutes. I understood Father's objection because so many family members think they can, at such an emotional time, stand and talk extemporaneously without having prepared remarks ahead of time.

After the funeral, several family members returned with me to Oakdale Street. I could see in their faces their concern for me now that Mom was gone. Throughout the past few years, as her health was declining, family members would express concern for me as the primary caregiver. How would I adjust to her passing, when the time came? My answer was always the same. "I have done all I could while she was alive. I will not have any regrets when she has left me."

I was thinking of so many people I knew, who upon the death of a loved one, expressed regret that they had failed to do or say something to the deceased that they now wished they had. I had none of that. For years now, Mom had been the reason I got up in the morning. My schedule was her schedule. I did not have a life of my own, but I did not regret one minute. I was doing what I promised I would do, see to it that Mom would never again be without her family. I had kept that promise, difficult as it sometimes was.

When everyone left, I put out the lights and sat in the dark in the living room. For years I had prayed that when the time came for her to be called, that it would be in her home, on her couch and in her sleep. That is exactly how it happened, and I was so grateful to God. I thanked him, not only for taking her as I asked, but also for having someone with me, not just someone, but a nurse. I did not ask for anyone to be with me. I did not think I would need anyone. I had years to prepare for this moment. But no matter how much time one has to prepare for death, one is not prepared when it happens.

Without Danielle with me, that time would have been much more difficult than it was. I did not have to inform the family. Danielle did it for me. I was so thankful I did not have to make those calls.

Sitting alone in the dark, I was reliving moments, the good ones and the not-so-good ones. As the primary caregiver, I was the one who had to endure the anger of my patient when she did not get her way. We were strong-willed individuals, guaranteed to produce fireworks. My sisters objected to her abusive manner and would tell her so. I told them that supporting me only made things worse.

Now I was alone, and how I wished that I could have just one more unpleasant moment.

• Chapter 34 •

A New Home, New City, New Life

The months passed by and oddly enough, I do not have any memories of that time. I do not know how I spent those days. My mind is blank. I think about those days now and wonder what did I do to pass the time? I knew that one day I would move from Oakdale Street and that I would buy a condo. I never liked owning property, too many problems I could not solve without outside help. But I was not ready to leave. Mom was in every room. It would be like walking out on her.

Sometime later, I saw an ad in the real estate section of the Sunday paper publicizing a senior condo complex, to be built in Berlin, just a few miles from my home. It was under construction and taking orders for units when completed. I thought it would be a good idea to at least investigate such complexes, just for information, for the time when I would want to relocate.

I mentioned the ad to Danielle and asked her to join me in looking over the complex. She brought her daughter Jessica with her. While I was asking a zillion questions of the representative of the complex, I could overhear Jessica talking to her mother. She was saying something about her brother, Jason, moving into Nana's home if I should buy a condo.

I walked over to them to follow-up on their conversation. At the time, Jason was living in Philadelphia and working in New

Jersey. He had married and wanted to return home with his wife, Christine, to raise a family. When they explained the idea to me, I was receptive and soon after I had a conversation with Jason to determine his interest in living in his Nana's home. Jason was the first great-grandson and had a special place in Mom's heart. He would visit her regularly and the sight of him brought a big happy smile to his Nana's face. If he was serious about wanting to live in his Nana's home, I would move out and make it available to him.

When I learned that Jason was shopping for mortgage money, I thought I had better start looking for a new home. Raymond Howell had many times suggested the Woodland House would be perfect for me, but Mom would never consider a 12-story, 237-unit property as her home. Now that I was alone, I could investigate that property for myself.

I was introduced to a real estate agent who lived at the Woodland House, and I asked him to keep an eye out for a two-bedroom unit for me. A week or so later, he called to have me look at a unit.

It was on the third floor. I thought it was too dark. I had decided I wanted wood floors and a modern kitchen. This unit had new wall-to-wall carpeting and there wasn't any reason to look further.

In the meantime, Jason changed his mind and bought a property in Windsor Locks, but he neglected to inform me. When I learned of his decision, I decided to forget about moving.

Sometime later, the real estate agent called again to say he had another unit to show me, it was on the seventh floor. I had forgotten to notify him of my change in plans and was too embarrassed to say so over the phone. I agreed to look at the property and then make some excuse for changing my mind about relocating. When he opened the door to the unit, I saw the beautiful parquet floor. Two steps away was a remodeled kitchen. The almost 1,200-square-foot unit was about the same size as Oakdale Street.

I called great-niece, Gianna, who was working in Hartford and asked her to look at the unit I wanted to buy. I wanted a female's opinion. She saw the unit that afternoon and called to say, "Uncle George, it is beautiful." That did it. I called the agent to finalize the sale before an Open House was to be held the very next day.

Now I owned two homes; Oakdale Street had to be sold, and soon, because I had agreed to move into the Woodland House in three weeks. I needed to sell and sell quickly. It was a good time in the real estate market and in three weeks I went from having no intention of moving, to buying and selling property and sleeping in my new home. The agent told me that was a record time for such a transaction.

That first evening in bed, I could look out my windows and since I was above the trees next door, I could dream I was anywhere in the world I wanted to be. The move had been made so quickly, I did not consider that I was really alone now. I did not know a single person in Hartford or in the Woodland House.

It was September of 2002, I was 72 years old and embarking on a new life, in a new home, in a new city.

Without property responsibilities, I had plenty of time on my hands and nothing to do. The Cathedral of St. Joseph was a short distance and I decided to attend daily the noon Mass, in appreciation for the manner in which Mom left this world. That filled only one hour each day. I had to find something to do. I informed the cathedral sacristan that I wanted to get involved in the church's activities and in no time at all, I had volunteered for six ministries in the church, including being a lector at daily and weekend Masses when assigned.

The Woodland House Board of Directors held meetings once a month and I attended, promising myself I would not get involved. At the beginning of each meeting, owners of units were permitted to speak. I sat there uncharacteristically silent throughout the meeting, which lasted about two hours.

I found the afternoons without something to do particularly difficult. I attended movies a few times but did not enjoy the film because small children were behaving like they were home watching TV. Up and down the aisles, back and forth to the concessions stands, rustling candy wrappers, throwing popcorn at each other and causing a disturbance which made it difficult to hear the movie on the screen. I wondered why parents took small children to R-rated films.

The University of Connecticut's women's basketball team was on a roll toward a perfect season. There was a community room with an oversized TV at Woodland House. The interest in a possible perfect season brought many residents to the room and I started to meet my neighbors. On the evening of the final game, a crowd gathered to enjoy the expectation of a perfect season. UConn won the game! After the game, the residents cleaned up what mess they had made with their refreshments.

While cleaning up, a resident threw an empty Pepsi can in the trash. I asked if he was throwing that item away. At that time, all soda and beer containers had a 5-cent deposit to encourage the return of the container. He answered that it was "only a nickel."

I was a Great Depression baby who did not understand anyone throwing away money. I was taught to save my pennies and the dollars would take care of themselves. I thought that maybe someone on staff was responsible for collecting and redeeming these returnable items but was told that they were picked up with the trash. With 237 families living in the building, that could add up to something.

The next morning, I visited the management office to verify the status of returnable items. When confirmed that they went out with the trash, I asked if I could collect them and was told I could. I was told that the trash was removed at 4 p.m. and midnight from compactor rooms on each floor. I planned my days so that I was home at 3 p.m. every day and would make the second collection before going to bed each evening.

At that time, there was much publicity in the area about families, suffering from the downturn in the economy, who were being fed by soup kitchens and food banks. The cathedral operated a food bank for the neighborhood, serving more than 150 families with groceries on a weekly basis. When I had raised $100, I gave it to the cathedral food bank and put a notice on the bulletin board of my action. The word spread quickly of my work, and I received numerous compliments for my efforts.

In my opinion, the Woodland House was what America aimed to be. People of all ages, nationalities, skin color, believers and non-believers, all living together in harmony. I was so proud to be a resident in that building. One day in the elevator a resident suggested that I give the money I raised to the "Loaves and Fishes," an organization on Woodland Street of which she was a volunteer.

It was a community organization that among other things operated a soup kitchen, which served walk-ins (about 150) every day with a hot meal. I visited the organization to meet the director and learned that they also offered food to take home when it was donated by food stores. They taught people to sew, to learn how to operate a computer, how to apply for a job, and other programs designed to assist the residents with their needs. One could only be impressed with their mission.

I planned to give future donations to this worthwhile endeavor and put a notice up indicating my plans. When I had $100 collected, I brought it to the director, who thought it was a one-time donation. I asked Alyce Hild, the director, to send me a notice of the donation that I could post on the bulletin board for all to see. I instructed her to credit the donation to the Woodland House residents and not to me.

When I had raised $500, I told the pastor at the cathedral of this activity of mine. I suggested we ask our parishioners to bring their returnable items to the church, and I would redeem them and give the money to the cathedral for parish activities. The cathedral was located in an area where many poor families resided. I believed more parish activities could be planned if funds were available.

The pastor was agreeable and said he would put a notice in the weekly church bulletin. I thanked him for his willingness to support my suggestion, but I told him I could do a better selling job than a notice in the bulletin. I asked if he would allow me to speak to the parishioners at our three weekly Masses. He approved my request.

Monsignor Bergin, like me, was new to the cathedral and did not know that such announcements from the pulpit were not permitted. But he was the pastor, and his approval overruled any policies of the past. There was concern that the empty bottles and cans would bring insects inside the cathedral and that the accumulation of items would be unsightly. I promised that I would remove the items on a timely basis.

The following weekend, I spoke at the three Masses. At the 11 a.m. Mass, I was applauded as I completed my appeal. I said to the pastor, who was pleased with my presentation, "You know why they applauded me, it was because I did not ask them for money." We both laughed. I received the same kind of approval from parishioners as I did from Woodland House residents.

It is now 2017, and more than 14 years since I began the program. The Loaves and Fishes donations have exceeded $13,000 and more than $20,000 has been donated for parish activities. I guess, like pennies, saving nickels the dollars would also take care of themselves.

❊ ❊ ❊

One day while I was doing my laundry, a resident apologized for not supporting the returnable items effort, saying she did not drink soda or beer. She suggested I conduct regular clothing drives which she could support. I asked Alyce Hild, the director of Loaves and Fishes, if she would accept clothing from the Woodland House. She would do so, but only on a seasonal basis. She said her clients are very mobile and spring and fall clothing drives would be helpful.

I cleared the matter with the management office and posted a notice in the mail room's bulletin board and twice a year the residents filled a large van with clothing. When we placed a framed sign holder in the elevator with a message of the next clothing drive, the residents filled two vans with their donations.

The drives became an annual event at the Woodland House.

❊ ❊ ❊

One day, it was exactly 4 o'clock in the afternoon, I suddenly had violent stomach pains. My doctor's office closed at 4 o'clock so it was too late to call anyone except 911 for an ambulance to take me to St. Francis Hospital, two blocks from the Woodland House. I was diagnosed with a gallbladder attack and surgery was necessary. While recovering in the hospital, I asked to see the director of volunteer services who visited me a few hours later.

Tobye Karl interviewed me to determine where I could fit in as a volunteer. I had only one restriction, I did not want to be involved with patients. After learning of my various careers, she said she would have to think about an assignment that could benefit from my experience in the business world. A week or so later, she called with news that I could be helpful in the St. Francis Foundation, which raised funds for the hospital.

The foundation staff was intrigued by my work experiences and asked if they could interview me for the hospital's monthly magazine. I agreed to the interview but requested that no photo accompany the article and the message should be that seniors in their 80s are not too old to volunteer. A year or so later I was invited to be a corporator of the hospital, which met only once a year at an annual meeting at the Connecticut Convention Center. Hundreds of corporators attended the luncheon.

At my first corporator's meeting, a woman named Joan Dauber came over to me and asked whether I would conduct a fundraiser for the food bank at the hospital, of which she was the director. Joan was a nutritionist at the hospital and was allowed one day each week to spend managing the food bank.

I asked Joan what fundraisers they had planned in the past and was told that they never had a fundraiser. I assumed the food bank was a recent undertaking by the hospital but was shocked to learn it had been in operation for 30 years with volunteers. When she needed funds, she said, she would walk through the hospital and when she saw someone she knew, she would beg for a donation. I agreed to plan an event for her. Having been hungry most of my childhood, feeding hungry people was something around which I could wrap myself.

I asked to meet with the top officials of the hospital so I could determine the restrictions that would be placed on anyone raising money in the hospital. Every suggestion I made to the group was denied with the explanation, "If we agree to your request, we would have to allow others who raise funds, the same opportunity."

I left the meeting discouraged and walked across the street to the foundation office, where I asked to meet with the president, Paul Prendergast. I told him of my failure to get approval for anything I wanted to do.

I had another idea that I suggested to him. Could I write a personal letter to all of the corporators (over 500 at that time) and tell them of the need at the food bank? He not only approved my suggestion, but also said he would write a cover letter to go with mine, supporting the idea. I

n the six years that followed, the annual letter raised almost $150,000 for the food bank.

• **Chapter 35** •

A Fairy Tale Life

In my eighth decade, I found myself over-extended and decided to resign from some of my commitments. Now 85 years old, I plan my volunteer work so that I am out of the Woodland House by 8:30 a.m. It gives me a reason to get out of bed in the morning. I still attend Mass most every day. I still travel the 12 floors of Woodland House collecting returnable items. I continue to serve as a trustee of the Loaves and Fishes organization. Most of all, I continue to attend all family functions.

As I look back, I believe I have lived a fairy tale. My first 19 years were unpleasant. I strongly believe that someone has been watching over me and that the early years formed a base of negatives that made me stronger. Nothing I faced later could compare to my earlier years.

I have lived by four words most of my life. One is "moderation" in everything, and the other three words are "Get Over It."

I have not let the negatives in my life rule me. I do not bear grudges or seek vengeance. I rise each morning with a clear conscience, ready to take on the day. I think anger is a waste of energy. I am a positive-thinking person, who, when he objects to something, offers solutions, not just complaints.

I have been blessed with energy, passion, perseverance and a triple dose of common sense. When I say that I believe someone has been watching over me my entire life, it is because I cannot explain what I did, or what I said, on so many occasions.

For example: There was my obsession with Ann Uccello's attempt at political office. I gave up five years of earning power during those years to volunteer for someone else's career. Was it a coincidence that every important idea I had in planning campaigns came in church? I believed after a few months in office, that one day Ann would be mayor of Hartford and I was driven to make it happen.

After elections, the pundits make statements that this group or that one is responsible for the victory. It was the women's vote, or the Black vote or the union members' vote that is credited with the victory. Each constituency demanding action for their particular issues, because, in their opinion, they were responsible for the victory. The truth is they needed each other to win.

But in the Uccello victories, without the volunteer effort, Ann would not have won her first victory for City Council. She was unknown and would run behind the other Republicans who would be elected to the two minority seats. (It was taken for granted that Betty Knox would win her sixth term.) Ann would then return to G. Fox.

In the mayoral election of 1969, the pundits saw it as a loss for the Democrats. It was the division within the party that caused her to win. They ignored the number of votes she received, far more than any other Republican candidate in years had received. Democrats crossed over to vote for her.

It is true that had the Democrats united behind one candidate, no Republican could beat them. But it is also true that voters had a choice, and they chose Ann over the Democratic candidates. The Democrats had been divided in other years, but no Republican was elected except to a minority position. Miss Uccello had wide appeal and that is why she was re-elected two years later, proving her previous election not a fluke.

❊ ❊ ❊

I say I was being watched over by someone. Take the two automobile occurrences that I came through without injuries. It was winter and I was driving on I-91, having just left downtown Hartford. That road was a parking lot all day long, a two-lane highway connecting Hartford with Springfield, Massachusetts. I hit a patch of black ice and my car did a 360-degree spin, landing an inch or two from the guard rail. I never touched another car. I merely waited until I could move back into the traffic and proceed as if nothing had happened.

Then there was the time when I was waiting for the streetlight to change to green so I could cross a busy intersection and continue on my way. When the light turned green, I proceeded across the intersection and my car was hit in the rear passenger area by a driver running a red light. My car again did a 360-degree spin and I landed in the only space that was not occupied by another vehicle.

My car had over $7,000 in damages and I did not have a scratch on my body. Coincidence? I think not.

What about the fall from the roof, where a half-inch could have meant brain damage or the loss of one eye? I was told that I was lucky to be alive. Someone was watching over me? You betcha.

In a three-week period, buying and selling property and moving to the Woodland House, where I did not know anyone there or in the city. A move that opened a new life for me following Mom's passing.

The empty Pepsi can that started me on a volunteer career that gave my senior years meaning. Again, coincidence? Too many such moments for all of them to be coincidences.

I was told repeatedly that resigning from G. Fox and remaining unemployed for five years, years that are said to be peak earning years in one's life, was absolutely idiotic. Yet that decision was the best decision I made in my entire life. It was something I had to do. I did not know why. The result was that every position I had after Ann went to Washington was as a result of my association with her.

Peter Savin, hiring me for a position for which I was totally unqualified, saying "Anyone who can beat the Democrats in the City of Hartford, not once but twice, can do this job." Then Mr. Savin suggesting me to Howard Baldwin when the football league failed. Leaving the Whalers to become Executive Director of the Multiple Sclerosis chapter, without even an interview, simply because of my reputation and the recommendation of Raymond Howell, a board member. I came to know Ray when he volunteered for Ann's campaigns. Leaving the MS Society when WRCH owner Enzo Dedominicis offered me a position as Community Relations Director. I met Enzo during the campaigns for Ann. Someone watching over me?

❊ ❊ ❊

Consider this: I was 74 years old when I began experiencing pain from my neck to my groin. I visited Dr. Pope. That began a series of examinations and I think all the tests known to medical science at that time. I kept being told "There is nothing wrong with you." The pain was real in spite of the tests. When you have lived 74 years in your body, you know when something is not

331

right. I went home after the latest "oscopy" test results, and for the first time in my life, terribly confused and depressed.

I sat down at my computer and my right hand was touching my phone book, opened to the letter "g." My middle finger touched Dr. Graydon's phone number. I had not considered an appointment with him because I had seen him recently for my annual PSA exam. I did not know what to do except that I could not ignore the pain. I wanted to talk to someone who would listen. I had a special relationship with Dr. Graydon, having been his patient for years.

I picked up my phone and dialed his number to make an appointment. After doing so, I put down the phone. The pain was gone. I knew I had found the answer. I knew that I had been led to make that phone call. Whatever caused the pain was serious, but I knew I would survive it.

It was prostate cancer. Those were just words to me. I did not react to the word "cancer" as most people would. No emotion whatever upon learning the news. I had expected it was serious, but I was going to win the battle and one day be cancer free. Radiation treatments, 40 of them were prescribed.

Routinely, for eight weeks, I walked to St. Francis Hospital for my radiation treatments. Those around me thought I was in denial because I just dismissed any concern about my condition. I was absolutely convinced that the treatments would be successful in curing my cancer. Five years later, Dr. Graydon said "You are cancer free. No need to see me in the future. Visit your primary doctor for your PSA test each year."

When I made the Dr. Graydon appointment and the pain disappeared, I knew I was led in that direction, and all would be well again. Because of that feeling, I did not react to the word "cancer" the way others might. Years later, in visiting a new doctor, I filled out a questionnaire that asked for previous surgeries or serious illnesses. When I saw the new doctor, he was reviewing my history on his computer and said, "It says here that you had cancer."

I answered, "Oh, I am sorry, I forgot I had cancer."

The doctor looked at me quizzically, "You forgot you had cancer?" he said.

"Yes," I replied, "there was nothing to remember. I had 40 radiation treatments, no pain, no discomfort, no change of lifestyle, there was nothing to remember." The doctor just shook his head.

❈ ❈ ❈

The most telling incident of all had to do with a conversation. Many, many times over the years, someone would ask me, "How does it feel not to be recognized for the work you have done?" Some expressed the same thought by asking, "What does it feel like when you learn others are taking credit for what you have accomplished?" I would merely shrug my shoulders, thinking what can I do about it? That is the way it is.

One day I was asked the same question and I answered, "The recognition I seek, is not of this world." I paused. Where did those words come from? I do not talk like that. In fact, I never thought about it that way.

I saw it as a message from the one watching over me. It certainly made sense. Why had I not thought about it that way? Everything I did, I did with the gifts that were given to me, energy, passion, perseverance and common sense. So, was it unreasonable to think that whatever I accomplished with those gifts, was really accomplished by the one who gave them to me?

If someone thinks that I thought I was special because I believed someone was watching over me, I do not. I would like to believe that we all have someone watching over us. In my life, I may have had more proof than others.

When I fell from the roof in December 1990, I was beginning to look for a new job. I had a disability insurance policy that was settled for enough funds to keep me solvent for over 10 years. I did not expect to live that long. Males in our family history were long gone by their 60s. When that money was spent, I was left a large sum in a will that would keep me solvent for at least another 10 years. Was someone watching over me? You decide for yourself.

I do not only think it, I believe it.

• **Chapter 36** •

Reflections

I regret that I will never know what it feels like to stand at an altar in church, watching someone in white walk toward me. One who will stay with me for better or for worse, until death us do part. That has to be a unique experience. Maybe that is why today so many people do it over and over.

I also regret that I will never know what it feels like to hold a newborn in my arms and know I had something to do with it being there. I think that must be the ultimate pleasure in this world and only duplicated when future children are born. But I temper that regret because I was blessed with dozens of nieces and nephews who have been a major part of my life. Men and women who have added so much joy in watching them grow from childhood into responsible adults, parents and grandparents.

I regret that I never knew my father. Being raised by a stepfather who wished I did not exist, and a mother lost in the pain of knowing she had two daughters out there somewhere, left me without parents when you need them ... and the love, I later learned, that comes only from parents.

I regret that I was sometimes abrasive and arrogant in my dealings with others. I have always had little patience with those who are satisfied with the status quo. I was never satisfied with the status quo. I preferred to adjust to the times, always looking

335

for a better way to do something that needs to be done or trying something new that had not been done before. Too many people in responsible positions do not want to rock the boat.

I sometimes wonder if I had made more of an effort to work with the Republican Party if it would have made a difference. I saw them as the enemy of my candidate and avoided contact as much as possible. I do not think I could have persuaded them to accept a woman as an equal. That attitude did not come until much later.

I think I would have resigned years earlier, for the second time, from the Whalers, had it not been for Gordie Howe's encouragement. He was there, in person or by mail, when a pat-on-the-back was helpful. No wonder I remember him as a personal friend instead of the super sports star that he was.

Having been employed as a traveling auditor, a resident auditor and a budget director, I was trained to look at a situation and almost immediately see its flaws and many times its solutions. Those who wanted to study the issue, just to delay change, found little support from me.

❈ ❈ ❈

I wish sometimes I could have been satisfied with success. I was always bored with success, needing a new challenge to get the juices flowing.

I wish I were 6-feet tall. My father was 6 feet, 4 inches. My growth was stunted by rickets, a deficiency of Vitamin D, which later led to malnutrition. I was always hungry and wanted more to eat at mealtime. My stepfather decided what amount of food would be placed on my plate.

I think tall people get more respect than short people. I doubt I would have been "picked on" as a child if I were taller.

When I chose my major in college, I wish I would have thought to learn what "marketing" was and not chosen "finance" just because I would receive a free copy of the Wall Street Journal.

I wish I had asked more questions about my mother's and father's early years. Mom would not talk about those days, and remembering my conversation with Aunt Lilly, I did not press for answers.

I think sometimes that humans say very stupid things. I think that the most stupid words ever to come out of humans' mouths are those that say, "You know everything you need to know about a person just by looking at the color of one's skin." The color of one's skin tells you absolutely nothing about that person.

I pray that someday we will accept people as they are, and cease being critical or judgmental of those who think, look and act differently from others.

I believe I have lived during the best years of our country's existence. I have lived through an economic Depression, saw my country save the world from Hitler, become the world's superpower and become the world's watchdog for peace.

I am proud that I lived in a country that conquered its enemies and never took a foot of land for its own. We did it because it was the right thing to do. We restored Germany and Japan after World War II and today they are free and successful countries. What other conqueror ever did that?

I was fortunate to live during the time of fabulous entertainers: Al Jolson; Judy Garland, who I saw in person three times; Frank Sinatra, who I saw four times. Others who I saw in person include Ella Fitzgerald, Sammy Davis Jr., Nat King Cole, Dinah Washington, Andrea Boccelli, Johnny Mathis, Mae West,

Barbra Streisand, Ethel Merman, The Ink Spots, Mills Brothers, Michael Jackson and so many others.

In the movies: Bette Davis, Ingrid Bergman, Elizabeth Taylor, Paul Muni, Katherine Hepburn, Marilyn Monroe, Shirley Temple. I should not have started this, too many to list.

※ ※ ※

As for the title of this book, I had several choices. One, I could have named it "My Fairy Tale of a Life," but I thought it might be considered a children's book. I could have named it "The Phone Call" because so many of my high-profile positions were the result of a phone call. And I could have named it "Nobody" because the political people, football people, hockey people and non-profit people considered me a "Nobody."

This "nobody" made a difference. If you feel you are a "nobody" just remember, you too can make a difference.

And finally, my most important thought to leave you with ... If you cannot change it, if you cannot control it: GET OVER IT!

CPSIA information can be obtained
at www.ICGtesting.com
Printed in the USA
BVHW051923190722
642501BV00017B/162

9 781792 381225